D1007327

WHO REALLY
RUNS THE
WORLD?

Conspiracy Books is a topical range of titles dedicated to publishing the truth about all conspiracies—whether ancient or modern, theoretical or real. The series is informative, entertaining, subjective, and incisive, and will endeavor to bring the reader closer than ever before to the reality of the conspiracies that surround us.

WHO REALLY RUNS THE WORLD?

THOM BURNETT
ALEX GAMES

disinformation

© 2007 Conspiracy Books

Published by The Disinformation Company Ltd.
163 Third Avenue, Suite 108
New York, NY 10003
Tel.: +1.212.691.1605
Fax: +1.212.691.1606
www.disinfo.com

All rights reserved. No part of this book may be reproduced, stored
in a database or other retrieval system, or transmitted in any form,
by any means now existing or later discovered, including without
limitation mechanical, electronic, photographic or otherwise,
without the express prior written permission of the publisher.

Library of Congress Control Number: 2007925563

ISBN-13: 978-1932857-58-0
ISBN-10: 1-932857-58-3

Printed in the USA

10 9 8 7 6 5 4 3 2 1

Distributed in the USA and Canada:
Consortium Book Sales and Distribution
1045 Westgate Drive, Suite 90
St Paul, MN 55114
Toll Free: +1.800.283.3572 Local: +1.651.221.9035
Fax: +1.651.221.0124
www.cbsd.com

Contents

Introduction

On September 11th, a new world order was declared by President George Bush. Earth-shattering events had ushered in a new period of history where security would become paramount. This new world order was born out of chaos, and tough measures would have to be carried out to ensure its survival. But this is not what it seems. The president was George Herbert Walker Bush and not his son, George Walker Bush, and the date was September 11th, 1990 and not September 11th, 2001.

Bush 41, and not Bush 43 (using the numbering system of US presidents), declared to the US Congress that "out of these troubled times, our objective, a new world order, can emerge. Today, that new world is struggling to be born, a world quite different from the one we have known." The new world he was referring to was the post-Cold War one, where the old bipolar system of the United States and the USSR had been reduced to only one superpower by the complete Soviet collapse. The enormous military and intelligence resources of the Cold War machine had to be redeployed elsewhere. In the Soviet case, this seemed to involve a rapid decline into organized criminality and corruption. In the American case, the focus switched from waging war against the Great Enemy to waging economic war against the rest of the world in the name of market share for American products. In 1995, a special report on the future of US intelligence prepared by the immensely influential New York think-tank, the Council on Foreign Relations, recommended that the intelligence-gathering capabilities should be used for industrial espionage to the benefit of US corporations.

Then, a new enemy emerged. The terrorist attacks by al-Qaeda against American targets escalated during this period until the dramatic events of September 11th, 2001, when a synchronized hijacking of four passenger jets resulted in the horrors forever to be known as 9/11. The new world order of Bush 41 came crashing down along with the Twin Towers of the World Trade Center. But that was not the only crash in the financial markets. There was the record-breaking bankruptcy of the Enron Corporation and the record-breaking bankruptcy of Argentina. There were plenty of signs that the globalization of the new world was corrupt at its core. The new world order was in need of firmer management. This book asks the question *Who Really Runs the World?* and attempts to give some answers.

Gone are the days when all that was needed to run the world was access to the cabinets of governments. Now access is also needed to the boardrooms of global corporations. Who are the people that can move freely in both these worlds? In Part One of this book, Thom Burnett supplies a list of the usual suspects familiar to conspiracy theorists. From the Freemasons to the Skull and Bones society, from the Illuminati to the Bilderbergers, the shadowy world of political puppet masters is revealed and assessed. He concentrates the search by assuming that whoever controls the White House now controls the world of the solitary superpower. The result is a secretive group that has guided American foreign policy since the final year of World War I, creating the League of Nations and the United Nations along the way.

The greatest of global unifying forces is money, and the management of the world's finances is crucial to the general health of the planet. Alas, as with all money transactions—from the smallest personal payments to the largest national and international payments—there are always opportunities for criminals to abuse the system. Theft is not an activity restricted to the dark alleyways of the world, but is all too common among the boardrooms of secretive off-shore banks, and the amounts are almost too incredible to believe. Trillions of dollars disappear in a global financial market that is woefully unregulated. Attempts to track the whereabouts of these lost funds have involved the utilization of state-of-the-art electronic surveillance technology that originally snooped on the USSR and its allies. Since 9/11 the same techniques are being deployed in destroying the terrorist-financing operations. The price that is paid for such successes is the erosion of personal liberties and rights to privacy. The National Security Agency monitors the entire world, reading e-mails and listening in on telephone conversations. Finance and intelligence are linked, and governments have to get dirty in the fight against terrorism.

In Part Two, Alex Games catalogs the trail of corporate crimes, corrupt political influence, and financial disasters. From the largest corporate bankruptcy in history (Enron) to the largest accounting fraud in history (WorldCom), the motive is profit, totally unearned profit at the expense of the ordinary shareholders. Yet WorldCom transforms itself into something else and gets offered a lucrative government contract in the rebuilding of Iraq. There are further examples of US government links with American multinational corporations in the former George Bush war zones. Defense contracts are big business, and conspiracy theorists often claim that the smell of oil and natural gas leads America into the regional conflicts.

Yet the United States does not act alone. It has its allies, both politically and militarily. The Group of Seven (G7) and the now enlarged Group of Eight (G8)—the seven largest industrial nations "plus Russia"—are claimed to be the managers of the world economy, and as such are held responsible for all the inequalities of the world's trading system. This has produced violent public demonstrations at their regular get-togethers. The whole concept of globalization has attracted much criticism, and the major writers in the anti-corporate field, such as Naomi Klein, George Monbiot, Howard Zinn, and Noam Chomsky, are given their due. Reference is also made to the origin of globalization in a secret meeting in Geneva in 1967, when a small country's economy was rebuilt under the guidance of one of conspiracy theory's giants, puppet-master David Rockefeller.

The views on globalization and the International Monetary Fund (IMF) from an "insider" come in the shape of George Soros. As well as being a phenomenally successful financial speculator, he is a member of the secretive group that may well really run the world. Although the IMF's own secretiveness and apparent unaccountability cause concern for those worried about the seriousness of its efforts in developing "Third World" trade, its bailouts during financial crises have often exacerbated the situations.

With the bulk of the world's media controlled by only a handful, literally, of multinational corporations, are we ever going to find out who really runs the world? The reporting of events is already heavily censored by those who control the strings. The best indicator of who they are is to look at the boardrooms of those media giants. They consist of members of the same secretive group that created the United Nations and wrote that 1995 report on the future of US intelligence.

PART ONE

Chapter One: All Conspiracy, No Facts?

Of all the suspects for world domination behind closed doors, the elite Bilderberg group is one of the most popular, attracting the attention of conspiracy theorists from its formation. This assembly of eminent Americans and Europeans first came together in 1954—taking its name from the small hotel that hosted the meeting—and ever since has been regularly convening at secret locations to decide on the management of the world's political and economic future. The quality of the members and their guest speakers, and the high security surrounding their meetings, has conjured up images of a secret cabal running the world.

The group was born from a belief that leading citizens from both sides of the Atlantic could come together one or twice a year to have frank, informal discussions to clear up any differences or misunderstandings that challenged the Atlantic alliance. In 1952, a former wartime Polish intelligence officer, Joseph Retinger, had approached Prince Bernhard of the Netherlands with the idea of such a gathering. There was a rising tide of anti-Americanism within Europe, prevalent among left-wing circles but also felt by the general population, and something needed to be done to maintain the West's defenses against the threat of Communism. There was a distinct feeling that Europe was acting irrationally in the face of American military and economic assistance such as NATO and the Marshall Plan. Was it really a case of biting the hand that feeds you? Or did the Europeans have very real grievances?

Prince Bernhard agreed to the idea and organized a confidential survey to be carried out among his international contacts, taking two contrasting political viewpoints from each of the countries in Europe. From this survey, Bernhard and Retinger drew up a summary document and sent it confidentially to some of the prince's American friends, who were invited to respond. Not that 1952 was the best year to ask for American frankness. It was an election year.

The next year, once the new president, Eisenhower, was inaugurated and settled down into the White House, Prince Bernhard traveled to Washington and paid a visit to his old friend Walter Bedell Smith, the director of the CIA. Smith directed him to C.D. Jackson, a special assistant to the president, who passed him further on to John S. Coleman, a member of the newly formed Committee for a National Trade Policy. It was left with the committee to draft an American reply to the European criticisms. One of those invited to respond was a figure central to all serious conspiracy theories about secret rulers of the world—David Rockefeller.

The two sides eventually met in May 1954 at the Hotel Bilderberg, near Arnhem in Holland. The group of statesmen, financiers, and academics spent three days surrounded by security guards and kept away from journalists. They pledged not to reveal publicly anything that was discussed, and this confidentiality allowed them to state their true feelings. The Europeans were concerned that a conservative Republican Party had won the election for the first time in 20 years and a soldier was now in the White House. The rants of Senator McCarthy and the book-burning actions of his anti-communist followers had reached into the US embassies of Europe. There was a genuine European fear that America was turning into a fascist state. The critics had seen enough in Europe over the last few decades to know the signs.

C.D. Jackson was given the opportunity to explain the McCarthy phenomenon. It all boiled down to freedom of speech and lack of party discipline. He made a prediction that proved to be correct: "Whether McCarthy dies by an assassin's bullet or is eliminated in the normal way of getting rid of boils on the body politic, I prophesy that by the time we hold our next meeting he will be gone from the American scene."

If McCarthy had been assassinated, one wonders how the

Bilderberg group would have coped with the unfortunate sense of being part of a plot. One thing the group did not want to be was a Mafia-style Murder Incorporated. McCarthy's swift fall from grace convinced the Europeans that some good had come of the meeting, and annual conferences were planned. The pattern has not changed in over 50 years. The Bilderberg group take over an entire hotel in a secret location and surround it with tight security. Heads of state and future heads of state attend, and the press play games of cat and mouse, trying to glean gossip of the proceedings.

The key to understanding what goes on at the Bilderberg conferences is to always remember why the first one was called. It was to give the opportunity for Americans to hear European criticisms of their foreign and economic policies. The criticism has not always been one way; the 1956 Suez crisis, when France and Britain attempted to wrest back control of the Suez Canal, which had been nationalized by President Nasser of Egypt, caused great hostility between the American, British and French delegates. On the whole, though, the Americans always feel that they have to defend their policies. That is why there is little difference between the discussions at the beginning of the Bilderberg era and the most recent ones concerning the war in Iraq.

In 2002, the Bilderbergers met at Chantilly, Virginia, near Washington. The Europeans were angry at the US preparations for the war in Iraq. The Secretary of Defense, Donald Rumsfeld, promised the delegates that war would not occur that year. That pledge was honored, but it did occur the following year.

In 2004, they met at the five-star Grand Hotel des Iles Borromees in Stresa, Italy, and there were angry protests about the bloody occupation of Iraq by American troops. These European complaints were paralleled by the European opposition to US military action voiced in the United Nations for all the world to hear. The Bilderbergers urged that the United Nations should be given a greater role in all future outbreaks of violence.

Does the Bilderberg group constitute a secret society bent on running the world? The evidence suggests that it is primarily a forum for some pretty frank criticism of the American way of doing business in the world—but if they are no more than a debating society, who else could be pulling the strings?

Disunited Nations

To answer the question of *Who Really Runs the World?* one should have to look no further than the United Nations headquarters in New York. Here is an international institution that deals with issues affecting every nation on the planet. Because of the interconnectedness of countries, events unfolding in one part of the world will have knock-on effects elsewhere. Wars are monitored and, if necessary, contained from the UN, with its own military force, and peace is theoretically kept. Certain nations have superior voting rights, such as those on the Security Council (the US, the UK, Russia and China, for example), but less powerful nations are given the opportunity to exert certain degrees of influence. Nevertheless, the elite's right to veto votes that they don't like preserves the realistic power relationships. The debates and voting are open to public scrutiny. A very good example was the UN Security Council debates on whether to force a regime change in Iraq when Saddam Hussein was refusing to cooperate with UN weapons inspectors. The worldwide TV coverage allowed the public to witness the decision-making process live.

Although great patience was displayed by the US, it eventually brushed aside UN reservations, and led a coalition invasion of Iraq. The UN may be an honorable institution set up to discuss global management problems, but the United States has the military and financial might to do whatever it deems necessary in pursuit of international stability as viewed through its star-spangled glasses. The eventual public exposure of dirty tricks being played behind the scenes of the UN Security Council voting, with secret surveillance of critical nations' voting intentions, only confirmed suspicions that the world was being run in a very different way from the popular TV perception.

The United Nations had acted very differently just over ten years before, in 1991, when it sought support for an international military operation to liberate Kuwait from Saddam's illegal army of occupation. President George H.W. Bush rallied the international troops with speeches impressing the importance of victory in establishing a new world order. The old world order had recently crumbled with the fall of the USSR and the disappearance of the old bipolar world of the Cold War years. The United States, as the only surviving superpower, would have to take on a role of international policeman, but it was not going to do it alone. Other nations were given the opportunity to sign up for the ride and share in the glory of defeating a true villain on the international stage. The evil Saddam's Iraqi forces were kicked out of Kuwait in a fast display of US military might, but amazingly, he was allowed to keep control of his own country. That foreign policy error was rectified in 2003 by the next generation of high-tech US weaponry and the next generation of Bush presidency, George W.'s.

The change in international support for the two military operations against Iraq reflects the changing world we live in. The United States was now perceived as an empire-building bully, reacting violently to a bloody nose received on 9/11 courtesy of Osama bin Laden. Immediate, justifiable revenge on Afghanistan for harboring the al-Qaeda culprits was now being extended to other troublesome spots on the newly redrawn map of the world. For all its valiant attempts at holding back the bloodlust of the United States, the United Nations failed. Its only consolation was the postwar failure of the US to find the weapons of mass destruction in Iraq which had been used as the moral justification for invasion.

Had America and its small group of allies been hoodwinked by some unseen forces who were secretly bent on the removal of Saddam for their own reasons, or was the question of WMDs really irrelevant? When history unfolds in a chaotic way, conspiracy theorists step in to try to unravel the true forces at work, and these forces are invariably secret ones. What were the real reasons for attacking Iraq? Was it for the world's second largest reserves of oil? Or was it simply the case of a son wrapping up his father's unfinished business? If it was either of these—or bearing in mind the Bush family's oil interests, a combination of these—why is it so hard to admit it? "Yeah, we did it for the oil and I wanted to make my dad proud."

The reasons are because politicians never reduce international relations to the level of childhood truths. Politicians on the international stage are diplomats, a word originating from the ancient Greek meaning "two-faced." They are always wearing two faces, one for the foreigners and one for their own country. They say one thing but probably mean another. Conspiracy theorists are aware of this, but their general unwillingness to believe what politicians say leads them to view all politicians as two-faced, not just the ones dealing with international relations.

There was a time, during the 1980s, when the United Nations headquarters in New York was popularly viewed as a hotbed of Soviet spies working for the destruction of the United States from within its enemy borders, yet protected by diplomatic immunity. The United Nations became the target of the American militia movement, which used the Posse Comitatus Act as justification for bearing arms against the imminently perceived UN attack. As a conspiracy-based movement, the militia must surely have taken no comfort in the subsequent decreased threat of the UN as the USSR collapsed and the UN took a supporting role in the first Gulf conflict, yet found renewed evidence supporting their suspicions in the most recent war. The militia are given as an example here of the more extreme views on the danger of a new world order. They seem to ignore the fact that their own country is the single most powerful component of the United Nations, and any attempt to govern the world would be an American one, not a foreign one. The militia have problems with the federal US government, believing it to be under foreign control, and that the first step in taking over the United States is to outlaw the private ownership of guns. The constitutional right to bear arms is one that they will defend with their lives. As the new Islamic terrorist threat enters the militia's mindset, perhaps the United Nations will be spared any further involvement in their conspiracy theories.

When promoting the concept of the new world order, President George H.W. Bush dedicated the freedom of Kuwait to the men who created the United Nations. It may be significant that he was not dedicating it to the United Nations itself, but to its founders. It is my view that the men to whom President Bush was referring are indeed the architects of the new world order, and their influence is still felt today, some 60 years after the founding of the UN. But they are not members of the United Nations organization. They are the single most powerful cabal working behind the scenes, and their pedigree is second to none. Are they the ones pulling the strings?

Puppet masters

There is a popular belief that all politicians are puppets. They are controlled by puppet masters who, like the puppeteers on stage, are hidden from sight of the audience. But the strings being pulled are still visible. Some of the audience ignore the strings and accept the puppets for what they really are. It allows them to enjoy the show. But there are also some people who cannot ignore the strings and spend more time wondering what the puppeteers really look like. Conspiracy theorists are like those who cannot ignore the strings. In fact, they sometimes look for strings where none are visible. For these people, politicians become part of the illusion of theater. They are the stars of stage, performers who have learned their lines of script written by others. They are out in the open, backed up by a team of manipulators who work off-stage. The apparent willingness of these controllers to stay out of the limelight intrigues conspiracy theorists. There must be sinister reasons why these people do not seek the limelight themselves. What makes a puppeteer perform the way he or she does? What are they themselves hiding from? Too ugly for the stage? Lacking in the confidence to face the public? Or are they pulling the strings to make the puppet perform actions that they know are beyond their own capabilities?

When the greatest nation on Earth elected to have a relatively unknown peanut farmer as its president, followed by a former Hollywood B-movie actor, conspiracy theorists could not help but look for the strings. Jimmy Carter introduced us to the influence of the Trilateral Commission (more on in Chapter Four), and Ronald Reagan confused us with his Pinocchio-like ability to act without any strings at all.

Whoever the incumbent, he occupies the most powerful position on the planet. Any individual or group bent on world domination should be capable of pulling the strings on the US president.

Skull and Bones

In the most recent presidential election, in 2004, secret powerful forces were at work behind the scenes to get their man into the White House. As George W. Bush was seeking re-election against John Kerry, Republicans and Democrats operated huge party machinery to achieve their respective aims, but in a small crypt-like building on the campus of Yale University in New Haven, Connecticut, a very old secret society had supreme confidence that one of their old boys would win. In fact, the rather spooky Skull and Bones society could not fail in its quest for power and influence, since both the presidential candidates had passed through its doors. George Bush had been initiated in 1968 and John Kerry in 1966.

Actually, far from being a secret, this affiliation with the Skull and Bones society was well known, thanks to conspiracy theorists' exposure and the general public's increasing awareness of this rather sinister and powerful fraternity at Yale through its previous presidential initiate, George H.W. Bush. It is extremely rare for father and son to be elected to lead a nation, but not rare in the secret world of the Skull and Bones, where family tradition of a Yale education ensured that succeeding generations became "tapped" as Bonesmen and given the official invite, wrapped in a black ribbon and sealed in black wax with the skull and crossbones emblem of the order. The father and grandfather of these presidents, Prescott Bush, was also a member of the Skull and Bones, and was involved in the theft of Geronimo's skull from the Apache leader's grave at Fort Sill, Oklahoma in May 1918. Such criminal pranks are typical of university fraternities the world over, so nothing too sinister should be read into it—unless, of course, you happen to be a member of the Apache tribe or a conspiracy theorist.

The Bush family represent the strongest influence the Skull and Bones have yet wielded upon American politics. There have been a few instances in the past when the crypt at Yale, known to initiates as "the Tomb," has produced nearly the same degree of power in the White House, and these will be looked at in detail. But if we are to search for signs of an organization that pulls strings, then the two Bushes must not be treated as a unity, since there was an eight-year interregnum of the Democrat Bill Clinton. How does he fit into the conspiracy of the Skull and Bones? Although he graduated from Yale, he was not a member of the Skull and Bones, or any of the other secret societies on campus (and there are several, including the almost equally influential Scroll and Key). Could the Yale connection actually be more important as a source of influence? It does become more significant when yet another Yale graduate, Gerald Ford, is added to the list. That's four presidents over a thirty-year period: four out of only six men who held the most powerful position in American and world politics. Is this evidence of a Yale conspiracy? No, for the simple reason that there is no secretive element to it, whereas the Skull and Bones has it in spades.

Its origins were revealed after a rival group calling itself "The Order of File and Claw" broke into the Tomb on September 29th, 1876 and reported its discoveries. They found a room numbered 322 furnished with red velvet and a pentagram on the wall. On the west wall there was an old engraving of a burial vault. In the picture is a stone slab upon which rest four human skulls among a fool's cap and bells, some mathematical instruments, an open book, a beggar's scrip, and a royal crown. Above the vault was inscribed in Roman letters: "Wie War Der Thor, Wer Weiser, Wer Bettler Oder Kaiser?" (Who was the fool, who was the wise man, beggar or king?) Below the vault is engraved in Gothic script the sentence "Ob Arm, Ob Reich, im Tode gleich." (Whether poor or rich, all's the same in death.) Accompanying the picture of the vault scene was a card on which was written "From the German Chapter. Presented by D.C. Gilman of D.50."

Research shows that this D.C. Gilman was a Yale graduate and Bonesman of 1852, Daniel Coit Gilman, who went to study philosophy in Europe at the University of Berlin. He returned to the United States and incorporated the Skull and Bones as the Russell Trust Association in 1856, with William H. Russell as president and himself as treasurer. Russell had been one of the original founders of the Skull and Bones back in 1832. The break-in revealed the history of the order. It was a chapter of a corps in a German university, and Russell had been in Germany before his final year at Yale. During this stay, he had formed contacts with a leading member of the German society, who gave him authorization to found a chapter when he returned to Yale. Along with 14 other students, Russell founded the Order of Scull and Bones, which later changed to the Order of Skull and Bones, and this number of 15 has been preserved by succeeding generations of Bonesmen.

Each year 15 new recruits are "tapped" during their junior year and initiated in the Tomb. At any one time there are believed to be about 600 Bonesmen alive. One of the original founders, Alphonso Taft, became the Secretary of War under President Rutherford B. Hayes in 1876, the same year as the tomb break-in. His son, William H. Taft, became a Skull and Bones initiate in 1878 and followed in his father's footsteps, becoming Secretary of War from 1904 to 1908 and then attaining greater glory when he was elected President of the United States in 1908. Taft selected fellow Bonesman Henry Lewis Stimson as his own Secretary of War in 1911. Stimson himself would serve under seven presidents: Theodore Roosevelt, William Taft, Woodrow Wilson, Calvin Coolidge, Herbert Hoover, Franklin Delano Roosevelt, and Harry S. Truman. Once again, he was Secretary of War under the last two, Roosevelt and Truman. It is perhaps deeply significant that President George H.W. Bush was constantly seen referring to a biography of his Bonesman idol Stimson during the first Gulf War, as if seeking inspiration.

Stimson's special assistant and a key person in the Manhattan Project to develop the atomic bomb was fellow Bonesman Hollister Bundy, whose own two sons, William and McGeorge, were initiated in 1939 and 1940 respectively. They would go on to occupy important positions in the CIA, and the Departments of Defense and State, and become Special Assistants to Presidents Kennedy and Johnson.

One Yale student who was not "tapped" was Ron Rosenbaum. As a classmate of George W. Bush, he has spent the last few decades investigating the Skull and Bones. Reports of naked mud wrestling and confessional masturbations in an open coffin only compound his fear that there is something very dark about the whole ritual side. The mystical number 322 on the emblem and its use in the Tomb to identify the order's inner sanctum are supposedly either a reference to the date of the death of the famous Greek lawyer and patriot Demosthenes in 322 BC, whose fraternity the Skull and Bones models itself upon, or a cryptic reference to its German origins. Rosenbaum found the pamphlet published by the Order of the File and Claw, which described the interior of the Tomb and its history, among the old papers of the Russell Trust Association kept in the Yale library. It claims that the number 322 is to be read as the order's founding date, '32 (i.e. 1832), and its rank as the second chapter of the German society. Whatever the truth, the identification of the room within the Tomb has to be considered: furnished totally in black velvet, it is identified as Room 324. Rosenbaum speculates that the German connection is ominous and could represent a secret connection with the dreaded Illuminati.

The Illuminated Ones

In any study of secret organizations that are supposed to rule the world, the name Illuminati blazes forth as the one group that everyone else wants to belong to or be linked with. Why is it that this Bavarian group of scholars has such a magnetic hold on the modern conspiracy theorist's imagination? What made the "fairy tale for paranoids," *The Illuminatus! Trilogy* by Robert Shea and Robert Anton Wilson, such a cult classic in the 1970s and 80s, when its success lies within its science-fiction genre and not in real history? The fascination is still with us, as shown by Dan Brown's *Angels and Demons*, the prequel to his phenomenal bestseller *The Da Vinci Code*. Perhaps it is time to put the Illuminati in its proper context.

Much is made of the fact that it was created in 1776, the same year as the Declaration of Independence in the United States—as if the two were linked in some secret way. Some conspiracy theorists view the 13 stages of the pyramid on the US $1 bill as the 13 degrees of Illuminism and the all-seeing eye as an Illuminati symbol. The Latin date on the base of the pyramid is 1776 and the "Novus Ordo Seclorum" is the new secular Order of the Illuminati. Yes, there are links between the Illuminati and the United States, but these were forged at a later date; 1776 is too early. Likewise, Ron Rosenbaum's link between the Illuminati and the Skull and Bones in the 1830s is too late. There are very strong links between Freemasonry and the United States which survive to this day, but the Illuminati were a short-lived phenomenon. They took on Freemasonry and lost. Their illuminating flame had been extinguished by the end of the eighteenth century.

To raise doubts about the influential power of the Illuminati, one has only to study its leader, Dr. Adam Weishaupt. He was a professor of canon law at the University of Ingolstadt in Bavaria who had fought for the introduction of non-Catholic books into the Jesuit-controlled library and scientific subjects of the Enlightenment into the University curriculum. Frustrated by the Jesuit control over thinking, he was forced to consider other avenues of knowledge sharing, and turned to Freemasonry. Unfortunately for Weishaupt, he did not have the financial resources to become a Freemason, since it was at that time an even more expensive hobby than it is today. However, the secrets of Freemasonry were already generally known outside the brotherhood, and Weishaupt set about creating his own pseudo-Masonic lodge, with its own three degrees of initiation. The Order of the Illuminati was launched on May 1st, 1776 with only five members, and the three degrees were given the titles Novice, Minerval and Illuminated Minerval. A Minerval was supposed to recruit young impressionable men from the ages of 20 to 25 and keep the identity of his fellow Minervals a secret. The Novices were told to prepare a very detailed report on themselves, including a complete list of books that they owned. After a probationary period of two years, where they identified their enemies and tried to recruit other novices, they would become raised to the grade of Minerval. Only then would they be introduced to other Minervals and attend Illuminati gatherings.

In the first four years of its existence, the Illuminati membership rose to about 60. Weishaupt eventually found enough money to buy his way into Freemasonry. In 1777, in a move apparently designed to acquire the secrets of the higher degrees of the craft, he joined the Theodore of Good Counsel lodge in Munich. Accessing these higher degrees and their revealed mysteries was a way of allowing him to plagiarize them and offer comparable ones as higher degrees in the Illuminati. Weishaupt knew that he was in competition with the established lodges, so he set about infiltrating them. By 1779 the situation in the Munich lodge was such that it was now considered dominated by Weishaupt's Illuminati, and other lodges viewed it as part of the new order. Yet the Illuminati were going nowhere until they recruited the established Freemason and North German diplomat Baron Adolf Knigge in 1780. When Knigge asked Weishaupt about the higher degrees of the Illuminati, Weishaupt had to embarrassingly admit that there weren't any. During those first four years, the great Weishaupt had not been able to create a series of rituals for his own order. What does that say about the qualities of the man? Here was a supposed leader of the most "illuminated" individuals in Europe who hadn't been capable of creating the "secrets" of his own cult.

Baron Knigge introduced a far superior marketing plan, ignoring the young men who were starting out in life and concentrating on the older, established professional men of influence. In other words, his fellow Freemasons. Through Knigge's effective networking and Masonic knowledge, the Illuminati started to become a far more influential force. Knigge had the experience of higher degrees to be able to write equivalent ones for the Illuminati. He expanded the organizational structure and put Freemasonry at a higher level of entry into the Illuminati. The sequence of advancement within the order became Novice, Minerval, Illuminatus Minor, the three grades of Freemasonry (Apprentice, Fellow and Master), Illuminatus Major, Illuminatus Dirigens, Prince, Priest, Magus, and King. (Note how there are only 12 grades, not 13 as sometimes claimed.) Yet even Knigge was not able to find time to write the final two grades.

The leaders of the Illuminati were also known as the Areopagites, and Knigge found that the upper ranks were very critical of Weishaupt's attempts to run the Illuminati as a dictatorship. This internal division and unrest within the order was holding the Illuminati back from further expansion, and Knigge's reorganization was welcomed among the Areopagites but resented by Weishaupt. A vote taken by the Areopagites on July 9th, 1781 to adopt Knigge's proposed organizational changes effectively ushered in a new era and represented a substantial defeat for Weishaupt.

German Freemasonry was open to attack from the Illuminati and its new teachings on the Enlightenment, because up until Knigge's campaign, its members had succumbed to the childish mysteries of alchemy and thaumaturgy so prevalent in French Freemasonry. Science was now taking over from magic, and revolutionary political concepts of freedom and equality were being discussed rather than continually harping on the Temple of Solomon. The Illuminati, under Knigge's direction, expanded by recruiting nearly 3,000 new members among German society's elite. In its competition with German Freemasonry, the Illuminati scored decisive victories in the enlistment of the two most important characters in German Freemasonry, Duke Ferdinand of Brunswick and Prince Carl of Hesse. All looked set for the complete takeover of Freemasonry, until the intense rivalry between Weishaupt and Knigge exploded in April 1784, resulting in the resignation of Knigge and the beginning of a very swift decline in the power of the Illuminati. Within a few months, the ruler of Bavaria, Carl Theodore, issued edicts that banned all secret societies and brotherhoods in his land. Weishaupt and his order soon learned that the power they had over German Freemasonry did not translate into real political power at all. Boasting of their immunity from prosecution did not aid their case in the slightest, and served only to annoy the authorities even more.

In March of the following year, 1785, the monarch specifically targeted the Illuminati in a second edict. All of its financial resources were confiscated and half given to the poor and half to informers against the order. This was very effective in producing numerous former members of the Illuminati to provide evidence against their leadership. Knigge had managed to leave at the right time, but Weishaupt showed a streak of cowardice by fleeing two weeks before the second edict even appeared. The excuse he gave for the sudden abandonment of his order is an incredible one and needs to be stated clearly. He had had an argument with the librarian of the University of Ingolstadt over some books that Weishaupt had needed for his classes. The refusal of the librarian to purchase these books was what drove this leader of the Illuminati to travel across the Bavarian border and luckily escape persecution.

The government of Carl Theodore demonstrated a certain degree of ruthlessness in its dealings with the order. Its aim was the complete destruction of the secret society, and this it achieved. It must be said that the severity of the legal actions against the Illuminati was partly caused by the continual writing of propaganda pamphlets by Weishaupt in exile. Other documents were discovered within Bavaria which painted the Illuminati in a completely different light, planning international revolution against governments and religion, willing to use poison and forgery to achieve their aims. A third edict was issued to prevent future recruitment, sanctioning the use of execution for those found guilty. Warnings were issued to other governments to outlaw Illuminati refugees. By 1787, the Illuminati were gone.

Proofs of a Conspiracy?

Of course, conspiracy theorists would not let their flame die. The Illuminati were the perfect example of a secret society with aims of world domination, and although they had brought most of their trouble upon themselves, the leadership showed an amazing lack of determination to fight back. If an organization intends to run the world, it must first be able to run itself. This the Illuminati evidently could not master. And as far as rulership of the world was concerned, the Illuminati only ever concerned themselves with trying to rule Bavaria. It was up to later commentators to spread the false-hood that they constituted a great threat to other governments. Conspiracy theory is not a new subject, as the case of the Illuminati will soon show. The historical reality of the order would soon be replaced with a paranoid reinvention of international proportions.

In 1797, there appeared a book written by a professor of natural philosophy at Edinburgh University named John Robison. Its long-winded title was *Proofs of a Conspiracy Against All the Religions and Governments of Europe, Carried on in the Secret Meetings of the Free Masons, Illuminati, and Reading Societies.* The book became an instant bestseller and laid bold claims that the Illuminati had been the secret organization behind the French Revolution of 1789. Although Robison was himself a Freemason, the English lodges with which he was acquainted supplied him with nothing more than "a pretext for passing an hour or two in a sort of decent conviviality." The European lodges he visited were altogether a different experience, and their revolutionary debates concerned him greatly. Robison believed he had found evidence that the Illuminati had survived their destruction at the hands of Carl Theodore by transforming themselves into other secret societies. As the title of the book announces, he suggested that the innocent-sounding reading soci-eties were part of the conspiracy. One in particular, known as the German Union, was none other than the reincarnated Illuminati, according to Robison.

A *reading* society? Are we to believe that members of some book club were now the hidden manipulators of history? Judging by Weishaupt's argument with the Ingolstadt librarian, one can see how important books were to the Illuminati leader in his mission to disseminate the latest Enlightenment thinking in Jesuit Bavaria, but are there grounds for believing that a group of bookworms were capable of orchestrating the French Revolution? Robison's informa-tion on the Illuminati was gleaned from the Bavarian government's trial documents and other virulent pamphlets in circulation. Robison admits that his knowledge of the German language was far from perfect and that his original intention had been to write a book attacking the Freemasonry conspiracy, but he got sidetracked by the

Illuminati. There are errors in his work, such as the most unfortunate blunder over the date of the Illuminati's founding, which he places in 1775, not in 1776.

Robison stated that "their first and immediate aim is to get possession of riches, power, and influence, without industry; and to accomplish this, they want to abolish Christianity; and then dissolute manners and universal profligacy will procure them the adherence of all the wicked, and enable them to overturn all the civil governments of Europe; after which they will think of further conquests, and extend their operations to the other quarters of the globe, till they have reduced mankind to a state of one indistinguishable chaotic mass." The pinnacle of its subversion on moral standards, in Robison's eyes, was the proposal to introduce women into the lodges. "There is nothing in the whole constitution of the Illuminati that strikes me with more horror." Weishaupt's own immorality was obvious in the case of his sexual relationship with the sister-in-law of fellow Illuminatus Xavier Zwack, whose secret papers were not consigned to the fire but found their way into the hands of the Bavarian prosecutors. Robison would have been more outraged if his German language had been more accurate. It was Weishaupt's own sister-in-law that he had the affair with.

Robison struggled to show the links between the Illuminati and the French Grand Orient Lodge, and through them the Jacobin revolutionaries responsible for some of the most radical and bloodthirsty action in 1789. Almost at the same time, another conspiracy theory book came out in France, entitled *Mémoires Pour Servir à l'Histoire du Jacobinism*, written by the Jesuit priest Augustin Barruel, which appeared to agree with Robison's speculations. It was this apparent independence of two sources describing the same Illuminati influence on the French Revolution that gave each writer a further boost in confidence about a real conspiracy. Both authors gave serious warnings to the United States. Robison included a table of Illuminati lodges that had been established before its dissolution in 1786. There were five lodges in Strassburg, four in Bonn, 14 in Austria, eight in England, two in Scotland, and "several" in America. Barruel had this to say:

As the plague flies on the wings of the wind, so do their triumphant legions infect America. Their apostles have infused their principles into the submissive and laborious Negroes; and St. Domingo and Guadeloupe have been converted into vast charnel houses for their inhabitants. So numerous were the brethren in North America, that Philadelphia and Boston trembled, lest their rising constitution should be obliged to make way for that of the great club; and if for a time the brotherhood had been obliged to shrink back into their hiding places, they are still sufficiently numerous to raise collections and transmit them to the insurgents of Ireland; thus contributing toward that species of revolution which is the object of their ardent wishes in America. God grant that the United States may not learn to their cost, that Republics are equally menaced with Monarchies; and that the immensity of the ocean is but a feeble barrier against the universal conspiracy of the Sect!

The distribution of both books in America raised fears that the Illuminati were conspiring against the government of George Washington and John Adams. In 1798, a full-blown Illuminati scare erupted in New England, with Thomas Jefferson accused by some of being the head of the American Illuminati. Chief among the conspiracy theorists was the Reverend Jedidiah Morse, pastor of the First Church, Charlestown, Massachusetts, who published three sermons and numerous newspaper articles promoting and defending his theories. Two academic heavyweights added their support in the shape of the Reverend David Tappan, a Harvard professor of divinity, and the Reverend Timothy Dwight, the president of Yale College. On the Fourth of July celebrations in New Haven, Dwight called upon his fellow Americans to stand up against the secret society and prevent their daughters becoming "the concubines of the Illuminati."

A copy of Robison's book was sent by the Reverend G.W. Snyder to President George Washington, who replied with a letter dated September 25th, 1798: "I have heard much of the nefarious and dangerous plan and doctrines of the Illuminati, but never saw the book until you were pleased so send it to me. It was not my intention to doubt that the doctrine of the Illuminati had not spread in the United States. On the contrary, no one is more satisfied of this fact than I am."

George Washington was a famous Freemason, and his comments on the enemy Illuminati are significant. On February 4th, 1789, Washington had been elected as the first President of the United States. At the inauguration on April 30th, the oath was administered by Robert Livingston, Grand Master of New York's Grand Lodge, using the Bible belonging to St. John's Lodge No. 1 of New York. The laying of the cornerstone of the Capitol occurred on September 18th, 1793, with the whole event serving as a very public display of the influence of Freemasonry. Washington and his fellow Masons marched in procession, wearing the full regalia of their respective lodges.

Jefferson, on the other hand, thought little of Barruel's theories. They were the "ravings of a Bedlamite." His views on Weishaupt were revealing: "Weishaupt seems to be an enthusiastic philanthropist. Weishaupt believes that to promote the perfection of the human character was the object of Jesus Christ. His precepts are the love of God and love of our neighbor." Jefferson's Republican press ridiculed the charges being made by the likes of the Reverend Dwight. New England, with its history of Puritan witch trials, was portrayed as a place where Church and State still conspired to keep the population docile and uneducated. The Illuminati were the targets of a modern witch hunt, which Republicans did not want to see repeating. The conspiracy theory had been successfully turned back upon the "political priests" of New England, such as Timothy Dwight. He was portrayed as the "Pope" who suppressed people's freedoms and protected the tax-supported Congregational churches. With the election success of Thomas Jefferson in 1800, the Illuminati conspiracy faded from Federalist propaganda.

Digging up the Truth

Curiously, another Timothy Dwight was elected president of Yale in 1886. He too was a professor of divinity, a grandson of the first.

Was this a case of history repeating itself? Certainly not: this one was a member of the Skull and Bones, tapped in 1849, and a colleague of the treasurer and donor of the engraving in Room 322, Daniel Coit Gilman.

Following on from the Illuminati conspiracy theory, what are we to make of Ron Rosenbaum's theory that the Skull and Bones are an offshoot of the Illuminati? Room 322 of the Tomb certainly displayed a Germanic origin of the Yale secret society, but does that make it an Illuminati one? As already shown, the Bavarian Illuminati were destroyed by the actions of Carl Theodore in 1786, and the Illuminati conspiracy theory was promoted by the books of Robison and Barruel in 1798. Are we to believe that the Illuminati survived at least up to the 1832 visit of Skull and Bonesman founder William Russell to the University of Berlin? Or the visit of Daniel Gilman and Timothy Dwight to the same university in the early 1850s?

Rosenbaum, in his September 1997 article for *Esquire* magazine, gives the reasons why he believes in a connection. He found the Skull and Bones slogan "Who was the fool, who the wise man, beggar or king? Whether poor or rich, all's the same in death" remarkably similar to the Illuminati sayings in the Regent (Prince) degree ritual. Towards the end of the ceremony, the initiate is shown a skeleton with a sword and crown at its feet. He is asked whether the skeleton belongs to a king, a nobleman or a beggar. As the initiate is undecided, the president of the meeting informs him that it is the character of the man which is important.

Rosenbaum equates these two sayings as proof of the link between the Skull and Bones and the Illuminati. But, as has already been shown, the Illuminati higher degrees were composed by Baron Adolf Knigge, and he drew from his extensive experience of German Freemasonry. It is in all likelihood a general German Freemasonry idea and, if anything, points more to that as the source than any specific Illuminati connection. What was the fascination with Germany for the founders of the Skull and Bones? It is probably less to do with the mysteries of a banned secret society and more to do with the dominance of German philosophy at the time. The founders were philosophy students who spent some of their academic time at the University of Berlin. Much has been written about the influence of Hegel on modern philosophy, and before him, Immanuel Kant. Hegel had been a professor at the University of Berlin until his death in 1831, the year William Russell arrived. Hegelianism would be responsible for the future development of both fascism and communism, stressing as it did that the supreme duty of the individual is to be a member of the State. This, of course, is in sharp contrast to the cultivation of a secret elite, which the Skull and Bones became.

As time went on, and Germany developed into a far-from inspirational source, the links with that country would be severed. Despite the dark desires of some conspiracy theorists to have the Skull and Bones evolve into a secret Nazi enclave, this is very unlikely. The death's head symbolism, though popular in Germany, is far more recognized as the flag on a pirate ship, suggesting highly illegal adventures on the high seas. Is it a coincidence that William Russell's uncle, Samuel Russell, established Russell and Company in 1823, and made the family fortune by acquiring opium in Turkey and smuggling it to China?

The re-election of George W. Bush in 2004, and the defeat of his fellow Bonesman, John Kerry, ensures that the Skull and Bones continues to enjoy another four years of influence in the minds of conspiracy theorists. When one asks what shape this influence could take, the ideas run dry. What does the Skull and Bones actually do when its former initiates are in positions of power? Does it try to guide foreign policy? Are there sinister experts wearing robes who plan the future of the world in a velvet room? The image is farcical. What influence the Skull and Bones had on their initiates in 1966 and 1968 was likely to have been very short-lived. A weekly trip to the Tomb was possible only when they lived on or near campus. Are we to believe that George W. Bush, a man known to be in bed by nine o'clock in the evening, crises permitting, would make the trip to Yale to confer by torchlight with his fellow Bonesmen? For such dedication, the rituals have to be far more interesting and far grander.

If You Go Down in the Woods Today...

Most secret societies conduct rituals that outsiders would have difficulty comprehending, and of which insiders understand the significance only after advancing through several degrees of initiation.
Sometimes, no amount of initiation instruction prepares the
member for what is nothing more than grand horsing around.
An example of this is the infamous pseudo-Druidic rituals carried
out at the Bohemian Grove celebrity summer camp, 75 miles north
of San Francisco in California. Apart from men in red hoods and
black robes marching in a procession up to a giant statue of the
Great Owl Moloch and public displays of drunkenness, the "Grovers"
are usually entertained by serious speakers at the so-called "lakeside lectures." There is a famous photograph taken in 1995 of past
and future presidents George H.W. Bush and George W. Bush,
casually dressed, giving one of these lakeside lectures to their
fellow campers.

It is claimed that every Republican president since Herbert
Hoover has been a member, and most, but not all, Democrats. In his
memoirs, Herbert Hoover described the scene at Bohemian Grove
in 1927 when, on learning of Calvin Coolidge's announcement that
he would not be running for re-election, hundreds of Grovers came
over to his camp and demanded that he announce his candidacy.
The following year, he was again at Bohemian Grove when news
came that the Republican Party had chosen him as its candidate. In
1964, Nelson Rockefeller abandoned his bid for the Republican nomination after a poor reception at Bohemian Grove. In 1967, a deal
was struck between Richard Nixon and Ronald Reagan, while they
stayed in the same camp, that the latter would stay out of the con-
test. It is at Bohemian Grove that politicians mix with industrialists, financiers, and stars from the entertainment world in a
relatively secure theme park that pays homage to the college
fraternities these powerful men obviously so sorely miss.

Claims are made by conspiracy theorists that some of the major
decisions concerning the military industrial complex have been
made at Bohemian Grove, citing the case of Grover Edward Teller,

the father of the H-bomb. Somehow the association of thermonuclear weapon systems and drunken urination in the woods of California seems too surreal. Theorists become too sidetracked on the bizarre aspects of the Owl ritual and its simulated human sacrifice, and seldom delve into the origins of the summer camp and who exactly controls the event.

The Bohemian Grove began as the Bohemian Club in San Francisco in 1872, founded by a group of journalists as an excuse for late-night drinking. With the likes of Mark Twain, Bret Harte and Jack London, these bohemian boozing sessions soon attracted the most un-bohemian members imaginable—rich businessmen who would gladly pay for the hacks' champagne. Eventually, journalists would be banned entirely, and the Club acquired 2,700 acres of redwoods to turn into a businessmen's retreat. As an organized gathering of powerful men who want to get drunk, dress up as prostitutes with fake breasts and fishnets, and let off steam in crazy, fraternity-style antics, Bohemian Grove is without equal. As a source of secret control over the United States' domestic and foreign policy, it has to be consigned to its own funeral pyre.

Evangelical Christians who subscribe to the dangers of a new world order are understandably appalled by the use of the biblical name Moloch for the Great Owl. In the Old Testament, Moloch or Molech was an Ammonite deity that had an altar dedicated to it on the south side of Jerusalem where children were sacrificed in its honor. But, apart from the name, there are no signs of Ammonite theology in the Bohemian Grove rituals. As the name "Grove" implies, the ritual is basically Druidic. There are important links with the trees and the natural environment. The return to the wild explains the frequent public urination in the woods and not in the portable toilets provided.

The ritual that has caused so much intrigue over the years was finally captured on video by conspiracy theorist broadcaster, Alex Jones, in July 2000, and almost immediately disseminated through the internet. The "Cremation of Care" is nothing more than an outdoor nocturnal staging of pure theater with impressive pyrotechnics and Death punting across a lagoon in a gondola, carrying an effigy of Dull Care towards its eventual burning. Whatever Dull Care really represents, it is denounced as the arch-enemy of Beauty. Though distinctly pagan, the ritual is not satanic as several conspiracy theorists have warned. Children are not kidnapped and sacrificed to the Great Owl. First-hand accounts of sex slaves used in mind-control programs who have performed at Bohemian Grove are nothing more than pornographic fiction feeding into the mainstream conspiracy theories through the genre of cult deprogramming "confessions."

Bohemian Grove certainly opens itself up for this kind of perverse speculation masquerading as fact, and some of the Grovers may even welcome such outrageous stories about their yearly holiday break. But are we to seriously consider the organizers of Bohemian Grove as wielding an all-year-round influence on the decision-making process of the White House and, through it, the world?

Freemasons

When one also asks the question: "What the hell are Druids doing in California in the first place?" one needs to realize that the modern Druidic movement is an offshoot of the Freemasons. Suddenly, it starts to make sense. People are familiar enough with the strange handshakes and rituals of the Freemasons to readily accept the possibility of Freemasons getting drunk and doing business deals in the urine-soaked forests of Bohemian Grove. America has a long relationship with Freemasons and owes part of its independence from Britain to the lodges of New England. Two out of the five original drafters of the 1776 Declaration of Independence, Benjamin Franklin and Robert Livingstone, were Masons, with a third, Roger Sherman, listed as a possible but unconfirmed one. Nine of the signatories, including George Washington and John Hancock, were Masons and a further ten are believed to have been.

The Constitution Convention of 1787 was fully aware of the dangers faced by all republics, and sought to rule out the possibility of allowing dictators or dynasties to emerge. Two main principles were devised to achieve this aim, and both were based on how Freemasonry ran its organization of lodges. The first was that power was to be vested in the office of the president and not in the man. He was to be replaced in office at regular intervals by vote. This was exactly the system by which Masters and Grand Masters were elected. If they became deemed as unworthy of office, they could be impeached or deposed. There was no need for violent, bloody revolution. The second principle was an equal distribution of power between the Executive (i.e. the Presidency) and the Legislature (the two houses of Congress) where the possible excesses of power of one could be checked and balanced by the other. This reflected the Masonic structure of the lodges and the Grand Lodge.

The secret societies and groups mentioned here are just a few of the usual suspects that appear in the conspiracy theorist's universe. As far as secrecy is concerned, a lot of them are remarkably open about their activities and beliefs. Some have been in existence for hundreds of years, but others are just transitory. Those new ones are obviously hoping that their existence will continue after the demise of their founders, but this is far more difficult than they may imagine.

Since the end of the Cold War and the break-up of the USSR, the world has entered a new phase where there is no longer a bipolar rulership. The United States now rules supreme. Europe and China may think otherwise, but American military muscle exerts the kind of control achieved only by empire builders. How they choose to exercise this power will be an interesting lesson for future historians growing up within the process. When conspiracy theorists attempt to discern the hidden hands pulling the strings of political puppets, they would be wise to concentrate their search on American hands. Any belief that the world is still run by the Queen of England, acting through secret power structures that survived the break-up of the British empire, is just ludicrous. That the royal family are shape-shifting alien reptiles from another dimension, as claimed by David Icke, is just plain lunacy. Conspiracy theory does encompass a very wide range of belief systems, but such ideas belong in either conspiracy stand-up comedy, or science fiction comics.

Any foreign influence on the running of American policy is also likely to be an unrealistic supposition. Some of the secret societies have their roots in foreign countries, but this is only a reality imposed upon a young nation seeking secret traditions extending back in time before its own founding. The European origin of American Freemasonry does not necessarily mean that European grand lodges continue to exert power and influence over their younger American brethren. The American War of Independence was a sure sign that freemasons were willing to break their prime oath, and fight against fellow members of the craft. Freemasons are now spread throughout the world, but there has been the inevitable dilution of power. This is exactly the opposite of the conditions required to run the world. The quality of people becoming Masons has obviously dropped since the early days when the secrets and mysteries were available to only a select few. But with expansion of membership, the conspiratorial power has understandably weakened. One has only to gain access to the House of the Temple in Washington DC to see the true caliber of 33rd Degree Freemasonry in America. The last real man of influence in world politics who was a 33rd was President Gerald Ford. Senator Bob Dole made an attempt but failed. Otherwise, who else among their ranks could run the world? Golfer Arnold Palmer? Or that actor from *Seinfeld*?

Like most secret societies, there were times when matters were very different indeed. In the case of the 33rd Degrees, it was during the presidency of Franklin Delano Roosevelt. With a member running the country, and a fellow running the internal security in the shape of J. Edgar Hoover, the Freemasons appeared to be in control. This was only short lived, but there is a permanent testament to the influence of the 33rd at this time: the design of the Masonic seal on the back of the US $1 bill. Conspiracy theorists are correct in saying that the all-seeing eye and the 13-staged pyramid that feature on the bill are Masonic symbols; however, the conspiracists' claim that the Latin inscription on the bill—"Novus Ordo

Seclorum"—means new world order, is not. In fact, it translates as New Secular Order. The additional Latin text above the all-seeing eye, "Annuit Coeptis," means "Announcing the Birth of." The date at the base of the pyramid is also in Latin, MDCCLXXVI, and it trans-lates as 1776 (the date of the signing of the Declaration of Independence), while the 13-staged pyramid represents not some secret cabal, but refers to the original 13 colonies who signed the Declaration in 1776. So, although it was yet another high-ranking Freemason—future Vice President Henry Wallace—who was respon-sible for suggesting the image upon the dollar bill when it was intro-duced in 1935, the symbolism relates specifically and clearly to the founding of the United States. The inscription "Novus Ordo Seclorum" simply reminds every American of one of the key tenets of the new nation: that the United States was to be free both of Britain, and of Church control generally. Neither the founders of the United States nor President Roosevelt had any desire to establish a new world order. That desire would come a lot later.

Where the Real Power Lies

The secret societies mentioned so far have captured the conspiracy theorists' imagination since there are plenty of occult rituals and secluded places conducive to evil machinations. Powerful figures in government and, more importantly, presidents themselves, are involved in these secret activities. This is definitely not a Christian meeting of minds, in the modern sense at least. The original Christians had, out of necessity, to meet clandestinely during peri-ods of extreme persecution, and Roman accusations of evil prac-tices such as cannibalism and blood drinking were easily made. However, as Christianity became mainstream and its rituals toned down over the centuries, the desire for the macabre persisted. Freemasonry took up the slack and introduced biblical rituals involving murder, death and resurrection. The Skull and Bones has similar rituals. Conspiracy theory, because of its belief in hidden powers, populates its grand narratives with men in hooded robes. The secret manipulators are like the priesthood of old. They are the custodians of great secrets that endow them with wisdom and power.

Although the hooded robes still exist today, they tend to be worn by students as they graduate from the influential universities. These graduates from Yale and the like are destined to move into government and political power. The robes are abandoned for expensive business suits. Those who retain the robes and become academics themselves sometimes make the transition to politics at a later time. Examples of these are Henry Kissinger and Zbigniew Brzezinski.

Secret societies have their days of influence, when members are presidents of the United States, but these come and go and cannot be honestly viewed as effective manipulators behind history. There needs to be a certain degree of permanence behind the scenes. There has to be the power to influence those who are elected into the White House, no matter what political party they represent. When Jimmy Carter was president, the Trilateral Commission appeared to hold sway, but this was only for a short period. A more permanent, yet secret, organization, lies behind the Trilateral Commission. It is one which even the Skull and Bones acknowledge. It is the Council on Foreign Relations. John McCloy, the Assistant Secretary in charge of personnel to the Bonesman Secretary of War Henry Stimson, once admitted that: "Whenever we needed a man we thumbed through the roll of the council members and put through a call to New York [the headquarters of the CFR]." McCloy was himself a member of the CFR, as was Stimson. The CFR was more powerful than the Skull and Bones.

Could the CFR in fact be the most powerful elite in the world today? No secret organization has wielded more influence over succeeding US administrations. From its headquarters in New York, the Council on Foreign Relations exerts the kind of power that conspiracy theorists fear, yet perversely admire. Its ability to influence foreign policy of the United States is the single most important key to understanding how the most powerful nation on the planet can control the other lesser nations. There are no aliens, no members of the anachronistic British aristocracy, no secret satanic rituals in black crypts. To secretly run the world, one has to know how international relations actually work. The CFR has practically written the training manuals. We'll see in Chapter Four exactly why the CFR is able to wield such immense power.

Chapter Two: Money Does Make the World go Round

When the United States and the rest of the world were preoccupied with the immediate aftermath of 9/11, Argentina defaulted on its sovereign debts—a cool $100 billion. This was the largest-ever sovereign debt default, and much of the blame lay with Wall Street. Conspiracists saw the usual story of a small group of powerful financiers bringing an entire country to its knees for the sake of a fast profit. Economic and political ruin were of no concern to some of the wheeler-dealers in the bond markets because they'd already shifted the losses onto the naive, small-scale investors of another country.

Was this a crime? Not in the world of international finance. For every cent made, someone is losing that same cent. Winners and losers. Someone knows something that someone else doesn't and exploits that difference. Currency fluctuations on the world markets are the results of rumors—some true and some false. When the events materialize, the prices have already taken into account the likely effects of the events, so the markets ignore them. It is only when the truly unexpected happens that the prices react instantly. The attack on the Twin Towers was such an event...or was it? Certain stock price movements showed advance knowledge of the attack. This was a clear indicator, after the event, that Osama bin Laden was profiting in more ways than one from the terrorist attack.

Who Really Won the Battle of Waterloo?

The method of making money from rumors was finely exemplified in a story well known to conspiracy theorists: that of the

Rothschilds and the battle of Waterloo in 1815. The founder of the family banking business was Amschel Moses Bauer. (The future change of name to Rothschild is perhaps symptomatic of the deviousness with which the family would operate.) After an initial period of lending money to local governments, Amschel expanded into lending to national governments. In truly biblical fashion, he set up his five sons in banking houses spread throughout Europe: Nathan went to London, Meyer to Frankfurt, Solomon to Vienna, James to Paris and Carl to Naples. As a family, their great wealth was generated by playing one country off against another. The threat of war was a catalyst for greater lending and greater profits. As countries geared up their industrial output for war, they took on more debts. If the wars did not materialize, then the Rothschilds would still profit in the build-ups. When war did occur, the countries would borrow whatever was required to keep their individual sovereignty. The distribution of the brothers allowed profits to be made out of any regional conflict in Europe. In the case of the war between France and Britain, and the specific battle of Waterloo in June 1815, it was a manipulation of misinformation that produced the desired result for the Rothschilds.

The family had already set up a communications network throughout Europe, linking each of the banking centers and each of the brothers. An army of couriers carried secret information in specially identified pouches, which border guards of various nations were ordered not to detain under any circumstances, even if the courier came from an enemy country currently at war. The speed with which these couriers transported information allowed the Rothschilds to act on news before the rest of the financial markets, and make money on both good and bad news. Other bankers were fully aware of this system and kept a careful eye on Rothschild activities in the markets as indicators of what was really happening. In the case of Waterloo, Nathan Rothschild put on a performance to his audience of fellow bond dealers in London. Receiving advance news that Napoleon had lost the battle, Nathan gave the impression that the Corsican despot had actually won. His apparent despair at receiving the bad news fooled the London dealers into offloading British government bonds, which Nathan's agents snapped up at greatly reduced values. When the official news eventually reached London of Wellington's victory, the bond prices jumped back up. Nathan was nowhere to be found as his fellow bankers realized that they had been duped.

Such a display of deception in order to make market prices move in the desired direction may be viewed as unethical and almost criminally fraudulent. But bankers are in the business of making money, and money can only be made if prices are actually moving. Hopes and fears are what move these prices. It doesn't matter what the currency, stock, or commodity is. Hopes produce speculative bubbles and fears are pushed aside as more and more investors pile into the bonanza. At some point the bubble bursts and fear dominates the market, producing panics and price crashes. These are naturally occurring cycles of indeterminate lengths—the so-called "boom and bust" phenomenon. Bankers are prey to the forces too, and losses are inevitable, yet there exist groups of bankers who seem to outsiders to have an inordinate amount of luck in trading markets of unfathomable dangers. Conspiracy theorists attribute this success over many generations to inside information and market manipulation. The apparent ability to move markets in any direction requires vast amounts of money. As the financial markets became larger and more diverse, banking groups and families had to operate together in secret agreement. For every winner, there has to be a loser. The long-term winners make the losers into short-term winners and let them believe that their short-term gains are going to continue. Then, the winners bail out and pull the plug. As short-term gains evaporate and turn into losses, the losers suffer so that the winners continue to win. When the bankers are acting on commission of sales, the conning of unwary investors can become rampant.

Banking on Power

There has been a constant fear among conspiracy theorists that democracy is always threatened by a central bank. None more so than the American Federal Reserve. Since the early days of the new republic, America has struggled with the need for one and, when it had one, wanted to destroy it.

The first Bank of the United States was chartered by Congress in 1791 for 20 years with a capital stock of $10 million, of which $2 million was to be held in gold. Twenty percent of the stock was held by the government and the remaining 80 percent was in private hands. Although members of Congress subscribed for about a third of the stock, there were conspiracy theories that the Bank of the United States was secretly in the hands of foreigners, especially the Bank of England.

Thomas Jefferson wrote: "The Central Bank is an institution of the most deadly hostility existing against the principles and form of our Constitution...If the American people allow private banks to control the issuance of their currency, first by inflation and then by deflation, the banks and corporations that will grow up around them will deprive the people of all their property until their children will wake up homeless on the continent their fathers conquered." Although empowered to repeal the charter, President Jefferson did not, but did sell the government's stake in the bank. When the charter was automatically up for renewal in 1811, it failed by a narrow margin. The next year saw the outbreak of war with the British.

The large number of state-chartered private banks, nearly 250 of them, soon led to a position where the bank notes in circulation were far in excess of the amount of gold or silver redeemable. As a result the second Bank of the United States was chartered in April 1816 for a period of 20 years, with a larger capital stock of $35 million, and, once again, the government held 20 percent. During the re-election year of President Andrew Jackson, in 1832, the president of the bank attempted to get the re-chartering done four years earlier than it was due, and this was a fatal mistake. Jackson saw the bank as a British conspiracy to control American financial markets and was not going to let an election year cloud his judgment. He vetoed the re-chartering and then withdrew all the government's deposits. It was a replay of the first Bank of the United States. Subsequent investigations carried out after its eventual demise failed to identify any foreign influence on the bank's operations.

Andrew Jackson had been anti-British since receiving a wound from an English officer while he was a teenager fighting in the Revolution. He had grown up with a distrust of financial institutions, having read all about the South Sea Bubble. In 1836 a speculative bubble developed in American land prices and Jackson tried to deflate it by passing the Specie Circular, which demanded that all payments for federal land be paid for in either gold or silver. It was believed that this resulted in the 1837 crash in land prices. Computer research on economic models in the 1960s put forward the theory that the land price bubble was independent of the Bank of the United States closure and the real culprit lay with the soaring imports of Mexican silver. When this supply dried up in 1837, the crash occurred.

The speculative bubble attracted the interest of the Rothschilds, and a representative, August Belmont, was sent over from Europe. He soon bought up American government bonds and wormed his way into the White House, eventually becoming Andrew Jackson's financial adviser. John Reeves, in his authorized biography, *The Rothschilds, the Financial Rulers of Nations*, details a secret meeting in London in 1857 at which the International Banking Syndicate decided to cause a civil war in America for the purposes of forcing the creation of yet another central bank. This is just the sort of meeting that conspiracy theorists yearn for. When civil wars are reduced to the level of foreign financiers making profits by stirring up internal unrest, the theories become almost like Greek myths. The financiers are the gods up on Olympus, and the heroes on Earth are just pawns in some game or wager. This imagery pervades the work of conspiracy theorist John Coleman with his Committee of 300. He even calls his international puppet masters "The Olympians." It may be blasphemous to give god-like qualities to these secret rulers of the world, but the timeline is not persuasive. The American Civil War started on April 12th, 1861, four years after the meeting of the Rothschilds in London. That would seem to suggest that the Civil War had causes other than filling a bank ledger. But then again, patience and long-term investments are often rewarded, and, continuing with the Greek myth analogy, the gods did leave the Greek soldiers on the beach outside Troy for ten years before allowing them to sack the city.

President Abraham Lincoln believed that there were conspiratorial forces behind the South: "Combinations too powerful to be suppressed by the ordinary machinery of peacetime government had assumed control of various Southern states." He was also resistant to the call for creating a central bank. Instead, Lincoln issued the "greenback" in February 1862, a currency banknote that had been created with no backing of gold, and using no borrowed funds. This Fiat money was a direct snub to the international bankers. A year later, Congress passed the National Banking Act, creating a federally chartered bank with the powers to issue US banknotes. In 1875, Congress passed another act, bringing to an end the Lincoln greenbacks, in the Specie Redemption Act, where by 1879 the currency would be redeemed in gold. In the meantime, Lincoln had been assassinated—the first US president to be so. Needless to say, there are conspiracy theories out there that accuse the Rothschilds, the prime one being Paul Goldstein's *The Rothschilds' International Plot to Kill Lincoln*, but there is very little to persuade the skeptics.

The Rothschild family was accused of making another attempt to force the creation of a privately owned central bank in America in 1907. Acting as their agent in this conspiracy theory was the American banker J.P. Morgan. After spending a few months in Europe, receiving Rothschild instructions, Morgan returned to the United States to precipitate a banking crisis. He started rumors that the Knickerbocker Bank in New York was insolvent. Such was his personal reputation on Wall Street that other investors believed him and there was a run on the bank, followed by similar runs on others. The Panic of 1907 raised serious doubts about the trustworthiness of the state-chartered banks. Once again, the call for a central bank emerged. Morgan's activities were also criticized, but an interesting scholar came to his defense, the president of Princeton University, Woodrow Wilson. For a future president of the United States, he made a very curious comment about J.P. Morgan: "All this trouble could be averted if we appointed a committee of six or seven public-spirited men like J.P. Morgan to handle the affairs of our country." But Morgan was the man responsible for initiating the panic: are we to believe that he exposed the insolvency of the Knickerbocker Bank out of public-spiritedness, or out of competitive financial greed?

The Federal Reserve Conspiracy

The creation of the Federal Reserve, America's central bank, was shrouded in secrecy right from the start, as if something illegal was going on. The individual senator who was selected by the bankers to introduce the legislation was Nelson Aldrich, the future maternal grandfather of Nelson and David Rockefeller. He was appointed head of a National Monetary Commission and spent two years touring the great banking houses of Europe, learning the secrets of operating a central bank. In November 1910 he returned to the United States and boarded a special train in Hoboken, New Jersey, for Jekyll Island, Georgia. Fellow passengers on board the train were Piatt Andrew, Assistant Secretary of the Treasury; Frank Vanderlip, president of Kuhn-Loeb's National City Bank of New York; Paul Warburg, partner in Kuhn-Loeb and Company; Henry Davidson, senior partner of J.P. Morgan; Benjamin Strong, president of Morgan's Banker's Trust Company; and Charles Norton, president of Morgan's First National Bank of New York. Their final destination was the Jekyll Island Hunt Club, owned by J.P. Morgan.

Vanderlip later wrote of the journey: "We were told to leave our last names behind us. We were told further that we should avoid dining together on the night of our departure. We were instructed to come one at a time and as unobtrusively as possible to the terminal of the New Jersey littoral of the Hudson, where Senator Aldrich's private car would be in readiness, attached to the rear end of the train for the South."

Was this over-zealous security arrangement by J.P. Morgan really necessary? Or was it just the eccentric paranoid behavior of a fabulously wealthy man? Why was the creation of a central bank so in need of great secrecy? The previous history of US banking outlined above certainly shows that there was a perennial fear of central banks and possible foreign influence. Either J.P. Morgan or the US government, or both, was aware that the public had to be kept in ignorance of Morgan's involvement in the drafting of the banking legislation. He had, after all, been responsible for the Panic of 1907. Such was the fear of the dreaded words "central bank" that the conspirators came up with the name "Federal Reserve System" as an alternative. It would be owned by private individuals who would derive their profits from the ownership of shares. They would control the issue of money for the United States and be able to mortgage the nation in times of war. In order to protect the Federal Reserve from the accusation of being a central bank, there would be 12 districts, all under the control of a single Federal Reserve chairman. This deception shows how deep-rooted the fears of a central bank really were.

With the legislation written not by legislators, but by bankers, it would still have to go through Congress. Its passage through the House and the Senate would be in vain if the incumbent president was willing to veto the bill. Unfortunately for the J.P. Morgan secret group, such a president was in office at the time: William Howard Taft. He had gone on record as saying he would veto any such bill if it were presented to him to sign. Taft had been elected in 1908, and all the signs were that he would be re-elected for a second term in 1912. Taft, it must be remembered, was a Skull and Bonesman. If that Yale secret society had any power, it was about to come head to head with J.P. Morgan.

The campaign against Taft was three-fold. The conspiracy tried to prevent him gaining the Republican nomination by supporting ex-President Teddy Roosevelt. When this failed, they supported the Democratic candidate, Woodrow Wilson, the very same president of Princeton who had defended Morgan's reputation after the Panic of 1907; the very same scholar who had recommended that "a committee of six or seven public-spirited men like J.P. Morgan" should be appointed "to handle the affairs of our country." Was it a coincidence that the Jekyll Island group consisted of seven men like J.P. Morgan: Aldrich, Andrew, Davidson, Norton, Strong, Vanderlip, and Warburg?

When it was realized that Wilson would not get enough votes to defeat Taft, the conspiracy urged Teddy Roosevelt to run against both Taft and Wilson as an independent. They hoped that Roosevelt would draw Republican votes away from Taft without damaging any of Wilson's figures. The political ploy worked, and Wilson won with 45 percent of the vote, Roosevelt beating Taft into third place. With Woodrow Wilson in the White House, the Federal Reserve Bill was duly signed and the central bank that America had so long resisted came into existence. Congressman Louis McFadden, chairman of the later House Committee on Banking and Currency, stated: "When the Federal Reserve Act was passed, the people of these United States did not perceive that a world banking system was being set up here. A super-state controlled by international bankers and industrialists...acting together to enslave the world...every effort has been made by the Fed to conceal its powers but the truth is the Fed has usurped the government."

Conspiracy theory has been defined by Frederic Jameson as "a poor man's cognitive mapping," implying that it shows the same grasp of realism as a poor man has of international banking. The above account of the history of the Federal Reserve is commonly found in conspiracy theory works, but is it prone to an amateurish grasp of history? The meeting on Jekyll Island, described so conspiratorially in G. Edward Griffin's 1995 *The Creature from Jekyll Island*, did take place, but the outcome of it is significantly different. The so-called Aldrich Plan, named after the senator, failed to be passed by the House of Representatives. The idea that bankers would control the Federal Reserve found great opposition within the Democratic Party. The Aldrich Plan needed to be adjusted to allow private ownership but public control. The president would appoint officials to the Federal Reserve Board. The concept of a central bank was to remove power away from the handful of banks that had previously controlled the financial markets. This was in stark contrast to the conspiracy theorists' beliefs that the whole aim of a central bank was to increase their power. Control of the nation's finances would come not through the central bank, but through influencing the chairman and the publicly appointed officials.

The "Colonel"

As Wilson celebrated his election victory by vacationing in Bermuda, he read an anonymous work entitled *Philip Dru: Administrator*. It was such an influential book that his administration reorganized the United States' financial structure in accordance with that described in it. Wilson's legislative program similarly followed that outlined in the book, and public interest in finding out the real identity of its author continued into 1917.

Published in 1912, *Philip Dru* was a futuristic novel, set in 1925, and described the actions of a West Point graduate who leads a coup d'état against an oppressive American government by gaining control of both the Republican and Democratic parties and using them to create a socialist one-world government "as dreamed of by Karl Marx." In a violent civil war, Dru seizes control and installs himself as the "Administrator," a totalitarian dictator. The book was full of political, economic, and social policies that Woodrow Wilson subsequently adopted as his own. Dru created a central bank and introduced graduated income tax. One of the most startling influences was Philip Dru's creation of a "League of Nations." This would become one of Wilson's greatest political aims.

In 1918, Wilson's Secretary of the Interior, Franklin Lane, stated: "All that book has said should be, comes about." By then, the anonymous author had been exposed—it was Wilson's closest adviser, Colonel Edward Mandell House. He had written the book in the winter of 1911–12 and sent a copy to the future Wilson cabinet member David Houston. The economic principles in the novel were sound, but Houston recommended that the ideas would be better presented in a serious scholarly work. House ignored Houston's advice and published in 1912, using the popular socialist publisher B.W. Huebsch.

"Colonel" House held no military rank, but was extremely well connected with the financial giants of Wall Street and Europe. His father had been an agent for the Rothschilds' London branch. House was the "guardian angel of the Federal Reserve Bill" who acted as liaison between the J.P. Morgan group and Woodrow Wilson. His influence over Wilson was profound, and his influence over the bankers was more so. His ideals impressed the Rockefellers, the Schiffs, the Warburgs, and the Kuhns. He was once described by Jacob Schiff as the "Moses to their Aarons." His vision of a one-world government would become enshrined in a secret society of his own making. His disciples would be responsible for the creation of the United Nations...

Secret Bank Accounts

The creation of the Federal Reserve was not just a conspiracy theory; it was a conspiracy fact. Secrecy and banking go together, and the whole Swiss banking industry was built upon the anonymity it provided its clients. It was only natural that the secrecy offered safe havens for money made in criminal ventures. The financing and profits of the illegal trade in drugs, or weapons banned by international embargo, would be routed through banks that asked no questions. Since 9/11 there have been international attempts to tackle the financing of terrorism. As an acid test for the secret rulers of the world, their power to halt terrorist funding would confirm or deny the claims of the conspiracy theorists. For the US government to enter the secret world of terrorist funding and block its functions, it would have to know how the system actually works. As the following few examples show, the US government has had relatively recent experience in the shadowy banking of the criminal underworld. Lessons learned from tackling drug money transfers and other illegal activities are now being applied to dealing with the money flow of al-Qaeda.

During its brief existence, the League of Nations prohibited opium and cocaine products from being sold legally. This prohibition drove those commodities underground and created a clandestine banking network to deal with the enormous amounts of money involved. In 1944, the Bretton Woods agreement established a currency system whereby fixed exchange rates were based on the US dollar. By 1971, President Nixon decided to devalue the dollar, and brought the Bretton Woods agreement to an end. It was also seen by some as the end of the period when America ruled the financial world. With the opportunities for foreign banks to invest wherever they liked in a free, unregulated market, tax havens were set up which attracted criminal funds. They provided strict secrecy, and charged practically no taxes.

During the Cold War period, the major opium-growing regions of the world became strategically important enough to force unethical alliances between the United States and the local drug lords. Criminal activities were ignored by the US authorities if the political support of the drug lords aided the regional fights against Communism. Examples are the covert military action in Laos in the 1960s and 1970s, and Afghanistan during the Soviet occupation in the 1980s. It was one thing for the US to ignore those criminal activities; it was a completely different matter to aid in those same criminal activities. The CIA would give assistance in the transportation of drug harvests to market. With the drug lords being the only effective guerrilla leaders in the combat zones, the United States felt compelled to support these undesirables. Various branches of the US government would be on opposite sides of the law. The Drug Enforcement Agency would be blocked from investigating certain criminals and their drug syndicates because the CIA had them as assets in the war against Communism.

In the late 1970s, the American Internal Revenue Service (IRS) investigated the financial activities of a bank based in Nassau which had been set up by a retired CIA operative named Paul Helliwell. Castle Bank had branches throughout Latin America which offered his former employers the opportunities to make secret money transactions through a "friendly" bank. Other clients sought out Castle's skills in tax-evasion. Two mentioned in the customer list were porn magnates Hugh Hefner of *Playboy* and Bob Guccione of *Penthouse*. When the IRS started its investigations of suspected money laundering, the CIA blocked them. What could have become the biggest case of tax-evasion in history was thwarted by the invocation of national security. The CIA was using Castle Bank as a conduit for funding clandestine operations against Cuba and Latin America. Castle Bank collapsed, only to be replaced by an

Australian bank named Nugan-Hand, which took over some of the Latin American and European networks developed by Castle.

Nugan-Hand in the Till

The two founders who gave their name to the bank were an unlikely pair. Frank Nugan was a small-time, incompetent Australian lawyer, and Michael John Hand was a US Green Beret who had served in Laos as a CIA contract operative, advising the Hmong guerrillas in the north of the country. While operating out of Vientaine, Hand became friends with the local CIA station chief, Theodore Shackley, and his deputy, Thomas Clines. It was later revealed by Professor Alfred McCoy in his landmark 1972 *The Politics of Heroin: CIA Complicity in the Drug Trade* that the CIA's very own airline Air America (founded by Paul Helliwell) was flying Hmong opium shipments to market. This supposedly secret operation was just a continuation of what the French secret service, the Service de Documentation Extérieure et du Contre-Espionage (SDECE), had been doing when France had controlled the Indo-China drug trade up until the military defeat at Dien Bien Phu in 1954. Not that that justifies the action in the slightest, but there was a definite sense that covert control of the drug distribution was a political tool against Communism. Hand brought no banking experience to the relationship with Nugan, just intelligence and criminal contacts.

In 1973, Nugan-Hand Limited was formed through a straightforward banking fraud. With just $5 in paid-up capital and only $80 in the company's bank account, Nugan wrote his company a personal check for a staggering $980,000 to purchase 490,000 shares of its own stock. Utilizing the banking delay in clearing checks, Nugan wrote himself a company check for exactly the same amount. The transaction would appear in the company accounts as "proof" that the company had a paid-up capital of nearly $1 million. Further deception required that the bank have expensive offices, which it acquired at 55 Macquarie Street in the heart of Sydney's business district. Utilizing the part-time services of a reputable money market manager, a large volume of transactions gave the false impression that the bank was a busy one. On $2.4 million worth of transactions, the bank incurred a loss of over $18,000. Making a legitimate profit in any way seemed to be an impossible task. By 1976, the bank claimed to have assets of $22 million, and also claimed to be part of the Nugan-Hand Group with worldwide turnover of US$1 billion per annum. All these claims were false. Money was moving through the Nugan-Hand bank, in large amounts, but it was all illegal.

As Nugan concentrated on bank fraud and money-laundering for Australian crime lords, Hand re-entered the secret world of CIA operations. He opened up an office in Pretoria, South Africa, and handled the "private" shipments of arms and ammunition for the anti-communist guerrilla forces in Angola. When the CIA covert operation folded in Angola, Hand moved to Hong Kong to run the newly chartered Nugan-Hand Bank, registered in the British colonial tax-haven of the Cayman Islands. What makes its criminal business fit into the conspiracy theorists' universe is the make-up of its board of directors. Hand managed to recruit Admiral Earl Yates, retired chief strategist for the US Pacific Command, as the president of Nugan-Hand Bank; General Leroy Manor, former counter-insurgency specialist at the Pentagon; General Edwin Black, former OSS officer and commander of US forces in Thailand; Dale Holmgren, former chairman of the CIA's airline, Civil Air Transport; and most extraordinary of all, former CIA Director William Colby as the bank's legal counsel. With the demise of the Castle Bank in Nassau, Hand saw the chance to take over the role of the CIA's banker. The granting of the Cayman Island charter was certainly fortuitous.

With William Colby drawing up the legal contract, Hand used the bank's money to buy a former US naval base in the Turks and Caicos Islands in the Caribbean as a probable way-station for cocaine smuggling between Columbia and the United States. That was the likely purpose, according to the Australian banking investigators who started looking into the secret activities of the bank. Nugan-Hand was soon found to have handled $4.3 million in identifiable drug deals between 1976 and 1980.

On January 27th, 1980, Frank Nugan was found dead in his

locked car by the side of a road outside Sydney. He had apparently shot himself in the head with a rifle. Police found a calling card from William Colby in his wallet. Within six months the Nugan-Hand Bank collapsed. In true conspiracy theory style, Michael John Hand was exfiltrated from Australia by none other than former CIA officer, Thomas Clines. Safely hidden away from the Australian police and banking investigators, Hand has not resurfaced.

What are we to make of all this? After successful careers in the CIA and other elements of the US intelligence community, do retired spooks all gravitate to a life of crime? With no real experience of banking, they still become directors on the boards. What exactly are they bringing to the long table? Years of experience of clandestine operations in which criminals and murderers are allies and drugs are nothing more than a commodity? It is easily conceivable that a tolerance to drug-dealing had built up in the characters of these men. These retired officers were experts in the art of corruption. Acting as case officers, they recruited foreign assets through criminal activities: sexual entrapment, bribery, and blackmail. These are all perceived as moral activities when the greater good dictates. The enemies were viewed as evil and, sometimes, a greater evil was required to defeat them. With Soviet Communism vanquished, a new enemy emerged in Afghanistan—the very same Mujahadeen who took their liberation from the Soviets to bring in the Taliban with its extreme militant Islam and faith in terrorism.

Bank of Crooks and Criminals International

Just as the Nugan-Hand Bank took up the torch from the dying Castle Bank, so another took it from Nugan-Hand. This was the BCCI, the Bank of Credit and Commerce International—or, as it became known in the CIA, the Bank of Crooks and Criminals International. In 1972, Bank of America, then the world's largest bank, wanted to expand its international division. It chose to invest $2.5 million to acquire a 25 percent stake in a new bank set up by

Pakistani financier Agha Hasan Abedi. Bank of America was not deterred by the fact that Abedi had just been put under house arrest after his recently nationalized United Bank showed evidence of fraud. Abedi brushed this aside and succeeded in raising the rest of the BCCI finance from Arab rulers such as Sheik Zayed bin Sultan al-Nayan of Abu Dhabi and Saudi officials such as the former chief of Saudi Arabia's intelligence service, Kamal Adham, and the bin Mahfouz family who controlled Saudi Arabia's largest bank. From this relatively small start of $10 million, over the next 18 years BCCI grew into a $21 billion bank with over 400 branches in over 75 countries and 1.2 million customers.

On July 5th, 1991, a team of bank regulators from several countries shut down BCCI and charged the top executives with stealing as much as $15 billion from the bank's deposit accounts.

Like other shady banks before it, BCCI had difficulty making profits legally. Between 1979 and 1986, BCCI lost $849 million trading US Treasury bonds. BCCI also would give loans to its directors that would never be repaid. An example is the total of $313 million lent to Sheik Kamal Adham. According to the *Washington Post*, Kamal was the CIA's "liaison man" in the Middle East. In the late 1960s he acted as the CIA's intermediary for payments to Vice President Anwar Sadat of Egypt. Hundreds of millions of dollars flowed into Egypt after Sadat took power. Is it any wonder that Sadat expelled the Soviet military advisers in 1973?

BCCI was able to con respectable international institutions into using its services to deal with the Third World debt crises. Under a scheme promoted by the IMF, the World Bank and the United States, a debtor country would agree to honor its debts in full if a debt-purchaser would invest the money repaid in the debtor country or buy a company that the country was trying to sell. According to Jack Blum, a former counsel for the Senate Subcommittee on investigating the BCCI scandal, an example of such a financial scam was the case in Argentina. In the late 1980s, BCCI bought some of Argentina's debt for an unknown discount, though thought to be 79 cents in the dollar. BCCI bought the Argentine debt for $30 million and, under the IMF scheme, sold it back to Argentina for $38 million, making $8 million legally. BCCI was then supposed to use the entire $38 million to purchase Argentine assets. It announced its intention to invest the $38 million in a hotel and farm, but actually spent only $10 million and kept the rest. One can see how BCCI contributed to the downward spiral of the Argentine economy that contributed to its historic debt default.

BCCI was not only plundering Third World banks, but attempted to do the same in America. In 1977, BCCI launched a hostile bid for the largest bank in Washington DC, Financial General Bankshares. The US Securities and Exchange Commission (SEC) launched an investigation and uncovered widespread corruption within the private investors being used by the bank as front men for the deal. Such a history of corporate bribery scandals would normally have disqualified these investors from handling any federally insured deposits. BCCI employed the considerable legal talents of Clark Clifford, former Secretary of Defense and adviser to four presidents, to convince the Fed to give the deal its approval, on condition that BCCI did not try to control the bank. Similar acquisitions of a controlling interest in the National Bank of Georgia and the Independence Bank of Encino, and a minority stake in CenTrust, were carried out for wealthy Arabs, but the real investor was BCCI, using complex financial maneuvers through offshore tax havens. As an example, Ghaith Pharaon, a BCCI front man and the person responsible for the Argentine debt fraud mentioned above, was loaned $220 million by Financial General Bankshares, now called First American Bankshares, so that he could purchase shares in the National Georgia Bank.

With the whole deregulation of financial markets, securities firms were becoming banks and vice versa. Savings and Loans associations were allowed to speculate in the commercial real estate market—with disastrous results. When the property bubble burst and the market crashed, many investors went bankrupt. One of those was John Connally, the former governor of Texas who had been shot by Lee Harvey Oswald as he rode in Dealey Plaza with President Kennedy on November 22nd, 1963. In the late 1970s he owned a Texan bank with none other than BCCI front man Ghaith

Pharaon. Through him he met fellow BCCI shareholders, the bin Mahfouz family, the owners of the largest bank in Saudi Arabia. In this secret world of conspiracy, Connally then introduced Pharaon and the bin Mahfouz family to the infamous Hunt brothers of Texas. Pooling their immense financial resources, the group attempted to corner the world's silver market. The illegal manipulation failed and all parties lost heavily. The Hunt brothers lost their $10 billion fortune. Connally's personal bankruptcy during the property crash shows that even a former US Secretary to the Treasury had no idea about how speculative markets work.

Surely the best example of blowing bubbles was in the so-called "junk bonds" market. The Federal Deposit Insurance Corporation (FDIC) filed a $6.8 billion suit against BCCI-linked CenTrust and other Savings and Loans who operated "illegal and secretive trading activities." The junk bond dealers of the group would trade between themselves, creating a false impression that the junk bond market was very liquid and growing in volume. The market was totally bogus, with artificial prices to attract unwary investors. When the bubble burst, it cost US taxpayers $6 billion in insurance claims; thus the FDIC lawsuit.

The examples above are pure financial crimes, but the deregulation of the markets also allowed ordinary criminals to launder their ill-gotten gains through the new offshore havens. Since the Bank Secrecy Act of 1970, the United States has made it a criminal act to handle drug money. Panamanian dictator Manuel Noriega set up a $25 million account with BCCI, using his kickbacks from the Medellin drug cartel. It is believed that Noriega eventually laundered at least $90 million through BCCI. No wonder the bank issued him credit cards for both his wife and mistress and took him on $100,000 shopping sprees in New York. The US House Banking Committee investigating BCCI estimated that over $1 billion of Medellin drug money was laundered through the bank in the 1980s.

The CIA took advantage of the offshore banks. It allowed them to fund covert action operations outside the Congressional oversight and appropriations committees. This produced a foreign policy capability that could be carried out by the White House independently of Congress and against the American public's wishes. Such an example was the Iran-Contra affair, with its support of the White House-backed Contra rebels, in defiance of Congress legislation refusing aid. Jose Blandon, a former Noriega aide, admitted that the CIA advised the Panamanian dictator to use BCCI as his bank. The agency was depositing as much as $200,000 a year in Noriega's BCCI account. In return, Noriega assisted Oliver North in the setting up of dummy corporations and secret bank accounts to fund the Contra rebels. BCCI provided the finance for the clandestine arms shipments from Israel to the Contras and the allied weapons transfers to the Iranians in return for the release of US hostages.

BCCI's status as the CIA's banker increased with the war in Afghanistan between the Mujahadeen rebels and the Soviet armies of occupation. The founder of BCCI, Agha Hasan Abedi, had strong links with the Pakistani military and intelligence officials, and his bank was the obvious choice to handle the immense transfer of US dollars into the region. Since Afghanistan was a major producer of opium, the CIA operations would run along the lines of the previous covert operation in Laos: the agency would aid the drug lords of Afghanistan in their shipment of opium in return for their continued fight against the Soviet forces. The Saudis matched the CIA dollar for dollar, and within that complex alliance stood Osama bin Laden, a future source of trouble to both. The fight against the Soviet Red Army was a jihad—a holy war. With the removal of the Soviets, the new government of Afghanistan became controlled by the Taliban, Islamic scholars flooding in from Pakistan, bent on establishing a true theocracy. America rejoiced in the defeat of the Soviets and the success of the biggest, most expensive covert war in CIA history. The United States moved its attention away from Afghanistan and set its sights on Iraq, allowing bin Laden to build up his power base, al-Qaeda.

Bankrolling Saddam

During the ten-year war between Iraq and Iran, the latter's anti-Americanism and the embarrassment of the hostage-taking in

Tehran at the end of the 1970s led US secret foreign policy to finan-cially support Saddam Hussein's Iraqi war machine. Although a trade embargo was in existence, the CIA arranged to provide weapons to Iraq through typically devious routes. Money was loaned to Saddam so that he could illegally buy the arms. The source of this secret funding was Italy's largest bank, the Banca Nazionale del Lavoro (BNL), which channeled the cash through its Atlanta, Georgia, branch. Between 1985 and 1989, BNL loaned over $4 billion to Iraq. Some of that money came from BCCI, via Bank of America. Harking back to the old days, J.P. Morgan (the New York bank, not the man) acted as the clearing agent for the BNL loans to Iraq.

As with most Cold War alliances that the US engaged in, the sands of time would often blow up into a sandstorm that produced a radically different landscape within a few years. This is no more so than the case with Iraq. From backing the weapons build-up of Saddam Hussein during the war with his militant Islamic neighbor Iran, the US soon found itself waging war against Iraq. The pattern would be repeated later with Afghanistan.

In 1989, an FBI raid on the BNL offices in Atlanta found evidence of the "off-books" lending operations to Iraq since 1987. The records of the secret transactions were kept in separate account-ancy books where the money laundering was euphemistically called "commodities financing." The US Department of Agriculture offered short-term credit guarantees through its Foreign Agricultural Service, and Iraq was abusing this system. It falsified the amounts and types of agricultural commodities it was purchasing. Once Iraq invaded Kuwait in 1990, all the agricultural loans to Iraq were stopped.

Congress launched a House committee investigation under the leadership of Representative Henry Gonzalez (Democrat, Texas). BNL had made over $3 billion in unauthorized loans to Iraq. For political reasons at the Justice Department, the blame was put squarely on the BNL local office in Atlanta and not on the BNL headquarters in Rome. The reason for this was the fact that 96 per-cent of BNL was owned by the Italian government. Representative Gonzalez discovered that his requests for information from the CIA were blocked by the attorney general on the well-trodden grounds of national security.

It was claimed that the suicide of the former Italian military attaché to Iraq was directly related to the BNL scandal. There were also rumors that the collapse of the Italian ambassador in Iraq was due to stress over the truth behind the BNL links. A CIA report contradicted the Justice Department's theory that the whole corrupt affair was a rogue operation carried out by the BNL branch in Atlanta, totally behind the back of its Rome head office. Yet this report was suppressed. As Iraqi tanks thundered across the border into Kuwait, diplomatic pressures forced the case to be pushed aside. The new government of Prime Minister Andreotti was rocked by the scandal and, after the resignation of the chairman and vice chairman of the Rome head office, American damage control was requested by the Italians. And that was exactly what the US Justice Department did.

Gonzalez viewed the whole indictment as a whitewash. CIA evidence showing Italian knowledge of the deals with Iraq, and authorization of higher valued loans, was ignored and the Atlanta branch was blamed for a rogue operation. American taxpayers had to cover the losses through the insurance payouts. The diplomatic relationship between the United States and one of its allies, Italy, was worth far more than the $3 billion loss.

When the conspiracy theorists look for corruption in cover-ups, the BNL case is relatively simple. The United States covertly armed Saddam Hussein during his war with Iran, because he was the "lesser of two evils" and there was a far stronger hatred of the Iranians. When Saddam became the number one enemy of the United States, it was obvious that previous dealings with him would become politically embarrassing. The invasion of Kuwait would have to be responded to with force from a coalition of countries. The Italian government was in a weak state and the BNL scandal had erupted when Andreotti had been in office for only three months. With the parallel BCCI scandal, and the links between the two banks, taking place in the United States (in fact, in the same city, Atlanta), it was only reasonable to let the BNL Atlanta branch take all the heat. The attorney general of the United States showed all concerned where the power lay.

When the Reagan and Bush administrations were deeply involved in covert action against the communist threat, they used the secretive banking channels to fund the operations without Senate approval. The Iran-Contra scandal and the BCCI collapse brought out into the open the White House's willingness to deal with criminals and dictators. The fight against the USSR was won during this period, and the disintegration of the enemy empire could be seen as ultimate justification for the immoral acts carried out to bring it about.

The Third World is notoriously corrupt. Foreign aid goes through the greedy hands of the ruling elites and never reaches the people it is meant for. The deregulated financial markets opened up the markets to unbelievable criminal opportunities. The sheer scale of the frauds and thefts, running into billions of dollars, makes one wonder if there are any good guys out there. The profits of these banks are derived solely from criminal activities. Time and time again, when they try to operate legally, they incur enormous losses. Although the answer may be simplistic, perhaps ordinary, law-abiding investors should avoid offshore banks and therefore reduce their exposure to criminal elements. If they keep their hard-earned funds in respectable banks, and pay their due taxes, then the only investors placing funds offshore will be the criminally inclined. If the directors of the banks disappear with their money, then that's the dog-eat-dog world of crime.

The problem is that the players in these offshore banks were the fabulously wealthy Arabs of the Middle East, and their oilfields were, and still are, of strategic importance to the greatest oil-consumer in the world, the United States. Allowing rich Arabs to steal funds out of a whole plethora of shady banks was the price the United States was willing to pay in order to maintain cordial relations with the powerful men in robes who sat upon the majority of the world's oil supply. But what happens when a whole country is doing the stealing?

Don't Cry for Me, Argentina

In the 1990s, Argentina was being touted on Wall Street as one of the world's hottest economies. Investment bankers, fund managers, and brokers were advising their clients to invest heavily in the second largest economy in Latin America, buying up Argentine stocks and government bonds "like there was no tomorrow." How dangerously close that phrase came to being true. It has been estimated that over the decade 1991–2001, nearly $1 billion in fees went to Wall Street firms involved in underwriting the government bonds. Extremely bullish reports were produced by those same firms' analysts, and Argentina became yet another bubble like Enron Corp and WorldCom Inc, sucking in foreign investors with no clue as to the inherent nature of bubbles—they always burst.

As foreign interest developed into over-enthusiasm, the Argentine government continued to issue more and more bonds, increasing its debt levels to over $100 billion. The government of President Carlos Menem had introduced reforms into the previously stagnant economy, deregulating it and privatizing former inefficiently state-run enterprises. Bouts of hyperinflation and frequent currency devaluations appeared to be a thing of the past as the Argentine economy grew. One of the key reasons was the decision to fix the exchange rate between the peso and the mighty dollar. Set at parity, the stability that this afforded allowed Argentine manufacturers, businessmen, and consumers to become confident for the first time in several generations. As the economy produced an impressive growth rate from the mid-1990s, Wall Street analysts started to heavily promote the Argentine market to private investors. All the major Wall Street firms sent down sales teams to Buenos Aires, and each new bond issue was eagerly grabbed.

With the banking crises in Asia and Russia causing fund managers in those zones to be twiddling their thumbs, Argentina became the top-priority location for making money hand over fist. Its rise to dominance of the emerging markets sector was apparently based on sounder economics than the rest. It was not thought of in the same category as the Asian countries or Russia, whose respective meltdowns should have rung alarm bells. Yet its level of debt, which had stood at 29 percent of gross domestic product (GDP) in 1993, had leapt to 41 percent by 1998. Argentina's only hope of surviving the inevitable was if the world's investors continued to have faith in the government's ability to service its debt and did not start dumping the country's peso.

There is a belief that the world's markets are self-regulatory, in an almost biological way akin to homeostasis. If a country does not deserve foreign investment, the free flow of globalized funds will not be drawn into it. There has to be a natural attractiveness based on prudent economic principles for money to flow in. That's the theory anyway. But in reality, money often gets pumped in for short-term profits. The owners of the money are purchasing far from short-term government bonds, for many are of 20-year duration, but the brokers who buy and sell on commission are doing it for the fast buck.

When the neighboring country of Brazil had a financial crisis in 1999, the knock-on effect sent the Argentine economy into recession. Doubts were starting to be raised about Argentina's ability to service its debt repayments, but Wall Street sought fresh sources of funding outside the United States, in parts of Europe where legislation protecting the small investor was not so strict as in America. Almost $24 billion of Argentine government bonds were sold to wrongly advised clients. As Argentina's economy went into a downward spiral of recession and its debt burden reached 50 percent of its GDP, the only thing keeping its head above water was this infusion of new investor money. In November 2000, the cabinet of President Fernando de la Rua (who had replaced Carlos Menem as leader in 1999) was torn apart as interest rates rocketed in a futile attempt to stem the flood of money leaving the country. The International Monetary Fund provided a $14 billion loan to Argentina, but this was quickly absorbed to no avail. The markets rallied briefly then quickly resumed their downward spiral.

Wall Street came up with a "debt swap" deal whereby Argentine debt-holders would be given the opportunity to swap their short-dated bonds, which were unlikely to be honored, with longer-dated ones. This would, in effect, give Argentina some breathing space to try and get its economy back in order. Although there was a great deal of skepticism that it would work, $30 billion worth of new bonds were swapped, and the seven Wall Street banks involved earned themselves a cool $100 million in fees. Before they could finish congratulating themselves, the Argentine markets resumed their freefall, and even a second IMF loan had no effect. In a desperate attempt to stop the outflow of cash, Argentine authorities shut down the banks, and this led to riots in the streets and the resignation of the de la Rua government in December 2001. The new president, Eduardo Duhalde, declared default and abandoned the fixed peso–dollar exchange rate. For several weeks the entire banking system was shut down and trading in the peso was halted.

It was the largest sovereign default in history but, because of its timing, world attention was diverted to the aftermath of 9/11. Argentina's problems were caused by over-aggressive selling of its government bonds. There are concerns that "banking improprieties" of banks such as the world's largest, Citigroup, contributed to the bubble, just as that bank contributed to the Enron and WorldCom bubbles. If Citigroup is one of the secret rulers of the world, one would have expected it to have escaped a bloody nose from the affair, but it had to write off about $2 billion in bad debts.

Three years after the default, Argentina offered to restructure the $100 billion debt by swapping the old debt for a new one at a loss of up to 70 cents on the dollar. Over two-thirds of the 700,000 bondholders were required to accept in order to make it happen. This majority was easily reached, and Argentina pulled off one of the most amazing financial deals in banking history. For once, a debtor was able to dictate terms to its creditors.

Where does this event, combined with the original default, fit within the conspiracy theorists' view of how the banking world is run? On a simplistic level, Argentina had conned foreign banks out of at least $70 billion. It is the biggest bank robbery in history. The IMF had always refused to accept any attempt by Argentina to pay off only a small proportion of its debt. Its enforced economic policies were viewed by Argentina as too strict for their economy to handle. It could pay only what it could afford to pay. Simple, real-life accountancy. The majority of creditors were willing to gain at least some chance of getting repaid some of what they were owed. Argentina's break with the dollar, a massive recovery in its domestic stock market, and general expansion of the world economy has allowed Argentine exports to compete in the world marketplaces.

The IMF faces a worrying future as the Argentine decision to do a private deal with its creditors, and appear to get away with it, might give similar ideas to other countries with heavy debt burdens. The whole world of international finance may be about to enter a new world disorder.

Terrorist Finance

Everyone seems to be hiding their money. Instead of under the bed, it's under the regulatory radar in offshore accounts. The interest rates offered for their deposits are almost as bad as that offered under the bed. Yet it is not interest rates that concern the depositors, but the secrecy of the accounts. The funds are either ill-gotten gains or are to be used for illegal activities. The United States has plenty of experience operating in this shadowy environment. Its covert operations around the world were often authorized without Senate approval, and therefore required independent financial resources. As we have seen, when the war against drugs was declared, the United States used some of the same assets it had used against Communism to disrupt the supply. Measures were taken to block the funding of the trade and sequester the bank accounts of known cartels. When 9/11 brought al-Qaeda to the fore-front of American concerns about the make-up of the new world order, anti-drug financing operations were upgraded to become anti-terrorist financing operations.

Al-Qaeda has four main sources of finance: the personal wealth of Osama bin Laden, direct funding from al-Qaeda supporters, contributions from Islamic charities, and profits from criminal activities. Bin Laden is said to have inherited between $250 million and $300 million from his Saudi family in the early 1990s. Up to 9/11 it was invested in bank accounts and businesses throughout the world. Arab financiers of al-Qaeda are thought to supply about $16 million annually. Islamic charities are big business. They raise billions of dollars each year because of *zakat*, the Islamic duty to make charitable contributions. How much of this is transferred to al-Qaeda is unknown, and the religious nature of the charities makes outside investigation a sensitive subject. Criminal activities involving the prime cash crop of Afghanistan, opium, would have provided millions to the revenue of al-Qaeda.

Since 9/11 more than 150 countries have joined in the international fight against terrorism, and blocked terrorist finances. President George W. Bush signed Executive Order 13224 and the United Nations Security Council passed Resolutions 1363 and 1390 to enforce greater powers to tackle the problem. About $112 million in assets were frozen worldwide, with $34 million of those within the United States. Through Operation Green Quest, the US shut down several American-based Islamic charities found to have links with al-Qaeda. Although action was taken swiftly against sources of finance in the US and its allied nations, the money moved fast out of reach into zones of the financial world where there is apparently no respect for international law. The Gulf States are particularly guilty of this. Despite signing agreements on tackling money laundering and terrorist financing, such as recommended by the Financial Action Task Force (FATF), some of these oil-rich states have refused to accept that Islamic charities are funding al-Qaeda and are failing to track funds known to be involved.

When terrorists are blocked in one country, they will always find another desperate or corrupt enough to accept their money. Some of the Third World banks do not have sufficient regulation to monitor illegal activities even if they so desired. The *hawala* system, from the Hindi word meaning "in trust," involves unwritten credit arrangements, and this form of underworld finance is rife throughout the Islamic world. When no paperwork exists, there is no paper trail for investigators to follow. The US has attempted to clamp down on domestic *hawalas* by forcing them to register as money service businesses. They would be legally bound to report suspected cases of money laundering to federal authorities. Attempts to introduce similar restraints on the *hawala* system internationally have met with great resistance.

Al-Qaeda's response to these worldwide attempts to block its flow of money has been to decentralize and economize on the costs of operations. It has been estimated that the 9/11 attacks cost only about $500,000. Smaller-scale terrorist attacks will be harder to anticipate from the study of money transfers. Whereas in the past, when terrorism was state-sponsored, the financing would be relatively simple, 9/11 brought in a new world order of terrorism itself. Al-Qaeda was found to be privately funded. Its sanctuary in Afghanistan, protected by the Taliban regime, was swiftly destroyed, but its worldwide network still exists, and at the time of writing, Osama bin Laden is still on the run. The overall amounts of sequestered funds have topped $100 million, but what this represents as a percentage of the financial resources of al-Qaeda is unknown. The initial successes in destroying the financing network have been replaced with legal problems over extending the control to parts of the world where the enemy is likely to be hiding. One has to hope that the United States and its allies who are the targets of al-Qaeda are using the same clandestine methods of the last few decades mentioned earlier in this chapter, to disrupt and corrupt the financing of terrorism from within. That would be the true sign of the secret rulers of the world at work.

All terrorist organizations are prone to fragmentation and ultimate disintegration caused by suspicions, paranoia, and infighting. Earlier evidence has shown how massive amounts of money go missing in the international banking system through the corruptness of financiers. It is most likely that al-Qaeda itself suffers from missing funds. The secret rulers of the world know full well that the best way of destroying the financing of terror is not to officially seize assets and freeze accounts, but to steal the money instead.

With the US Department of Justice estimating between $500 billion and $1 trillion circulating the world's financial system as dirty money, the secret rulers have an impossible task of controlling it. This does not mean that there is no "new world order" in banking—

only that the controllers have to exert their power through monitoring the transactions. Through software such as PROMIS, developed by the NSA to apply its ECHELON surveillance technology to the financial markets (see Chapter Three), secret flows of money can be tracked and criminal prosecutions secured when necessary. Financial intelligence picks up on insider trading and old familiar scenarios are replayed. A recent example was the case of former Deutschebank executive Kevin Ingram, who pleaded guilty to conspiracy in 2001 to launder $2.2 million of drug money and arranging secret arms sales to Pakistan and Afghanistan. Deutschebank was also involved in the Pakistani and Afghan opium smuggling operations of former CIA ally, Pakistani intelligence chief Brig Imtiaz, who was jailed for eight years less than two months before 9/11. The same bank was chiefly responsible for the pre-attack put-options taken out on United Airlines and American Airlines, which jumped in value as their prices plummeted after the attack. The monitoring of the markets did not need to be extremely sensitive, since the volume in trades on the airlines' parent companies soared way beyond normal levels. In the case of United Airlines' parent UAL Corp, the volume of put-options bought just before the attack surged by 285 times the average! Ironically, all records of the US branch of Deutschebank were destroyed as the Twin Towers collapsed. But Deutschebank is a global bank. It held the personal accounts of the bin Laden family, and, with a former president of the US branch now serving as the number three man in the CIA, one would assume that the secret rulers are keeping a close eye on the bank and its transactions.

Chapter Three: All-seeing Eyes

On May 16th, 1973, President Richard Nixon was up to his neck in trouble. The Watergate scandal had broken and the new White House aide for internal security, John Dean, had recently defected with a gift to the prosecution. It was a secret report authorizing the illegal domestic surveillance of US citizens known as the Huston Plan, and Dean was obviously using it as a bargaining chip in his quest for immunity. Nixon summoned his lawyer, J. Fred Buzhardt, to the Oval Office and asked him straight:

"What in the name of God is this? Why do you think he's played this game?"

"I have no idea, Mr. President, but we have managed to identify from his remarks—I have found a copy of this thing, at NSA...Now, I'm fairly sure NSA..."

From the taped evidence, Nixon then interrupted and said: "What is the NSA?"

After more than four years in office, President Nixon had no idea what the NSA was. If ever there was a testament to the reasons why the NSA was known as "No Such Agency," it would have to be Nixon's comment recorded on his infamous tapes. Nixon was under a lot of stress, and selective memory loss may have been an advantage considering the Watergate prosecutions, but he may very well have had no real idea what the NSA was. He did, after all, go on to ask Buzhardt: "What kind of action do they do?"

"I don't know the specifics," replied Buzhardt. "They pick up communications stuff."

Nixon had completely forgotten a meeting nearly three years

before in the Oval Office, which the then director of the NSA, Vice Admiral Noel Gayler, had attended with DIA Director Lieutenant General Donald V. Bennett, CIA Director Richard Helms, and FBI Director J. Edgar Hoover. With a preponderance of three-letter abbreviations, perhaps Nixon was confused as to who was who. The Central Intelligence Agency (CIA) and the Federal Bureau of Investigation (FBI) were well known to most American citizens by then. The Defense Intelligence Agency (DIA) and the National Security Agency (NSA) were part of the Pentagon intelligence structure and therefore relatively unknown to anyone outside of uniform. The group of government spy chiefs had been called into the Oval Office to bear the brunt of Nixon's anger over domestic opposition to the Vietnam war. Not enough resources were being allocated to the collection of intelligence on the revolutionary groups involved in the protests. Of the four intelligence organizations present, only one was officially authorized to carry out domestic civilian surveillance, and that was the FBI. Nixon's request that they all band together to spy on the dissidents opened up the other three to a radical change in their operational parameters. The NSA and the CIA were being asked to conduct surveillance operations within the borders of the United States, and the DIA was being asked to spy on civilians.

Old animosities existed between the CIA and the FBI over jurisdiction. The FBI had always handled domestic surveillance and the CIA, foreign surveillance. White House lawyer Tom Huston was also present at the meeting of the spy chiefs. His role was to coordinate the agencies and come up with a workable plan. The NSA came up with a memorandum entitled "NSA Contribution to Domestic Intelligence" and Huston drew up a proposal for Nixon to sign. The so-called Huston Plan authorized the NSA to intercept international phone calls or telegrams without a warrant or probable cause. The FBI could not object because it did not have the capability to tap international communications.

J. Edgar Hoover took one look at the Huston Plan and saw red. He viewed it as nothing less than an attempted takeover of his own personal territory, and demanded that Attorney General John

Mitchell withdraw the recommendation. Mitchell convinced Nixon that the whole operation was illegal. Five days after he had authorized it, Nixon was forced to cancel it. The Huston Plan was condemned to the private safe of John Dean, where it stayed until May 1973.

Although the Huston Plan sounded like a radical departure from the NSA's brief to spy only on foreigners, the agency had been spying on US dissidents for years. The Pentagon had drawn up lists of protesters against the war in Vietnam, such as the folksinger Joan Baez, actress Jane Fonda, civil rights activist Dr. Martin Luther King, and pediatrician Dr. Benjamin Spock. The NSA was tasked with monitoring all international communications to and from those individuals and many others. It was believed that the anti-war demonstrations, civil disturbances, and draft dodging were being encouraged by communists abroad as part of a destabilization campaign. As the Vietnam war became more and more unpopular, the domestic "watch list" program became ever larger. On July 1st, 1969 it became chartered under the official codename MINARET, and all links with the NSA were hidden. Up until its termination by Attorney General Elliot Petersen in 1973, Project MINARET produced nearly 4,000 NSA reports on "watch-listed" Americans.

J. Edgar Hoover showed his animosity and humor by demanding from the NSA a full surveillance of all Quakers in the United States, on the pretext that the religious sect was suspected of shipping food and general supplies to Southeast Asia. The fact that Richard Nixon was also a Quaker had nothing to do with it.

YUK

SHAMROCK

MINARET was not the only NSA program that spied illegally on US citizens. During the May 1973 White House meeting, Buzhardt brought Nixon up to speed on another one, codenamed SHAMROCK. This involved a conspiracy between the NSA and several of the largest US telegraph companies such as Western Union. The secret agreement was for the companies to give copies of every message they handled that was sent out of the country or into the country every day. From these copies the NSA drew up a list of more than 600 names of suspect US citizens who it considered warranted surveillance. Computers were programmed to spot these names when they occurred in the messages and select them for further analysis and distribution to whichever government department was interested in the names. When Nixon heard about SHAMROCK he dismissed it as a problem since, for once, it wasn't bad news linked directly to Watergate.

Two years later, with Nixon gone, the SHAMROCK program was exposed during the Senate investigations into the illegal activities of the US intelligence community. Its chairman, Senator Frank Church, warned the American public about the threat of such surveillance:

No American would have any privacy left, such is the capability to monitor everything: telephone conversations, telegrams, it doesn't matter. There would be no place to hide. If this government ever became a tyranny, if a dictator ever took charge in this country, the technological capacity that the intelligence community has given the government could enable it to impose total tyranny, and there would be no way to fight back, because the most careful effort to combine together in resistance to the government, no matter how privately it was done, is within the reach of the government to know. Such is the capability of this technology...I don't want to see this country ever go across the bridge. I know the capacity that there is to make tyranny total in America, and we must see to it that this agency and all agencies that possess this technology operate within the law and under proper supervision, so that we never cross over that abyss.

The "agency" that Church was warning against was the NSA. His Congressional investigators had hit a brick wall trying to request documents about SHAMROCK from the NSA, since the information was deemed too sensitive. Exposure of the project details would be against the interests of national security, and no organization knew better what was defined as national security than the National

Security Agency. An offer was made for Senator Church to be personally briefed on the matter, but an exposé in the *New York Times* soon made the allegations of illegal domestic surveillance a matter of public record, and the NSA decided to defend itself.

The new NSA director, Lew Allen, testified that project SHAMROCK had been started in 1945 with the cooperation of RCA, ITT, and Western Union, who between them represented almost all of the telegraphic traffic in the United States at the time. Their actions were purely patriotic and unpaid. First through the NSA's predecessor organization, and then through the NSA itself, microfilm copies of all incoming and outgoing telegraphs were made daily. In the early 1960s the cable companies started producing magnetic computer tapes that allowed the NSA to run all the messages through its HARVEST computer. Copies were made in an office in New York City, rented by the CIA under the codename LPMEDLEY. At its peak, the NSA was analyzing 150,000 messages per month. The cooperation with the CIA ended in 1973 when its lawyers had grave misgivings about the legality of the whole project. The NSA had to find alternative office space, but SHAMROCK was suddenly shut down by NSA Director Allen in May 1975, when Church's investigators started sniffing around.

When the Church Committee report was being drafted, arguments raged over whether the names of the telegraph companies should be given. They had, after all, broken the privacy of their customers. The NSA objected on the grounds that the companies were acting in the interests of national security and that public exposure would possibly result in lawsuits against them and definitely deter other companies from cooperating with the NSA in the future. With the strong urging of its chairman, the Senate Committee voted to make its final report public. President Gerald Ford attempted to personally intervene to change Senator Church's mind, but to no avail. All previous testimonies had been in closed sessions, but Church then made Director Allen appear in open session in front of the television cameras. It was the first time that the world got to see the head of the NSA.

Church raised the question about SHAMROCK but did not publicly identify the companies involved. Allen admitted that the project was illegal but that its disclosure did not harm national security. Republican members of the committee objected to the public disclosure, and Church had to agree only to discuss SHAMROCK in closed sessions. The final report ignored President Ford's pleadings and published the names of the companies involved. The whole episode introduced the NSA to the world and especially to conspiracy theorists. The NSA's Office of Security Services maintained reports on at least 75,000 Americans who appeared on NSA message intercepts between 1952 and 1974. The "No Such Agency" was now to become demonized as the destroyer of people's right to privacy, not just in the United States, but the whole world over.

The main result of the Church Committee report was a redefining of the NSA's role within the intelligence-gathering business. Whereas before, its existence and activities had been secret, it now had to act openly within the bounds of US law. If it wanted to carry out surveillance of an American citizen within the United States, it would have to apply for a warrant from the newly established Foreign Intelligence Surveillance Court (FISC). The NSA would have to provide evidence that the target was working for a foreign power or involved in either espionage or terrorism.

In reality, none of these conditions apply to the normal business of the NSA, which is to spy on foreign nationals or American citizens abroad. The SHAMROCK project should have been an FBI operation from the start, and it was even offered to the FBI at a later stage, but refused. Domestic surveillance on suspected spies and terrorists comes under the FBI's jurisdiction anyway, and it receives the vast majority of eavesdropping warrants granted by the FISC.

When Senator Frank Church was investigating the NSA, he learned the true scope of the surveillance technology, and it scared him enough to issue that warning to the American public. If a dictator wanted to monitor and ultimately control the American population, the technology was already available. The NSA itself needed to be controlled by Congress because its power was pervasive. What made him so scared of an organization that purportedly protected his own nation's security? Was it the sheer size of the behemoth that had lurked just beneath the waves for so long yet no one had ever seen it until he exposed it on national and international television? Since 1975, more information about this ultra-secret intelligence collector has come to light, and all of it has fed the paranoia of conspiracy theorists. It is the largest intelligence agency in the world, and its budget dwarfs any of its opposition. It is able to eavesdrop on communications anywhere on the planet and break the codes being used. As a source of world intelligence it reigns supreme. If one has to answer the question "Who really runs the world of intelligence?" one needs to look no further than the NSA.

Breaking Codes

When Skull and Bonesman Henry Stimson was appointed Secretary of State in the Herbert Hoover administration of 1931, he was shocked to learn that America's first civilian code-breaking organization, the Black Chamber, was not only eavesdropping on the enemy but also its allies. With the now-famous comment, "Gentlemen do not read each other's mail," Stimson closed down its operations. For a member of Yale's elite secret society, it is still unfathomable why Stimson took America out of the code-breaking business. The US army reacted by resurrecting the Black Chamber as the Signal Intelligence Service and kept its existence a secret from the State Department. Its head was William F. Friedman, a former member of the Black Chamber.

Despite the failure of the American intelligence community to give warning of the Japanese attack on Pearl Harbor, the US ability to crack some of the Japanese codes greatly impressed British Prime Minister Winston Churchill. With America's entry into the war, Churchill started to open up some of the secrecy behind various British scientific breakthroughs, but shared none of the details about the successful cracking of the German ENIGMA codes. This would have to wait until April 1943, when Friedman journeyed to England and was shown around the Government Code and Cipher School at Bletchley Park in Buckinghamshire. On May 17th, 1943, a formal agreement was signed between the code-breaking agencies of

Britain and the United States to cooperate on communications intelligence (COMINT). This pact between allies was known simply as the BRUSA Agreement and provided for the complete sharing of intelligence gleaned from deciphering foreign communications.

At the April 1945 San Francisco Conference to establish the United Nations, Lieutenant Colonel Frank B. Rowlett headed the operation to eavesdrop on the international delegates. Coded messages from the various delegations to their nations' capitals passed through the US telegraph lines in San Francisco. Western Union and other companies assisted in the collection by installing specially designed time-delay devices which allowed enough time for recorders to be switched on automatically. The intercepts were sent to Arlington Hall, headquarters of the Army Security Agency (ASA), where 46 special secure teletype lines were made available for the operation. The large number of messages in such a wide range of languages showed that the US was already leading the world in code-breaking. The decision to locate the United Nations headquarters in New York was the result of great pressure from the United States. It would allow the easier interception of international diplomatic communications.

The success of BRUSA allowed for the inclusion of two other English-speaking countries' code-breakers—those of Australia and Canada. New Zealand joined after the end of the war when the historic UKUSA Agreement set up the single most important alliance in COMINT history. The code-breaking agencies would go through several name changes, but are currently known as America's National Security Agency (NSA), Britain's Government Communications Headquarters (GCHQ), Canada's Communications Security Establishment (CSE), Australia's Defense Signals Directorate (DSD), and New Zealand's Government Communications Security Bureau (GCSB). The NSA, being the largest and most dominant, is designated as the "First Party to the Treaty" with the Commonwealth countries considered as joint members with Britain as "The Second Party to the Treaty."

The present-day NSA was established in 1952 as a last-minute act by the outgoing President Harry Truman. The Korean War had shown the deficiencies of the Armed Forces Security Agency (AFSA) in its SIGINT operations against the Chinese and North Koreans. Earlier successes in traffic analysis had provided an almost complete Chinese order of battle, but the North Koreans suddenly cut back on their radio transmissions and switched to the more secure land lines. This was the result of a warning that came from the Soviets based on secrets passed on to them by their mole within AFSA, William Weisband. AFSA struggled to crack the high-level codes and failed to impress the military commanders. For example, General James Van Fleet, commander of the US Eighth Army in Korea, complained: "Our intelligence operations in Korea have not yet approached the standards that we reached in the final year of the last war."

In December 1951, the director of the CIA, Walter Bedell Smith, complained to the National Security Council about the low standard of American COMINT. Internal security breaches at the AFSA headquarters in Arlington Hall had resulted in the sudden switching of all Soviet ciphers back in 1948, and the whole organization of COMINT needed to be shaken up. During an off-the-record meeting in the Oval Office at 3:30 pm on October 24th, 1952, President Truman scrapped the AFSA and issued a secret order creating in its place a new agency, the National Security Agency. It was to be hidden from Congress, the American public, and the world. The NSA first saw the light of day, or rather the shadows, on November 4th, 1952 as the nation elected a new president, Dwight D. Eisenhower. The US government did not officially acknowledge the existence of the NSA until 1957, and its presidential directive remains classified to this day.

Spies in the Skies

In 1962, President John F. Kennedy signed the Communications Satellite Act; a year later, the Communications Satellite Corporation (COMSAT) was formed. In 1965, eleven countries signed agreements to form a single global satellite network, the International Telecommunications Satellite Organization (INTELSAT), based in Washington DC. On April 6th, 1965, INTELSAT 1, also known as the "Early Bird," was launched into orbit and activated two months later, beaming telephone and television signals for the first time between the United States and Europe. One of the five INTELSAT earth stations was in southwest England, at Goonhilly Downs near Falmouth in Cornwall. Every few years, more powerful INTELSAT satellites were put into orbit, upgrading the forms of communications they could carry to include high-speed data and facsimile. Although the satellites carried mainly civilian traffic, they also carried diplomatic and governmental communications. GCHQ took advantage of the earth station in Cornwall by building its own set of satellite dishes, 30 meters (100 ft) wide, 60 miles north of Goonhilly, at Morwenstow near Bude in the same county. By this simple method, GCHQ would be able to eavesdrop on the INTELSAT signals, much the same way as the NSA did on the INTELSAT earth station at Etam, West Virginia, by building a mirror site in Sugar Grove, West Virginia. Since the Morwenstow station was practically funded by the NSA, and under the UKUSA Agreement, GCHQ passed all INTELSAT intercepts on to the NSA.

UKUSA members managed to cover the whole world in their INTELSAT satellite interception. Morwenstow covered Europe, Africa and western parts of Asia; Sugar Grove covered the whole of North and South America; the Yakima station in Washington State targeted the northern Pacific Ocean and the Far East; a DSD station at Geraldton, Australia, and a GCSB facility at Waihopai, New Zealand, covered the southern Pacific Ocean. As other commercial satellite organizations entered the market, the NSA started targeting them too. These non-INTELSAT satellites were monitored from the stations listed above as well as others located at Menwith Hill, England; Leitrim, Canada; Bad Aibling, Germany; Shoal Bay, Australia; and Misawa, Japan. Japan and Germany became "Third Party" members of the UKUSA Agreement.

In addition to spying on foreign communications on commercial satellites, the NSA went into partnership with the National

Reconnaissance Office (NRO) and the CIA to set up their own spy satellites. Most international communications before the 1960s were sent by high-frequency radio waves that were reflected back off the ionosphere and the Earth's surface and gave ranges of thousands of miles. With the introduction of microwave radio for intercity communications, relay ground stations were required to deal with the curvature of the Earth. Microwave radio signals are not bounced off the ionosphere, but carry on through into space. That, after all, is the reason why satellite communication works. But the NSA was interested in picking up the stray microwaves that were leaking out into space from the relay stations on the ground. It worked on the principle that only a tiny fraction of an original transmitted signal was picked up by each relay station, and the majority of the signals passed over the horizon and into space as "microwave spillage."

The first US COMINT satellite, codenamed CANYON, was launched in August 1968. It was controlled from the NSA ground station at Bad Aibling in Germany. In order to pick up Soviet signals, CANYON needed to be established in a geo-stationary orbit, but this was not achieved. The slight error caused the satellite to drift. Seven CANYON satellites were launched during the period 1968–77. The coverage of the USSR was aided by the fact that for thousands of miles over Siberia, permafrost restricted the laying of underground communications cables, thus forcing the construction of microwave radio relay stations.

After the CANYON series was proved to be a success, the NSA developed a new class of COMINT satellite, code-named CHALET. The ground station chosen to manage these surveillance satellites was Menwith Hill in England. The NSA invested heavily in the construction of the expanded facility, and after the launch of the first two CHALET satellites in June 1978 and October 1979, it wasn't long before Menwith Hill attracted media attention. When the CHALET codename was revealed in the US press, it underwent a name change to VORTEX. (This, too, was eventually revealed in 1987 and necessitated a further name change to MERCURY.)

Above and Below the Waves

Menwith Hill and the activities of the NSA in Britain were first exposed in a July 1980 article in the *New Statesman* by its editor Duncan Campbell and Linda Melvern, a reporter for the *Sunday Times*. In 1975, the Post Office, then in charge of national telecommunications, had established an underground coaxial cable link from one of its microwave towers at Hunter's Stone to Menwith Hill four miles away, to provide the NSA with direct access to the whole international telephone and telex network system running through Britain. Menwith Hill had been a joint American–British venture since the very beginning in December 1951 when the US Air Force and the British War Office signed a lease for the land. The NSA became the sole leaseholder in 1966, and its early work up until the mid-1970s was in intercepting International Leased Carriers (ILC) and Non-Diplomatic Communications (NDC). Using the most sophisticated IBM computers of the day, the NSA was able to sort through the telex communications of governments, businesses, and private individuals for anything that was of interest to national security. From 1974, Menwith Hill was upgraded to a satellite interception station with the addition of eight satellite communication dishes on the site. It would continue to expand as its role in coordinating satellite surveillance became more important. It would eventually become the largest spy station in the world, with over 25 receiving stations and 1,400 American NSA personnel working with 350 UK Ministry of Defense staff. It would earn several awards for the intelligence support it offered in the Desert Shield and Desert Storm military operations in the Gulf.

Its surveillance of the Middle East makes Menwith Hill the major NSA site for COMINT collection against Israel. Among its staff are linguists trained in Hebrew, Arabic, and Farsi. The NSA's relationship with Israel was indelibly stained by the deliberate attack by Israeli Air Force Mirage jets on the NSA spy ship, the *USS Liberty*, on June 8th, 1967 during the Six Day War. Although clearly displaying the American flag, the *Liberty* was allegedly mistaken for the Egyptian troop carrier *El Quseir* and attacked for entering Israeli waters, even though it was sailing in international waters. After the initial air attack, the Liberty was further attacked by Israeli motor torpedo boats. When the lifeboats were lowered into the water, they were immediately sunk by machine-gun fire. The combined attacks put more than 800 holes into the ship's hull, killing 34 men and wounding 172. The Israeli government always maintained that the attack had been in error, but, within two years, it paid $100,000 each to the families of the deceased and $20,000 for each of the wounded. Israel then spent the next 13 years haggling over how much compensation to pay over the damage to the ship. President Carter eventually accepted $6,000,000. The director of the NSA at the time, Marshall Carter, believed that the attack had been deliberate. Evidence from intercepted COMINT recorded high above the scene in an NSA EC-121 airplane mentioned the American flag being discussed by the attackers. For diplomatic reasons, President Johnson accepted the Israeli excuse, but the NSA will never forget the act of premeditated murder carried out on its analysts aboard the USS Liberty.

The Liberty was only one of several NSA surveillance ships that sailed the seas, eavesdropping on targets. But there were also operations being carried out beneath the waves. In October 1971 the US submarine, USS Halibut, sailed into the Sea of Okhotsk off the eastern coast of the USSR. Its top-secret mission, code-named IVY BELLS, was to record military communications being carried on the submarine cables to the Kamchatka Peninsula. The Halibut was equipped with a diving compression chamber welded to the outside of its hull, inside which deep-sea divers lived for a week to get ready for working at a freezing depth of 140 meters (400 ft). The Soviet submarine cable had "repeaters", signal boosters every 20 or 30 miles, and one of these was the target for the inductive wire tap. For 14 days the Halibut rested on its skis on the bottom of the Sea of Okhotsk, recording both encrypted and clear communications concerning military and naval operations. About 700 recordings were analyzed at NSA headquarters, Fort Meade, and the results were very impressive.

The Halibut was tasked to return a few months later after undergoing repairs. This time it laid a permanent pod that could be left for a year and then replaced. Over the next ten years the Okhotsk cable-tapping produced excellent COMINT. Another submarine, the USS Parche, traveled out of San Francisco, under the North Pole to the Bering Sea to lay a cable tap near Murmansk. For this achievement, the crew received a presidential citation. Alas, the IVY BELLS operation was compromised in 1982 when a former NSA employee sold details of it to Soviet intelligence, but the Bering Sea operation continued undetected until the end of the Cold War when it was terminated in 1992.

Modern submarine cables carry fiber optics, and the fact that they do not leak radio frequency signals rules out using inductive taps. However, the USS Parche would still be able to gain some data from the repeaters that are still needed to boost the signals over great distances underwater.

Out of the Shadows

With the NSA no longer being the "No Such Agency," its faceless character became fleshed out by a series of publicly identified directors. After the Church Committee hearings of 1975, the new "law-abiding" NSA emerged from the shadows under the new leadership of Vice Admiral Bobby Ray Inman. He was the youngest director in the NSA's history, and soon became the darling of Washington. Congressmen were given briefings that left them informed, impressed, and utterly seduced. Sharing secrets of even a mundane nature was a powerful aphrodisiac, and Inman cleverly turned potential enemies into friends. Senator Barry Goldwater, the chairman of the Senate Intelligence Committee, was typical in his praise: "You have my vote even before I hear your testimony." Inman also artfully managed to turn the Washington press corps into his private public-relations machine. Newsweek referred to him as "a superstar in the intelligence community." Howard Kurtz of the Washington Post described him as "the single greatest leaker of intelligence information."

Of course, the intelligence that Inman "leaked" was disseminated for a purpose. Not for nothing was he known as "The Smartest Spy."

As the most senior of the anonymous "senior intelligence sources" used by the press, his position was so important to the newspaper editors and executives that they didn't dare upset him. Through Inman's masterful manipulation of the media, the NSA managed to avoid any serious exposés. Even the mighty Bob Woodward at the *Washington Post* found that Inman had influence over his stories through his strong relationship with Woodward's superiors.

One journalist who resisted the charms of Inman was William Safire of the *New York Times*. When the NSA provided evidence from intercepts that President Jimmy Carter's brother, Billy, was working as a business agent of the Libyan government—the so-called "Billygate" scandal—Safire identified both Inman and the NSA operation in his article. Breaking the standard protocol, Safire incurred the wrath of Inman, but had the last laugh when he heavily criticized "the nation's chief eavesdropper" for "blabbing about sources and methods" on ABC's *Nightline*.

Inman's emergence from the shadows was a deliberate ploy to redefine the image of the NSA in the public's limited awareness. There was a battle going on within the US intelligence community over the dominance of the CIA. Historically, the CIA's director was also the Director of Central Intelligence (DCI), and, as such, acted as the single conduit for all the different intelligence agencies' information en route to the president. This gave the CIA an immense amount of political power. The NSA was about to change all that. In the "Battle of the Admirals," Vice Admiral Inman and the DCI Admiral Stansfield Turner waged war over satellite surveillance. The NSA wanted more ears in the sky and the CIA wanted more eyes. Both projects would require billions of dollars of funding, and Inman was determined to use his popularity to win over the relevant appropriations committees.

The CIA, used to an intense rivalry with the FBI, now found itself with an even bigger one against the NSA. Stansfield Turner suspected that the NSA was withholding some of its raw data from the CIA and the rest of the intelligence community. He objected to the NSA's increasing role in analysis, since it was only authorized to collect intelligence and not analyze it. Technically speaking, the NSA would have to do a certain degree of analysis in order to decide what to collect next, but this was just processing. What worried Turner was that the NSA was turning the processing phase of the intelligence cycle into full-scale analysis and thereby stepping very heavily on the toes of the CIA. In the secret world of the intelligence community, the NSA was being accused of withholding important information so that it could present it itself and look good. It was a definite sign that the NSA was aiming to take over.

One example of the harmful effects of a spy war between the NSA and the CIA was the Tehran hostage-rescue fiasco in 1980. When the American embassy employees were taken hostage by Iranian radicals and a Delta Force rescue operation was in the planning phase, the CIA provided all the intelligence support, deliberately cutting the NSA out of the loop. The CIA had tried to keep the operation secret from the NSA, but that proved a false hope since NSA COMINT picked up suspicious messages in its usual intercepts. Angered that the NSA had been cut out of the planning, Inman warned the chairman of the Joint Chiefs of Staff, Air Force General David Jones, that the NSA had discovered the planning because the communications security (COMSEC) was so pathetic. Whether General Jones's subsequent over-restrictions on communications contributed to the disaster in the desert, where the Chinook helicopters had to be abandoned and the Delta Force permanently embarrassed, is questionable. The NSA did manage to provide a minute-by-minute commentary on the disaster to the Pentagon chiefs and the Secretary of Defense, cutting out the CIA during the actual operation.

In the management structure of the US intelligence community, the director of the NSA is answerable to the Secretary of Defense. NSA directors seldom met the president, and this may explain why Richard Nixon had never heard of the NSA at the recorded meeting with his lawyer Buzhardt. Despite the NSA's massive budget, the political weight of the CIA's directorship with its leadership of the whole intelligence community as the director of Central Intelligence was too much for Inman to resist. On the election of Ronald Reagan as president, Inman left the NSA to become the deputy director of the CIA under William Casey. The relationship between the two men did not work out, and Inman resigned the next year. He would have to wait until the Clinton administration before re-entering Washington politics when Clinton nominated him as Secretary of Defense. After having accepted the nomination, the former "Smartest Spy" failed to survive the routine background checks. Ever since his days as head of the NSA, Inman had held his own dark secrets. There were continual rumors that he was gay, and the supreme hypocrisy would be to have a gay man leading the US armed forces that prohibited gays and lesbians from serving.

Inman was dumped by the Clinton White House, but instead of slipping back into the shadows, he showed extreme paranoid behavior by going on television and accusing Senator Bob Dole and his arch nemesis, the *New York Times* columnist William Safire, of conspiring against him. Clinton's aide George Stephanopoulos commented that Inman looked "like a man who was broadcasting instructions transmitted through the fillings in his teeth." It showed what can happen to media darlings when their star falls. The spymaster who trusted nobody and suspected everybody for a living was as prone to paranoia as any normal conspiracy theorist. The taunts over his sexuality and even, as he himself admitted, his name "Bobby Ray," were eventually to prove too much for the former NSA director.

Inman's replacement at NSA was Air Force Lieutenant General Lincoln Faurer. He was to oversee a massive expansion at the NSA Fort Meade headquarters as the new president Ronald Reagan plowed money into the intelligence giant. The secret facilities were taking on the appearance of a self-contained metropolis, and Fort Meade became known as Crypto City. Faurer's extravagant spending attracted Congressional criticism and attempts to constrain the NSA's budget. Fighting the cutbacks, Faurer warned of future intelligence failures if the NSA was under-funded. Faurer was pushed out slightly ahead of his retirement date and replaced by Lieutenant General William Odom, who had also served in the previous Carter administration as an adviser on the issue of the Tehran Embassy crisis. When Reagan took over, Odom had assumed the position of

the army's chief of intelligence. Now he joined the NSA and immediately clamped down on the level of leaks to the press, so important a tool in the hands of previous directors. Odom's obsession with
secrecy led him into direct conflict with President Reagan over the
Libyan terrorist bombing of the La Belle disco in West Berlin in 1986.
Reagan retaliated with an air strike against Tripoli and appeared on
television to justify this action.

> On March 25th, more than a week before the attack, orders were
> sent from Tripoli to the Libyan People's Bureau in East Berlin to
> conduct a terrorist attack against Americans, to cause maximum
> and indiscriminate casualties. Libya's agents then planted the
> bomb. On April 4th, the People's Bureau alerted Tripoli that the
> attack would be carried out the following morning. The next day
> they reported back to Tripoli on the great success of their mis-
> sion. Our evidence is direct, it is precise, it is irrefutable. We have
> solid evidence about other attacks Qaddafi has planned against
> United States installations and even American tourists.

NSA Director Odom was furious that President Reagan had given
such information from NSA intercepts on national television.
Qaddafi was now alerted to the fact that the NSA had broken his
codes. The state-sponsored terrorism of this period is different from
the current period where a non-state player such as al-Qaeda dominates international terrorism. The NSA had fixed targets such as
the Libyan People's Bureau to eavesdrop upon, whereas nowadays
the al-Qaeda cells are mobile and dispersed throughout the world.
Yet, there are similarities. NSA surveillance that fails to prevent the
terrorist attacks can be used as an investigative tool after the event.
Guilty parties can be tracked down and arrested. Modern techniques
will be discussed later.

Odom did manage to keep the NSA out of the Iran-Contra dis-
closures, despite the fact that the agency had provided Colonel
Oliver North and his fellow conspirators with KY-40 laptop computers with secure encryption chips that allowed them to communi-
cate with each other by e-mail while traveling. Odom's three-year

tenure at the NSA was not renewed in 1988, and his replacement was Vice Admiral William Studeman. He steered the agency through the dramatic end of the Cold War and warned them of future inevitable budgetary cutbacks. These enforced reductions in manpower were waiting on the desk of Admiral Mike McConnell when he took over from Studeman in October 1992. When once the USSR accounted for 58 percent of the targeting budget, by 1993 Russia was only 13 percent. Russian linguists were having to learn other, more "exotic" languages. The NSA, caught napping during President Clinton's wars in Bosnia and Haiti, needed to recruit Serbo-Croatian and Kreyol speakers from menial laborers working in downtown Washington. To correct this deficiency, Director McConnell forged stronger links with linguistic departments of American universities. Computer language translation was developed to optically scan foreign documents and automatically translate them.

As the new millennium approached, the NSA received a futurist as its next director in the shape of Air Force Lieutenant General Kenneth Minihan. His first announcement to the NSA workforce set the stage: "Now is the time for Team NSA to step forward and lead America's entry into the 21st century...We are no longer a world-class organization; NSA is the class of the world." He saw the future as being radically different—as one more akin to that portrayed within computer games. "Just as control of industrial technology was key to military and economic power during the past two centuries, control of information technology will be vital in the decades ahead...In the future, threats will arise and battles will be fought and won in the information domain. This is, and has always been, the natural operating environment of the National Security Agency...Information will give us the power to pick all the locks."

The enemies of the United States, Minihan claimed, were likely to be "electronic road warriors" or "techno-terrorists ranging from mischievous teens to sophisticated nation and state adversaries" whose targets would be information databases, power grids, emergency services, and communications systems. As Osama bin Laden was to show, however, the new millennium was not quite what Minihan had seen in his crystal ball.

A New Threat

In April 2000, David Ignatius of the *Washington Post* described a far more accurate vision:

> "Trust us" is the NSA's implicit message. Trust us to distinguish between the good guys and the bad guys, and to use our powerful surveillance tools for the good of mankind...The United States needs an NSA that...when necessary, can crack the codes and monitor the conversations of people who could get us all killed. But it is unrealistic to expect the rest of the world to be enthusiastic. People will be glad when the NSA bags that biological terrorist as he's about to deliver the anthrax bomb—even those dyspeptic European parliamentarians. But don't expect them to give the global policeman much help along the way or stop demanding the same privacy rights that Americans have.

The new world order that followed the fall of the Berlin Wall and the collapse of the USSR was one born out of necessity to redeploy intelligence assets once used against communist targets. If new targets could not be found quickly, there would be massive cutbacks in intelligence collection and analysis. It was obvious that the unipolar world would not rule out the need for surveillance and vigilance. It had been the same at the end of World War II. The defeat of the Axis powers did not make the world a peaceful utopia. In the case of the break-up of the USSR and the Warsaw Pact, it introduced a chaotic fragmentation that needed political management by the West to produce a soft landing. The all-encompassing centralization of power in Moscow was now removed, and the NSA found itself having to monitor many different targets as the former republics of the USSR gained independence.

As Moscow suffered economic collapse and the rise of organized crime, the NSA would find its own areas of surveillance move into financial and criminal intelligence. The move into law enforcement was the obvious choice from a marketing perspective. As former members of the disbanded KGB found new calls on their clandestine talents in narcotics trafficking and money laundering, former Soviet scientists found new employers for their expertise in nuclear, chemical, and biological weapons production. The threat of nuclear proliferation was far greater after the collapse of the USSR than before it.

Meanwhile, from the mountains of Afghanistan, the terrorist leader Osama bin Laden reached out into the world and attacked US property and its citizens. He wanted to take the fight to America itself after the first World Trade Center attack in 1993. In James Bamford's pre-9/11 *Body of Secrets*, he stated that the NSA regularly listened to unencrypted phone calls from bin Laden in Afghanistan. The terrorist leader was using a portable INMARSAT phone that transmitted and received calls over spacecraft owned by the International Maritime Satellite Organization. Bin Laden appeared to know that he was being listened to, but did not seem to care. Just before the August 7th, 1998 embassy bombings in East Africa, a suicide bomber, Mohammed Rashed Daoud al-Owhali, called a known al-Qaeda number in Yemen from a safe house in Nairobi. The NSA intercepted this and other calls. Osama bin Laden's satellite phone was used to contact the same number in Yemen, and this link established complicity in the Nairobi and Dar-es-Salaam bombings. As the NSA intercepts were being used in the case against bin Laden in the United States District Court in Manhattan, he was planning a far greater terrorist operation. The NSA analysts occasionally played audiotapes of bin Laden talking to his mother for any visitors to Fort Meade. That was before 9/11 and the latest in a series of great intelligence failures: an enemy attack on American territory that would rival that of Pearl Harbor.

Bin Laden had abruptly stopped using his satellite phone when he realized that the NSA was not only listening in to his conversations but was also able to home in on his signal and locate him. This he learned from CNN—yet another example of a strategic secret blown by the media for the sake of a scoop.

In the post-mortem of the 9/11 intelligence failure, the NSA came under scrutiny because its multi-billion dollar funding was supposed to prevent exactly this kind of event. Two messages were intercepted on the day before the September 11th attacks which had relevance. These were two separate communications between people suspected of being al-Qaeda members in Afghanistan and others in Saudi Arabia. The Afghan members were notifying the Saudi members that major attacks against the United States were imminent. "The match begins tomorrow," said one. "Tomorrow is zero hour," said the other. The NSA was unable to identify the two individuals who were announcing the attacks, and the translation from the original Arabic did not take place until the day after the attacks, September 12th. Investigators wanted to know why there was a two-day delay in translating the intercept. NSA Director Michael Hayden explained that the delay was standard since the agency collects a lot of information each day and it would be impossible to translate everything as quickly as critics would demand. The messages were only noted in retrospect since neither actually carries any firm clue as to what to expect. "The match begins tomorrow" and "Tomorrow is zero hour" were practically useless.

Indeed, some skeptics question whether the war against terrorism would be better fought using old, pre-technology methods. For decades the use of human intelligence (HUMINT) has shrunk and been replaced by signals intelligence (SIGINT). Spies in the skies rather than on the ground, in the dark alleyways of the world. Terrorist cells are so structured that they are nigh impossible to penetrate successfully. Intelligence on these groups often comes from only one source—an insider who has for various reasons become disgruntled with the cell and chooses to turn traitor to his cause. Most intelligence successes have been due to traitors defecting to the other side, not active recruitment. In fact, espionage history shows that several traitors have been either ignored when they first offered their services, or have not been believed when they did come over. During the Cold War, it was almost as if there was a great game being played; a game of chess. Psychological operations and disinformation flooded the espionage world to the extent that everything had to be viewed as a double cross. In the terrorist world, no such chess games are being played, so a defector needs to be instantly accepted and debriefed.

There is a natural propensity for terrorist movements to argue among themselves and splinter into increasingly smaller factions until they disappear. All that is needed to wage this kind of war is great patience and the willingness to take the long-term view. Al-Qaeda will become a different organization after the death or removal of Osama bin Laden. It is similar to George Kennan's theory of "containment" which, as we'll see in the next chapter, worked so well over the long term against the USSR. As terrorist movements are allowed to naturally fragment, NSA surveillance will hopefully be able to pick up calls from potential traitors.

Despite its multi-billion dollar satellite surveillance empire, the NSA also has its HUMINT side. Using the premise that it is far easier to steal a codebook than to try and decipher a code, the NSA joined forces with the CIA to form the Special Collection Service (SCS). Members are tasked to break into foreign embassies and steal foreign cipher materials, as well as recruit foreign cryptanalysts and communications personnel. Spy gadgets have made a welcome return with bugging devices now available in all shapes and sizes of camouflaged objects. All COMINT up until recently has been based on intercepting messages as they have been in motion, but now computers have provided the opportunity to access stored messages—messages "at rest" in disks and hard drives.

In August 2004 an English-speaking Pakistani computer engineer named Mohammed Naeem Noor Khan was arrested for running an al-Qaeda communications network, using e-mail and encryption keys. The public key cryptography available to all internet users is PGP (Pretty Good Privacy), which allows personal e-mails to be scrambled to a certain degree, which caused some concern at the NSA. During the 1990s, the NSA was frequently in court trying to keep PGP off the consumer market. The NSA tried to define PGP as a military product and therefore subject to export controls. When this failed in 1996, PGP became commercially available at low cost. The NSA had wanted to limit the length of keys in business ciphers, as the number of digits determined the time the agency would take to break the codes. All PGP codes could be broken by sequentially searching for the 1,024 digits that made up the key, but this could take a very long time indeed. The business and private customers wanted a secure system that protected their confidential information. Allowing the NSA with its Cray supercomputers to easily break the codes was not part of the deal. To this day, it is unknown whether the NSA has found a fast way of breaking PGP. But, if anybody were capable of doing it, then the NSA's large workforce of mathematicians and code breakers would be the ones.

Cyber Crime

As computer technology has advanced, more and more of the population are being drawn into cyberspace. Internet chatrooms allow communication to take place between complete strangers where false identities are the normal procedure. Sexual liaisons are arranged between consenting adults, but it is also an environment where criminals stalk their victims. Pedophiles masquerade as children in an effort to make real their sick fantasies. Police masquerade as children to ensnare the sick fantasists. Pornography of all types can be downloaded into any home with internet access. Buying and selling of anything from supermarket groceries to second-hand Soviet submarines is now possible. Goods are paid for through supposedly secure electronic transactions. Even personal bank accounts can be accessed through the use of passwords. The opportunities for fraud are enormous. Cyber crime is on the increase, and cyberspace needs to be policed, but the problem lies in the sheer scale of the internet and its global reach. If users are to be protected, and abusers tracked down and arrested, a very high level of monitoring must be established. The NSA already has this in place.

Back in the 1980s, the NSA and its UKUSA partners operated a secret communications network that was bigger than the internet of its day. Code-named project EMBROIDERY, this global network included the NSA's main computer network PATHWAY. As the civilian internet evolved from the military one, the NSA developed COMINT systems to collect, filter, and analyze the forms of data transmissions. Its task was made easier by the fact that most of the world's internet capacity either lies within the United States or connects to it. Communications within cyberspace from Europe to Asia would normally pass through intermediate sites within the United States, as do many other intercontinental routes. Any internet communication traveling through the United States would be easily intercepted by the NSA.

When a message is sent by e-mail, it is composed of packets of data known as "datagrams." These packets include numbers representing both the "IP addresses" of its origin and destination. These Internet Protocol addresses are unique to each computer that is hooked up to the internet. The packets of data are crucial for the working of the entire e-mail system, and the speed with which this system works when handling millions and millions of them each second indicates the level of processing power. This same rate of processing is achieved by the NSA as it extracts COMINT from the system. Due to its legal restrictions, the NSA is only supposed to examine communications that either start or finish in a foreign country. All the other data that is intercepted should, theoretically, be ignored by the computers unless a special warrant is issued. At times of terrorist threat, if the NSA is to effectively utilize its immense resources, then domestic surveillance is required. The presence of terrorist cells operating within the United States will make this an absolute necessity.

The FBI had attempted to operate a surveillance program to monitor e-mails and chatrooms, codenamed CARNIVORE. It was used in the immediate aftermath of the 9/11 attacks and was responsible for tracking down and detaining nearly 500 terrorist suspects. Of course, some innocents were falsely accused in the operation. On October 28th, 2003, three pickup trucks pulled into the driveway of a suspect identified as Norris and six federal agents piled out wearing body armor and carrying sidearms. When Norris answered the door, one of the men identified himself as a special agent for the United States Fish and Wildlife Service, a branch of the US Department of the Interior, and served him with a search warrant. Norris was a 65-year-old gardener who owned a business called Spring Orchid Specialities. The Feds showed him one of his e-mails from several years before, in which Norris was being offered plants smuggled from abroad. This was an example of the power of the FBI's CARNIVORE. Is it any wonder that the intercept system is now renamed DCS1000 (Digital Collection System) and all but retired? The FBI itself had no use for the system during 2002 and 2003 because a far more efficient method had been introduced into law enforcement. In the patriotic atmosphere of post 9/11, the Internet Service Providers were requested to contribute to national security and the fight against international terrorism, by conducting their own internal wiretaps on behalf of the US government.

The NSA tackled the software giants Microsoft, Netscape and Lotus over their cryptographic security levels in their software packages provided for customers outside the United States. All three companies offered to adapt their software for reduced levels on exports. In the case of Lotus, a subsidiary of IBM, the company limited the size of its e-mail encryption key to only 64 bits, allowing the NSA to break the key within a relatively short time if it needed to. It also built in an NSA "workfactor reduction field" (WRF) trapdoor to its Lotus Notes e-mail system. The WRF is 24 of the 64 bits of the encryption key which only the NSA can read. That leaves just 40 bits to be cracked, reducing the workfactor required to read the messages. The restriction of these WRFs to export-only software discriminates against the rest of the non-American world. The WRFs are basically devices to speed up decipherment in a battle against foreign enemies. When terrorists are home grown in the United States, the system has no advantage.

ECHELON

In conclusion, it can be seen from the evidence that the NSA reigns supreme in the world of intelligence. Other spy agencies and law enforcement agencies use its product. Its prime responsibility is to protect the national security of the United States and the shared security of its UKUSA partners. Yet Europe as a whole has great misgivings over the NSA and its secret surveillance of its member states. In January 1998, the European Parliament released a report published by its Scientific and Technological Options Assessment (STOA) committee, entitled "An Appraisal of Technologies of Political Control" written by Steve Wright of the Omega Foundation. It outlined the NSA's ECHELON communications interception system and exposed its surveillance of European Union (EU) citizens. The report was based largely on the few written sources on ECHELON—the Duncan Campbell *New Statesman* article from 1980 and the 1996 book written by Nicky Hager, *Secret Power: New Zealand's Role in the International Spy Network*. The NSA station at Menwith Hill attracted a lot of protest at its chief role in the spying on European citizens.

The European Parliament debated the issue of ECHELON violations of sovereignty and the privacy of citizens not just in Europe but throughout the world. During the debate on "Transatlantic Relations/ECHELON system," which took place on September 14th, 1998, Commissioner Martin Bangeman warned: "If this system were to exist it would be an intolerable attack against individual liberties, competition, and the security of the states." There was great concern that ECHELON was capable of being used by the NSA to give American companies an unfair knowledge of competitors' economic and business plans. The ECHELON system was capable of capturing virtually every phone call, fax, telex, and e-mail sent anywhere in the world. Using advanced voice and optical character recognition systems, NSA computers could extract messages that are flagged by certain words or phrases. These are known as the ECHELON "dictionary," and if a EU citizen's name were on that list, all messages referring to him or her would be separated from the billions trawled and processed for further analysis.

Former NSA Director Studeman gave a useful insight into the process of sifting through so much data, in a speech at a symposium in December 1992: "Just one intelligence collection system alone can generate a million inputs per half-hour. Filters throw away all but 6,500 inputs; only 1,000 inputs meet forwarding criteria. Ten inputs are normally selected by analysts and only one report is produced. These are routine statistics for a number of intelligence collection and analysis systems which collect technical intelligence."

ECHELON has become the buzzword for Big Brother surveillance in the conspiracy theorists' universe. All communications are read by the giant NSA. They may as well be broadcast in the clear, since encryption doesn't seem to bother the master code-breakers. They may as well be broadcast in English since the NSA now has advanced computerized language-translation systems that will soon eliminate the need for human linguists. There are no safe places to hide and conspire against the government. The NSA can bug you from space, in the air, on land, and under the sea. Senator Frank Church had seen the writing on the wall when he investigated the NSA back in 1975. In recent Hollywood films, such as *Mercury Rising* and *Enemy of the State*, the NSA has been portrayed as a sinister organization that chases the hero around with the aid of satellite technology. The image is not helped by the black Kevlar-clad armed security guards that patrol Crypto City. They are even known as the "Men in Black".

When Air Force Lieutenant General Michael Hayden took over from the futurist General Minihan as NSA director in 1999, it looked as though the soothsayer was about to be proved right. The future battlefield was going to be in cyberspace. As the new millennium approached, the NSA and the rest of the world had to prepare for the Y2K problem. Would the world collapse when the computers' internal clocks switched from 99 to 00 and took that to be from 1999 to 1900 and not from 1999 to 2000? Minihan warned that it would be "the El Niño of the digital age." Hayden knew that 94 percent of the NSA computers were Y2K compliant by July 1999. The remainder were ready by the end of September.

As in the rest of the world, the Y2K apocalypse failed to materialize at Fort Meade but, 24 days later, the entire NSA computer system crashed. Hayden held a town meeting in Crypto City and warned everyone not to say a word about the computer crash. "Our adversaries cannot know that our intelligence capabilities have been crippled." It took three days to repair the system, during which time much of the intercept traffic that would have gone to the NSA was diverted to Britain's GCHQ—a fine example of the UKUSA Agreement in action. It's a worldwide web in more ways than one...

Chapter Four: New Knights of the Round Table

Controlling America is the first step in controlling the world. Controlling America's allies is the second step. Who these allies are is best shown in times of war. It is only when a nation is called upon to put its own nationals in the line of fire for a common cause that true alliances are revealed. One has only to see the difference between France and the United Kingdom in their willingness to provide military support for American actions to understand the meaning of alliance.

The "Special Relationship" between the US and the UK is a curious reversal of the situation that existed a century ago. The British empire was dominant and a secret society existed which aimed to maintain its control over the world. This became the template for all future secret groups that never bothered themselves with the immature practice of dressing up in robes, but wore suits and wielded control over financial and commodity markets. It was called the Round Table and was the brainchild of the fabulously wealthy tycoon Cecil Rhodes. If costumes were to be worn, one would have imagined them to be Arthurian suits of armor. Our knowledge of the Round Table comes from a very interesting source: Carroll Quigley, a professor at Georgetown University's School of Foreign Service, who revealed the history of the secret society in a massive 1,300-page book entitled *Tragedy and Hope*. Although only 30 pages were devoted to the Round Table, Professor Quigley was to later comment that those 30 pages were responsible for the effective end of his government contracts to lecture.

Quigley's book was first published in 1966, when one of his

brightest students at Georgetown was future President William Jefferson Clinton. Quigley states: "I know of the operations of this network because I have studied it for 20 years and was permitted for two years, in the early 1960s, to examine its papers and secret records. I have no aversion to it or to most of its aims and have, for much of my life, been close to it and to many of its instruments. I have objected, both in the past and recently, to a few of its policies, but in general my chief difference of opinion is that it wishes to remain unknown and I believe its role in history is significant enough to be known." The information Quigley revealed would be picked up and used by other conspiracy theorists such as Gary Allen and Larry Abraham in their bestseller *None Dare Call it Conspiracy* and former FBI agent W. Cleon Skousen's *The Naked Capitalist* in 1970. The latter followed Quigley's *Tragedy and Hope* so closely that the Georgetown professor threatened to sue for infringement of copyright.

What was the Round Table? It was first written about by Quigley in an earlier book called *The Anglo-American Establishment*. Although written in 1949, it was not published until 1981, four years after Professor Quigley's death. It details the creation of a secret society "one wintry afternoon in February 1891" when "three men were engaged in earnest conversation in London...These men were organizing a secret society that was, for more than 50 years, to be one of the most important forces in the formulation and execution of British imperial and foreign policy." As well as Cecil Rhodes, the men involved were William T. Stead, the famous journalist; and Reginald Baliol Brett, friend and confidant of Queen Victoria and future adviser to King Edward VII and King George V. A fourth conspirator was soon added in the person of Alfred Milner. The aim of the Round Table was "to unite the world, and above all the English-speaking world, in a federal structure around Britain...The goal could best be achieved by a secret band of men united to one another by devotion to the common cause and by personal loyalty to one another...This band should pursue its goal by secret political and economic influence behind the scenes and by control of journalistic, educational, and propaganda agencies."

Upon the death of Rhodes in 1902, two things happened that bore great importance for the future of the Anglo-American "special relationship." Firstly, Alfred Milner took over leadership of the Round Table, and secondly, the massive fortune left in Cecil Rhodes's will enabled the setting up of the Rhodes Scholarships, which allowed certain selected students from all over the world to study at Oxford University. These students would each have "impressed upon his mind in the most susceptible period of his life the dream of the Founder"—one-world government. The most famous of these would be Bill Clinton.

Alfred Milner and the Round Table sought out anglophile Americans such as the Columbia historian George Louis Beer to correct the public misconception about British colonial policy they detected in American primary school textbooks. In an attempt to rewrite the War of Independence, Milner hired Beer as his American correspondent and honored him with the first non-British membership of the Round Table.

Beer became one of the most vocal supporters of early American intervention in the war against Germany. In 1916, the Round Table's Lionel Curtis met Beer in New York and proposed that an American group be set up within the Round Table. Beer rejected the idea. Although he was a strong anglophile, he knew instinctively that no American would join a movement to federate the British empire. Beer would soon be involved in the creation of an American version of the Round Table, totally independent of the Milner group. Its influence would eventually dwarf that of its British counterpart. It would be linked with modern, present-day secret groups such as the Bilderbergers (see Chapter One) and the Trilateral Commission (of which more later), and dwarf those too.

The Inquiry

The man credited with its actual creation in 1917 was Colonel Edward Mandell House, who as we saw in Chapter Three was the author of *Philip Dru: Administrator*. House was another anglophile, a first-generation American of English ancestry. He too was familiar with the Round Table and its leader Alfred Milner. Together with Supreme Court Justice Felix Frankfurter, House went to his friend and protégé President Woodrow Wilson with the idea of setting up an intelligence agency for foreign affairs. Wilson agreed and financed the agency through the secret President's Fund for National Safety and Defense. He stipulated that the agency should not be based in Washington DC, so a small office was found in the New York Public Library. James T. Shotwell, a fellow historian of Beer's at Columbia University, gave the agency its name, the Inquiry, which would be "blind to the general public, but would serve to identify it among the initiated." During the winter of 1917/18, the Inquiry moved to offices in the American Geographical Society at West 155th Street and Broadway. While here, House built up an organization of approximately 100 scholars who gathered information and discussed the likely future state of the world after the defeat of the Kaiser. They were a group of intellectuals committed to the concept of globalism with its removal of all economic barriers between nations and the creation of "a general association of nations." Walter Lippmann, a 28-year-old graduate from Harvard, was in charge of recruitment, and in his own words: "We are skimming the cream of the younger and more imaginative scholars...What we are on the lookout for is genius—sheer, startling genius, and nothing else will do." As far as intelligence was concerned, the scholars were restricted to the books, maps, and documents at the Library of Congress and the library at Columbia University. Among the Inquiry researchers was the young Allen Dulles, future head of the Central Intelligence Agency.

The Council on Foreign Relations

Elihu Root had once been the Secretary of State under Theodore Roosevelt, and was the recipient of the 1912 Nobel Peace Prize. In June 1918 he was the head of a select group of New York financiers and international lawyers calling itself the Council on Foreign Relations. With a membership of 108, the council provided dinner meetings for the purpose of entertaining "distinguished foreign visitors" and discussing commerce opportunities. Root led his small delegation to the Peace Conference at Versailles in 1918, where they operated alongside Edward House's Inquiry team in advising President Woodrow Wilson. Twenty-three of the Inquiry scholars had accompanied Wilson on his presidential cruiser, but were treated as amateurs by the diplomats of the Department of State and confined to quarters in the lower decks during the voyage across the Atlantic. While the major players handled the plenary sessions in Versailles' Hall of Mirrors, the Inquiry networked with other foreign experts over tea at the Quai d'Orsay. The Round Table were there as advisers to Prime Minister David Lloyd George.

Once the Peace Conference was over and the statesmen returned to their respective countries, members of the Round Table and the Inquiry remained in Versailles at the Hotel Majestic, the base used by the British delegation. The two secret societies met as equals with the view to establish a joint Anglo-American Institute of International Affairs.

The Charter of the League of Nations was signed by President Wilson on behalf of the US government on January 10th, 1920. He brought the treaty back to Washington and asked the Senate to ratify it. Wilson's hopes for a one-world government were about to come true, with he himself taking the de facto position of President of the World. However, remembering the advice given by the very first president, George Washington, to avoid foreign entanglements, the Senate refused to ratify the treaty. The League of Nations and further attempts to ratify its charter became the main issue in the 1920 presidential election. The Republican candidate, Warren G. Harding, went on record, stating rather awkwardly: "It will avail nothing to discuss in detail the League covenant, which was conceived for world super-government. In the existing League of Nations, world governing with its super powers, this Republic will have no part." The American people agreed and voted him in with 64 percent of the vote. The United States, after its brief foray into international war, retreated once again into isolationism. The power of Colonel House and the Inquiry suffered an early failure.

Since April 1919 the Council on Foreign Relations had dwindled down to almost nothing. Instead of completely folding, it became dormant until February 1921 when the Inquiry approached it with views to a merger. The academics had plenty of new ideas on foreign affairs but practically no finance to fund themselves. It seemed a logical move to combine with a group of Wall Street financiers, and negotiations continued for five months before a deal was made. The council's established headquarters at 25 West 43rd Street would become the headquarters of the new organization. There was a problem over the new name, since the "American Institute of International Affairs," which had been agreed upon with the British at the Hotel Majestic, was no longer such a popular idea. The British had left Versailles and returned to London to set up their end of the deal, the "Institute of International Affairs," at Chatham House, in St. James's Square. The post-Wilson isolationism of the United States now ruled out any joint venture with the British. The new American organization members were not keen on sharing any information with the British that might adversely affect commerce. Membership of the new organization would have to be "restricted to American citizens on the grounds that discussions and other meetings, confidential in nature, would be more productive if participants and speakers knew for sure that the others in the room were all Americans." This comes from the official history of the council.

Whitney Shepardson, the aide to Colonel House, was given the unenviable task of traveling to Britain and informing the Institute of International Affairs that the much-hoped-for Anglo-American venture, with one branch in London and the other in New York, was now dead in the water. There could be no exchange of membership, and the American academics appeared to have been won over to isolationism. Shepardson's embarrassment was saved by the British admission that similar views had been adopted by London, and the face-saving way of announcing it to New York had not been worked out. If we are to believe this, then the promises of a secret society spanning the Atlantic Ocean which were talked about in the Hotel Majestic were never a reality. On July 29th, 1921, the Inquiry became absorbed into the new Council on Foreign Relations, with a New York certificate of incorporation.

Conspiracy theorists who claim that the Council on Foreign Relations is controlled by the Round Table through the Institute of International Affairs are wrong and haven't done their research. This lack of agreement, and definite desire not to be linked, forces an enormous rift between these secret groups. Theorists tend to concentrate on the wishful thinking voiced at the Hotel Majestic without following the actual subsequent developments. Any sentence that combines the CFR and the IIS as co-conspirators must be viewed as false. By 1926, the British organization had been renamed the Royal Institute of International Affairs, the name by which it still goes to this day.

In 1928, one year before the Wall Street Crash, the Council on Foreign Relations liquidated most of its investment portfolio and purchased a five-story townhouse at 45 East 65th Street, next door to the family residence of the governor of New York, Franklin D. Roosevelt. In 1933, the CFR invited two foreign speakers to explain the motivations of two countries that would threaten the world's security in the next decade. One was a German journalist who warned them about the appeal of Adolf Hitler, and the other was a Japanese diplomat who offended his audience with Bushido propaganda. Present was the CFR member, Skull and Bones initiate, and Secretary of State, Henry Stimson. He was angered at the CFR allowing itself to be used as a forum for enemy propaganda. "The council existed for a rather more responsible purpose." The willingness of members to listen to the foreign points of view, no matter how offensive, was one of the main strengths of the organization. In order to understand foreign relations, one has to enter the foreign mindset. Similar comments of outrage had accompanied the heated debates on American isolationism from the very founding of the CFR. If the CFR was to become the influence behind the American government and behind the future world government, it needed to engage with foreigners. Obviously membership would be denied, but invitations to speak would always be open. The security surrounding the topics and speakers would insulate the CFR from official criticism. Through its journal *Foreign Affairs*, the CFR would go out into the world and engage more fully. A perfect example was the interview of Adolf Hitler by the editor Hamilton Fish Armstrong in April 1933. Less than a month after Hitler's rise to power, Armstrong was able to report back on a vision of a new world order totally alien and abhorrent to that of the council's.

This threat to their dream should have galvanized and united the council membership, but as fascism spread across Europe, the CFR split into two factions—interventionists and isolationists. The schism was shown no more clearly than the disagreement between brothers. Allen Dulles led the cause for intervention against the Nazis and John Forrest Dulles argued strongly for appeasement. Allen Dulles had beaten editor Armstrong to the Berlin Chancellory by a period of two weeks, and his impressions on Hitler appeared in a later issue. In 1934, Armstrong became the de facto leader of the CFR and established a study group to examine the US policy of neutrality, placing Allen Dulles as its head. The two men who had both seen Hitler face to face collaborated on a book, *Can We Be Neutral?*, in 1936.

In December 1937, with a $50,000 grant from the Carnegie Corporation, the CFR established smaller subsidiaries in eight cities throughout the United States. Though claiming to be autonomous, these so-called Committees on Foreign Relations offered an ideal network for disseminating policies and attracted the attention of the Department of State. The CFR's New York neighbor, Franklin D. Roosevelt, was now US President and the committees would provide efficient outlets for the discussion of his policies. Regional members were to be kept in the dark about the State Department source of the material. This early attempt of the government trying to influence the CFR stands in sharp contrast to the eventual reversal of the roles. The CFR aimed to be bipartisan and independent in its analysis as the fragile peace in Europe convinced the council that the League of Nations had been an opportunity lost. The CFR would soon put pressure on the State Department to give it a second chance.

A New Inquiry

That opportunity occurred on September 12th, 1939 as the Nazis invaded Poland. Hamilton Armstrong and Walter Mallory, the executive director of the CFR, took the train down to Washington to meet George S. Messersmith, the US assistant secretary of state, and proposed a venture similar to the Inquiry. They would provide the State Department with instant expertise in foreign affairs research and policy planning. The CFR's service would be of high quality, independent analysis which would greatly assist the foreign policy of the United States during the war and the years beyond, in exactly the same way that the Inquiry had provided useful guidance during World War I. The proposal was accepted by Secretary of State Cordell Hull but, like the Inquiry, was to be kept secret since there would be public outrage if it became widely known that the State Department was collaborating with a private, outside group. Once again, the State Department had been caught embarrassingly unprepared for such matters and eagerly accepted outside help. Whereas President Woodrow Wilson had funded the Inquiry project from his secret fund, the CFR project was funded by the Rockefeller Foundation, to the tune of $350,000.

The CFR project became known as the War and Peace Studies. For the duration of the war, almost 100 scholars and experts joined the project, dividing up into four specialist groups: economic and financial; security and armaments; territorial; and political. These groups would often meet over dinner and late at night to produce nearly 700 memoranda for the State Department, which would then disseminate the classified documents among the appropriate government offices. An example of the type of memo produced was the contingency plan in case Britain fell to the Germans and Churchill was forced to relocate to Canada. More farsighted was a study by the security and armaments group, led by Allen Dulles, on the need for an American army of occupation in defeated Germany.

When America finally did enter the war, the War and Peace Studies was absorbed into the State Department. Many of the CFR members were mobilized into uniform or into the Office of Strategic Services (OSS). Allen Dulles was one such member and he based himself in Berne, in neutral Switzerland where, once Germany was defeated, he was able to implement the very program his study group had proposed. Since many of the CFR memos were contingency plans that never materialized, it is difficult to assess the actual influence that the council had on wartime foreign policy-making. In effect, the CFR was producing scenarios of multiple universes where different outcomes of conflict were played out to determine the United States' probable response. As each alternative future collapsed, the CFR contingencies would be assigned to the wastebasket. Nevertheless, the CFR served its purpose in that it increased America's capability to respond to various different outcomes in the almighty fog of war.

In the spring of 1943, Armstrong and Norman H. Davis, a CFR director, proposed a plan to Secretary of State Cordell Hull for a "supranational organization" based on Woodrow Wilson's ideals of international liberalism. It was to be a second attempt at the League of Nations, but obviously under a different name. Secretary Hull asked Davis to present the proposal to President Roosevelt. Over a short period the charter was drafted, and Roosevelt took it with him to the Quebec Conference in August 1943. Churchill and Foreign Minister Anthony Eden made a few adjustments, and the agreed charter was taken to Moscow where delegates of the US, Great Britain, the Soviet Union, and China signed it on November 1st, 1943. This "Moscow Declaration," initiated by the CFR, became the document that pledged the establishment of "a general international organization, based on the sovereign equality of all peace-loving states and open to membership by all such states, large and small, for the maintenance of international peace and security."

The CFR emerged from the war a far bigger organization. The headquarters had moved from East 65th Street to a four-story mansion at the corner of 68th Street and Park Avenue, kindly donated by the widow of CFR member and director of Standard Oil of New Jersey, Harold Irving Pratt. John D. Rockefeller led a group of 200 members and companies who volunteered funds to refurbish the mansion into offices, conference rooms, and a library. A full-time staff of 20 researchers was housed there, and the number of Committees on Foreign Relations throughout the country had expanded from the original eight to 25. The circulation of the influential *Foreign Affairs* had grown to 17,000.

Allen Dulles returned from Switzerland to assume a leading role in running the CFR. One of his co-workers at the council was Alger Hiss, the Soviet spy. This is a revealing symbolism of the early postwar years, since although the CFR was unwilling to form any joint project with the Royal Institute of International Affairs in London, it was very willing to form one with the Soviets. Incredible as it may seem, the CFR approached the Soviet Embassy as early as January 1944 with an offer to do so. Its approaches were firmly rejected by Ambassador Andrei Gromyko. No Soviet spokesman would be allowed to attend such a venture. The new world order, as envisaged by the CFR, did involve coexistence with the USSR. The demise of world power for the British was evident by this action. The CFR was desperate to prevent the British dominating the postwar writing of history of the conflict, and CFR member William L. Langer of Harvard was commissioned to write an Americanized version as quickly as possible. This is another example of the CFR's lack of interest in a British alliance.

Just as the CFR's role in World War II had been a replay of its forerunner, the Inquiry, in World War I, so its role in the creation of a new world order following war was similar. This was the second chance to fulfill the plan first laid out by the Inquiry's founder Colonel Edward House. At the founding of the United Nations in San Francisco in 1945, forty-seven of the US delegates were CFR members, including Secretary of State Edward Stettinius, John Foster Dulles, Nelson Rockefeller, Adlai Stevenson, and the man who held the first position as Chairman of the United Nations, Alger Hiss. It was these men and their CFR colleagues to whom President George H.W. Bush was referring when he dedicated the liberation of Kuwait in 1991 to the "founders of the United Nations."

Containment

The CFR's attitude towards the USSR changed in January 1947 when an American Foreign Service officer named George Kennan took a sabbatical year at the National War College and wrote a report on his experiences which would become one of the most important documents in the Cold War. He expressed his concerns at the development of Soviet society to one of the small CFR study groups. One of the fellow members listening to Kennan's worries was George Franklin. The previous year Franklin had prepared a report for the council on the state of the USSR as could be gauged by the second-hand sources available. It recommended that "we take every opportunity to work with the Soviets now, when their power is still far inferior to ours, and hope that we can establish our cooperation on a firmer basis for the not so distant future when they will have completed their reconstruction and greatly increased their strength." The policy that Franklin advocated was "one of firmness coupled with moderation and patience." The CFR study group met at Harold Pratt House to vote on publishing the Franklin report. Of the 36 members present, fewer than half voted to accept the report. Nearly the same number could not make up their minds. Allen Dulles was one of those undecided. The sources used in the report were outdated. More up-to-date information was required.

When Franklin heard George Kennan's views in the discussion group in January 1947, he rushed to brief Hamilton Armstrong. The editor of *Foreign Affairs* invited Kennan to write his views down in the form of an article for the CFR's journal. Kennan was unsure about the legality of the authorship under his own name since he was a government employee. Armstrong gave him the pseudonym "X" and the article "The Sources of Soviet Conduct" appeared in the July 1947 issue of *Foreign Affairs*. The 17 pages contained a new political word, mentioned in only three sentences, which came to define US policy towards the Soviet Union for the next half a century—"containment." The article appeared in the same month as the introduction of the so-called Marshall Plan. Secretary of State George Marshall proposed an active engagement of the United States in the economic recovery of Europe, which was based on the 1946 CFR study "Reconstruction in Western Europe" co-written by Charles Spofford and a young man who was to dominate the CFR and several other secret groups for the next six decades, David Rockefeller. The committee created to formulate the Marshall Plan had as its chairman CFR Director and Skull and Bonesman Henry

Stimson. Its head in Europe was fellow Skull and Bonesman and CFR member Averell Harriman.

Key to the White House

The council's first recruitment of a future president of the United States occurred in 1950 when the temporarily retired General Dwight D. Eisenhower was briefly employed as president of Columbia University. The CFR appointed him to chair a study group to monitor the European aid program. Rarely missing a meeting, the general acquired experience in the economic policy-making process. One CFR member claimed afterwards that whatever Eisenhower knew about economics he had learned at the council study group. In December 1950, President Truman called him back into active duty as the Supreme Allied Commander in Europe.

As the Korean War raised the temperature of the Cold War, the United Nations got its first major chance to show its military might in attempting to maintain peace. As a direct confrontation between the United States and Communism, the struggle for a new world order was doomed to failure. The prerequisite for one-world government was one dominant power. In the bipolar world of the Cold War, that state of affairs would have to be won through world conflict. Or, according to George Kennan and the CFR, "containment" and great patience to allow the communist system to slowly bankrupt itself. Communism was rife within the United States government itself, if the rants of Senator Joseph McCarthy were to be believed. The CFR and its members became the targets as a direct result of the exposure of Alger Hiss as a Soviet agent by Whittaker Chambers. One politician who gained the most from the Alger Hiss case was the Republican CFR member Richard Nixon. As a curious coincidence, the CFR has only ever dismissed two of its members for non-payment of annual dues—Alger Hiss and Richard Nixon.

Eisenhower and Nixon became the first CFR members to be elected president and vice president in 1952. The defeated Democratic candidate had been fellow CFR member Adlai Stevenson. The council was starting to dominate American politics at the highest levels. The pattern would be repeated again four years later, with Stevenson again losing out to Eisenhower and Nixon. Although Nixon was to narrowly lose the next election in 1960 against John F. Kennedy, the charismatic Bostonian was also a member of the CFR. Nixon would return in 1968 to defeat fellow CFR member Hubert Humphrey, and win again in 1972 against George McGovern. Although not a member of the CFR in 1972, McGovern saw the light and joined afterwards.

Any image of a new world order would have to have nuclear missiles painted in the background. In order to fully understand the effect such weapons of mass destruction have on foreign policy, the CFR set up a discussion group entitled, appropriately, "Nuclear Weapons and Foreign Policy." In order to chronicle these discussions, CFR members Arthur Schlesinger Jr. and Skull and Bonesman McGeorge Bundy recommended a young scholar from Harvard named Henry Kissinger. Taking time off from his faculty, Kissinger spent the whole academic year 1955/56 working at the CFR headquarters. Using the discussion notes and his own ideas, Kissinger wrote the book that would make his name, *Nuclear Weapons and Foreign Policy*. It was the first CFR publication to become a national bestseller. Kissinger would go on to write 12 articles in *Foreign Affairs*, but it would be another 12 years before he entered government as President Nixon's national security adviser. Since then, Kissinger has become a giant in the field of conspiracy theory and is frequently associated with many nefarious plots to rule the world.

Another future national security adviser was recruited by the CFR in the shape of Zbigniew Brzezinski. The CFR published his analysis of Europe divided between East and West, *Alternative to Partition*, in 1965.

The CFR entered a new phase of its history in 1970 with the ascension to power of David Rockefeller, replacing John J. McCloy as chairman of the board. Rockefeller was the head of Chase Manhattan Bank and a CFR member since 1940, and he recruited Cyrus Vance to assist in the reorganization of the council. A new permanent position of president was created, with Bayless Manning being appointed in 1971. He came to lead a new CFR, radically different from its previous identity. There were now women admitted to the CFR membership. For nearly 50 years the Council on Foreign Relations had been a male reserve, like the secret societies of old. In 1973, Hamilton Armstrong retired from the editorship of *Foreign Affairs* and was replaced by Bonesman William P. Bundy. The public face of the CFR would change also. Its mission statement was no longer to "guide" American public opinion, but to "inform" it. Rockefeller also wanted to reduce the average age of the membership. In the early 1970s, the average age of the 1,600 members was 58. By 1975, through active recruitment of younger scholars aged between 21 and 27, the average age of new members was 47.

The Trilateral Commission

With the election of Jimmy Carter as president of the United States in 1976, something intriguing occurred among the puppet masters. While still a Democratic candidate, Carter had produced a book *I'll Never Lie to You*, in which he stated: "The insiders have had their chance and they have not delivered. And their time has run out. The time has come for the great majority of Americans…to have a president who will turn the government of this country inside out." The "insiders" was a reference to the CFR.

Carter's adviser Hamilton Jordan had this to say before Carter was elected: "If, after the inauguration you find Cy Vance as Secretary of State and Zbigniew Brzezinski as head of National Security, then I would say that we failed, and I'd quit." Although both of these men were members of the CFR, evidently Carter did not view them as "insiders" since he appointed them into the exact positions that Jordan had specified. Jordan himself failed to follow through on his threat and did not resign. Perhaps Carter was confused by the fact that Cyrus Vance and Zbigniew Brzezinski were members of his own secret society, the Trilateral Commission. They were "insiders" of a different breed, or so it might seem at first sight. In fact, they were of exactly the same breed as the CFR.

The Trilateral Commission was established on July 23rd and 24th, 1972 by David Rockefeller at his private estate. At the time he was the chairman of the CFR. All the eight founding members on the American side of the triangle were CFR members. Its aims were to bring together the three industrial engines of the world economy; the US, Europe, and Japan. Trilateral critic Senator Barry Goldwater quoted from its promotional literature in his own book, *With No Apologies*: "Close Trilateral cooperation in keeping the peace, in managing the world economy, in fostering economic re-development and alleviating world poverty will improve the chances of a smooth and peaceful evolution of the global system." He then gave his own interpretation: "What the Trilaterals truly intend is the creation of a worldwide economic power superior to the political government of the nation states involved. As managers and creators of the system they will rule the world."

Whereas the Bilderberg group was a US–Europe alliance, the Trilateral Commission was merely adding another region of the world economy, in this case the Far East sector represented by Japan. It was David Rockefeller's baby, and the dominance of CFR members could point to it being nothing more than an extended study group within that organization.

In December 1973, Jimmy Carter, an obscure peanut farmer turned governor of Georgia, appeared on the TV program *What's My Line?* and baffled the entire panel whose task it was to guess who he was. Zbigniew Brzezinski had obviously better observational skills. He knew not only who Carter was, but who he could feasibly become. He invited Carter to join the Trilateral Commission and spent the next three years tutoring him in the skills of modern foreign policy, along with fellow CFR member Professor Richard Gardner of Columbia University. Before the TV appearance, Carter had already been introduced to David Rockefeller in London.

Carter freely admitted that his success was due to the Trilateral Commission. In his 1976 book *Why Not the Best?* he wrote: "Membership on the commission has provided me with a splendid learning opportunity and many of the other members have helped me in my study of foreign affairs." Carter's reliance on the support of the Trilateral Commission is really a reliance on the CFR, a probable target of his "insiders" criticism. His presidential election campaign received financial support from the likes of Dean Rusk, Douglas Dillon, and Henry Luce, *Time* magazine's vice president. All were members of the CFR. Campaign advice came from Theodore Sorenson, W. Averill Harriman, Cyrus Vance, Richard Gardner, Paul Nitze, and Paul Warnke, all CFR men. When Carter gave a campaign speech at the Chicago branch of the CFR, he called for "a just and stable international order"—terminology which the CFR would fully appreciate. Yet Carter was not a CFR member. It would be only in 1983 that he joined the fold. For him, the CFR's "sister" organization was ample.

Once he received the Democratic nomination, Carter chose fellow Trilateralist Walter Mondale as his vice presidential running mate. After his successful election, Carter set about filling his administration with fellow Trilateralists. The *Washington Post* on January 16th, 1977 was quick to spot this undemocratic development. "If you like conspiracy theories about secret plots to take over the world, you are going to love the administration of President-Elect Jimmy Carter. At last count 13 Trilateralists had gone into top positions in the administration. This is extraordinary when you consider that the Trilateral Commission only has about 65 American members."

By 1980, when the team of Carter and Mondale were up for re-election, the Trilateral Commission was fielding another two candidates against them. First was the Republican George H.W. Bush and the second was John Anderson running as an Independent. Bush was not only a Trilateralist, but a CFR member and a Skull and Bonesman. The Trilateral Commission had tried to get a clean sweep of Republican candidates in 1978. George H.W. Bush and fellow Trilateralist, Illinois Governor James Thompson were talked of as a formidable pair to take on Carter and Mondale. Then Anderson was included in the race.

During the Florida primary on March 17th, 1980, candidate Ronald Reagan was asked if he would include any Trilateral Commission members in his cabinet if he was successfully elected. He replied: "No, I don't believe that the Trilateral Commission is a conspiratorial group, but I do think its interests are devoted to international banking, multinational corporations and so forth. I don't think that any administration of the US government should have the top 19 positions filled by people from any one group or organization representing one viewpoint. No, I would go in a different direction."

Ronald Reagan was neither a Trilateralist nor a member of the CFR. He was neither a Bilderberger nor a Skull and Bonesman. He was, however, a member of the Bohemian Grove. He belonged to the same camp as Richard Nixon.

When asked who really ran the United States, Reagan admitted: "I think there is an elite in this country and they are the ones who run an elitist government. They want a government by a handful of people because they don't believe the people themselves can run their lives...Are we going to have an elitist government that make decisions for people's lives or are we going to believe as we have for so many decades, that the people can make these decisions for themselves?" Quite which decades Reagan was referring to is hard to discern once one knows the history of the CFR. Reagan appears to be referring to the Trilateral Commission as the "elitist government" and not the CFR. It also seems that Reagan was thinking along similar lines to Jimmy Carter when he gave his pre-election promise to avoid "insiders" when selecting his cabinet.

After he was elected as the Republican presidential nominee, Reagan established a transition team that would act as a kind of recruitment agency for the major positions in the new administration if he won the race to the White House. Of the 59 people Reagan appointed for the team, 28 were members of the CFR, ten were Bilderbergers, and astonishingly, ten were from the dreaded Trilateral Commission! With George H.W. Bush as his vice presidential running mate, Reagan was not about to make the CFR or the Trilateral Commission or any other secret group into a campaign issue.

When Reagan entered the White House, he appointed 12 members of the Trilateral Commission into his administration, six of whom were also members of the CFR. As a sign of the true state of secret group influence, there were another 64 appointees who were only members of the CFR.

Increasing Influence

A former member of the CFR, Rear-Admiral Chester Ward USN (retired), exposed the sinister intentions of the council in the *Review of the News* during the campaign:

> The most powerful clique in these elitist groups have one objective in common—they want to bring about the surrender of the sovereignty and the national independence of the United States. A second clique of international members in the CFR…comprises the Wall Street international bankers and their key agents. Primarily they want the world banking monopoly from whatever power ends up in control of global government. They would probably prefer that this be an all-powerful United Nations organization; but they are also prepared to deal with and for a one-world government controlled by the Soviet communists if US sovereignty is ever surrendered to them."

That concept of Soviet supremacy in the Cold War sounded like one of those old CFR contingency studies that would quickly find its way into the wastebasket. Reagan was not about to let Kennan's "containment" fail after all this patience. By cranking up the military budgets on advanced weapons systems, Reagan would pile on the pressure and hasten the USSR's bankruptcy. Reagan appointed Alexander Haig (CFR) and George Shultz (CFR) as his Secretaries of State, Casper Weinberger (CFR) as Secretary of Defense, and Donald Regan (CFR) as Secretary of the Treasury. It was during the Reagan presidency that the "neo-conservatives" became a prominent force within the CFR, and they would exercise their influence on later Republican presidencies.

George H.W. Bush succeeded Reagan and appointed one of the rising stars of the CFR, Condoleezza Rice, as a member of his National Security Council. Brent Scowcroft (CFR) became National Security Adviser, Colin Powell (CFR) the Chairman of the Joint Chiefs of Staff, Dick Cheney (CFR) the Secretary of Defense, and Paul Wolfowitz (CFR) the Under Secretary of Defense.

When Bill Clinton (CFR) became president, he brought on board even more CFR members than Bush had—16 members of Clinton's cabinet were from Pratt House, chief among them the Secretary of State Warren Christopher and National Security Advisers Anthony Lake and Sandy Berger. Several key positions were filled by women, such as Madeleine Albright (US representative to the UN), Laura D'Andrea Tyson (chief economic aide), and Nancy Soderberg (special assistant to the president). All three were members of the CFR.

George W. Bush's team of advisers during his 2000 presidential campaign included the following CFR members: Condoleezza Rice, Brent Scowcroft, Colin Powell, Henry Kissinger, and George Shultz. Bush's running mate was Dick Cheney. The team was much the same as had served his father.

As we saw in Chapter One, both George W. Bush and John Kerry are members of the Skull and Bones secret society at Yale, and although Kerry is a long-time member of the CFR, Bush is not. He does, however, surround himself with advisers from the CFR.

The reason why the CFR is able to provide the bulk of the foreign and economic policy guidance to whichever president occupies the White House is because the CFR itself has its own partisan sections. Although its vision of a new world order is solid, the ways and means of achieving this are diverse. This fluidity allows adjustments to be made between administrations. The CFR's preferred candidate for the 2004 election appears to have been John Kerry. The CFR was all for the war on Iraq, as was Kerry. He believed, like Bush, that militarism and war was the main way to solve the world's problems. One of Kerry's advisers, CFR member Sandy Berger, the former national security adviser during the Clinton administration, published an article in the May/June 2004 issue of *Foreign Affairs* in which he laid down the Democratic alternative foreign policy strategy. "For the foreseeable future, the United States and its allies must be prepared to employ raw military and economic power to check the ambitions of those who threaten our interests. A posture of strength and resolve...are clearly the right approach for dealing with our adversaries." What Berger and the CFR were critical of was the "with us or against us" mentality adopted by Bush in trying to coerce foreign alliances. Berger saw the success of foreign policy in Iraq and Afghanistan threatened by the apparent waiving aside of UN authorization and involvement. The United States had alienated some of its natural allies in the process. The CFR did not want such alliances to be broken, since the whole one-world government hope would be threatened.

In order to mend the bridges, Berger and the CFR suggested that deals be made with the allies. Bush's major mistake was to refuse the sharing of the oil booty with allies such as France and Germany. Both countries had pre-existing oil exploration deals with Saddam Hussein, which were obviously cancelled when the United States invaded Iraq. The exclusion from the postwar oil deals played a strong part in the prewar objections from those allies. No one is willing to admit that the war was for oil, and the *Foreign Affairs* article vaguely referred to "geopolitical stakes," but the Democratic faction within the CFR differed from the Republican one over the type of world domination it envisaged. Bush's team sought unilateral domination by the United States, and the Kerry team preferred multilateral domination in cooperation with Europe.

With the defeat of Kerry at the election polls, the Bush strategy of "with us or against us" continues today. American foreign policy is being guided by those members of the CFR who believe that the new world order is one where America has moved beyond flexing its muscles and aims to dominate through brute force. The international criticism of bullying is justified. How long will it take until the United States burns off its anger over 9/11? The terrorist outrage against the Twin Towers was an attack against the World Trade Organization, and the death toll included many foreign nationals. It provided an opportunity to unite many nations in grief and desire for vengeance. There is nothing more unifying than a shared atrocity. If the aircraft had missed the targets and hit the United Nations headquarters instead, the new world order may have been a different animal. Yet the attempts to link Iraq with al-Qaeda were doomed to failure.

Who are They?

Who are the members of this modern-day secret society? Their membership is not a secret in itself, just the discussions and policy planning behind their closed doors. As with other secret societies, the membership is by invitation only. One has to be a US citizen and be nominated and seconded by other CFR members before the final election by the board of directors. A recent breakdown of the 4,200 membership reveals that 31 percent come from the corporate sector, 25 percent from academia, 15 percent from charities, 13 percent from government, eight percent from law, six percent from the media, and two percent from other professions. CFR members are on the boards of the following sample of corporations: Citicorp, J.P. Morgan Chase, Boeing, Conoco, Disney, IBM, Exxon Mobil, Dow Jones, Viacom/CBS, Time Warner, Carlyle Group, Lehman Brothers, Morgan Stanley, Goldman Sachs, Merrill Lynch, Credit Suisse First Boston, Chevron Texaco, Lockheed Martin, Halliburton, Washington Post/Newsweek.

The CFR prohibits its members from disclosing anything that has been said within its closed meetings to outsiders. It is this confidentiality that allows controversial subjects to be discussed within the council and which helps define the CFR as a secret society. The CFR defends its confidentiality clause in its own internal history: "Discussions at the Harold Pratt House remain confidential—not because they deal with secret information, but largely because members and invited guests often use the occasions to test tentative opinions they have not yet fully thought through and developed." This is backed up by article II of the CFR by-laws, which requires that the meetings of the membership remain secret, and anyone publicizing the contents of the closed sessions is subject to instant dismissal from the CFR.

Although membership lists are freely available nowadays, this was not always the case. The further back in time we go to the days of its early operation, the more secretive the CFR was. The atmosphere of secrecy was well suited to certain members. Since Allen Dulles left his position as president of the CFR in 1950 and became the director of Central Intelligence, almost all of the subsequent CIA directors have been CFR members: Richard Helms (1966–73), James Schlesinger (1973), William Colby (1973–6), George H.W. Bush (1976–7), Stansfield Turner (1977–81), William Casey (1981–7), William Webster (1987–91), Robert Gates (1991–3), James Woolsey (1993–5), John Deutch (1995–6), Porter Goss (2004–6) and Michael Hayden (2006-).

The Real Secret Rulers?

If the world today is run by any secret society, the most likely candidate would be the Council on Foreign Relations. Why them, though, and not for example the Bilderbergers? First, the Bilderberg group includes many non-Americans, and the Bilderbergers' criticisms of the US intentions and eventual military action in Iraq reflected the general European stance so obvious within the General Assembly and Security Council of the United Nations. The non-American members of the Bilderberg group were anti-American and did not evidently act as manipulators behind the scenes of history, since the military action went ahead despite their objections. So, as long as the Bilderbergers continue to take an anti-American stance, their ability to influence the only superpower in the world will be non-existent. Second, today the power lies with the Americans and so, if secret hands are pulling strings anywhere, they will be American and not foreign ones. The CFR is exclusively American.

The CFR is also a breeding ground for future presidents of the United States and their administrations. Whether Republican or Democratic, the men and women in power will have been schooled in foreign relations by the council. The number of bright young talents working their way through the council will ensure that when it comes to choosing top quality advisers, future presidents will need to look no further than the membership roll of the CFR. It has reached the point where if someone wants to exert influence in Washington, they have to pass through the doors of Pratt House.

The new world order has become a brave new world order,

where the chaotic aftermath of the old, stressfully secure bipolar world is still being studied by international relations scholars for signs of a totally new model. Until one is agreed upon and the chaos is explained, conspiracy theorists will continue to assume that everything is going to plan. If John Kerry had won the 2004 presidential election, the CFR would have had a husband and wife team in the White House. Teresa Heinz-Kerry, as controller of the Heinz foods fortune, has been a member of the CFR for many years. She is one of several powerful women to have joined the ranks of the elite since it opened up to the female sex at the end of the 1960s. (Up until then, members had been worried what their wives might think if they attended dinner meetings with unattached "ladies" present.) With the Kerry failure at the polls, the most powerful woman in America continues to be CFR member Dr. Condoleezza Rice. With the resignation of CFR member Colin Powell as Secretary of State, she moved over from her position as National Security Adviser to become, without doubt, the most powerful woman in the world.

Other members of the Council on Foreign Relations form the power nexus in present-day Washington. There is the current vice president, Dick Cheney; the current director of Central Intelligence, Lieutenant General Michael Hayden; and the current secretary of defense, Robert Gates; and the current president of the World Bank, Paul Wolfowitz. Conspiracy theorists do not have to look far to see the CFR at work. Its members control the world's banking, the world's largest intelligence-gathering apparatus, most of the media giants and most of the dominant American-based multinational corporations. With such a global coverage, anti-CFR press reports are unlikely to see the light of day, and that may be why the general public is unaware of its influence. That's the theory, anyway.

PART TWO

Chapter Five: Corporate Conspiracy

In December 2000, some revealing statistics were published by the Washington-based Institute for Policy Studies. As well as describing, in the starkest possible terms, the chasm between rich and poor countries, the report had another, even more pressing, message. Of the world's 100 largest economic entities, 51 were now corporations and only 49 were countries. Furthermore, the world's top 200 corporations accounted for over 25 percent of economic activity on the globe while employing less than one percent of its workforce. The tipping point, in terms of world power, had been reached. National governments have lost their grip on the reins of world power. In addition, those same top 200 corporations' combined sales surpassed the combined economies of 182 countries. And yet, far from improving working conditions in the countries over which they hold such influence, the top 200 have been net job destroyers in recent years. Workers' wages have languished while executive salaries have skyrocketed. Between 1980 and 1992, the 500 biggest corporations in the US saw their assets rise 227 percent, from $1.18 trillion to $2.68 trillion. Over the same period the number of people they employed fell 28 percent from 15.9 million to 11.5 million.

It is easy to draw the conclusion from these findings that globalization, or the rampant spread of corporate power, is dragging the world down. But globalization still has its defenders. One of its most eloquent apologists is *New York Times* columnist Thomas Friedman. In his recent book *The World is Flat* he argued that globalization, as well as making the world a smaller place, was also making it safer. His starting point was that the Dell computer he was using had been manufactured from parts shipped from all over the world. Arguing that "If Wal-Mart was a country, it would now be China's eighth-biggest trading partner, ahead of Russia, Australia and Canada" and "When multinationals 'outsource' work to developing countries, they typically not only save 75 percent on wages, but also gain a 100 percent increase in productivity," he went on to postulate Friedman's Dell theory. With tongue only slightly in cheek, he stated: "No two countries that are both part of a major global supply chain, such as Dell's, will ever fight a war against each other as long as they are both part of the same global supply chain, because people embedded in major global supply chains don't want to fight old-time wars any more."

This argument was a development from Friedman's earlier Golden Arches Theory of Conflict Prevention, in which he had argued that "when a country reached the level of economic development where it had a middle class big enough to support a network of McDonald's, it became a McDonald's country. And people in McDonald's countries didn't like to fight wars any more. They preferred to wait in line for burgers."

So much for Friedman's brave new world. One person who would not find himself nodding in agreement with Friedman is the writer John Raulston Saul. In his book *The Collapse of Globalism and the Reinvention of the World*, he argues that globalization is now, officially, dead, and that the nation state is making a comeback. Saul would argue that the rejection of the proposed new EU constitution in the 2005 French and Dutch referenda reflected a resistance among key groups to globalization and the laissez-faire capitalism that, for all but the urban elite, globalization represents. Saul discounts the "rising tide" theory of global economics, in which the increase in international trade would bring economic benefit to developing countries. "If you raise tides," he says, "a lot of crafts capsize."

The problem with the optimistic Friedman assessment of world economics is simply that his global network of Dell suppliers is actually quite limited. He name-checks Taiwan, Thailand, China, South Korea, Japan, Malaysia, Singapore, the Philippines, India,

North America, and even Israel. Not mentioned were any countries from South America, Africa, or Europe. Some are benefiting while others are not. And who gains most from this production drive? The corporations—such as Dell, Sony, Toshiba, Samsung, and other lesser-known names. These corporations can open a factory or parts base anywhere in the world. They pay employees minimum wages, and the governments are so desperate for jobs that they consent in being played off against other governments.

And how do companies make more money by operating abroad? Here is one way they do it from the website www.centristcoalition.com. "A multinational has two 'captive corps' plants in different countries, both operating at the same internal profit levels. But both plants use materials made by the other plant. One country has a 40 percent tax rate and the other has a 10 percent tax rate. So the company inflates the price of materials sold by the 10 percent plant to the 40 percent plant to reduce the profits of the 40 percent plant, effecting a *de facto* 'transfer' of those profits to the 10 percent plant, and thus paying lower taxes for the multinational as a whole."

It is, writes the blogger, illegal almost everywhere, on grounds of tax evasion, but it's almost impossible to prosecute and convict those companies that try it on. The result is, as John Ralston Saul says, that fewer and fewer people want to go into government, because that's not where the power is. "So you have this bizarre situation where there are more people in public life than ever before, but only a small proportion of them are democratically elected."

In fact, if it's real power you're after, go and work for a sneaker company, or a fast food organization, since these are the organizations that really control us these days. The trend towards corporate power began in earnest after World War II and can be inferred from the economic histories of companies like International Telephone and Telegraph (ITT). ITT's phenomenal growth—spearheaded by its legendary chief executive from 1959 to 1977, Harold S. Geneen—seemed to underline the progressive weakening of the authority of traditional national governments. Geneen built the company from a medium-sized telecommunications firm to a conglomerate, using leveraged buy-outs to buy over 300 companies in the 1960s, from Sheraton to Avis Rent-a-Car. Over the course of that decade, ITT's profits grew from $29 million to $550 million, but in the 1970s high interest rates ate at its profits, and public anger erupted about its influence in US elections—particularly about ITT's funding of pressure groups and payments to political parties.

That was just one of the many companies that grew so big that their power and influence threatened to outshine elected governments. These days, the problem has become greater, and the corporations have become ever more canny at disguising their real objective: power. Shell, the oil giant, claims: "We have an essential role in finding new ways to meet present and future energy needs in environmentally and socially responsible ways." Yet for all that, Shell is a major oil and gas company which employs more than 112,000 people across the world with a capital investment fund of $15 trillion. The petroleum business is notoriously unsentimental, and no pictures on the Shell website of contented workers picking flowers can disguise that fact.

In the 1970s, in the last flowering of old left political thinking in the West, no corporation wanted to be seen as wielding too much power in the world. But the rise to power of Ronald Reagan (1980–9) and Margaret Thatcher (1979–90) changed all that. In the yuppie 1980s, greed was good, and corporate conscience was for wimps. Manufacturing industries went to the wall, union power was smashed, and there was "no such thing as society"—Thatcher's statement of ultimate individuality. Stock markets woke from centuries of deep sleep, and suddenly a job in the City became sexy. The only question was whether or not a product stood or fell in the market. Britain's Tory government pushed forward an aggressive policy of privatizing publicly owned industries. It began in 1984 with British Telecom, and was followed by gas in 1986 and electricity in 1990. These newly privatized companies were supposedly "freed" by the liberal economics mantra that prevailed during that period. It was presented as radical, a new means of employee enfranchisement. In fact, something much more sinister was taking place.

Until the 19th and very early 20th centuries, expansion was the favored foreign policy initiative of many European countries. But after World War II, colonialism fell heavily out of favor, and by the end of the 20th century, the policy was being reversed all over the globe. For corporations, however, the opposite holds true. There are no brakes on a global corporation's ambitions, annexations, or invasions. The process is unregulated, and seemingly unstoppable. These corporations can continue to slice up the globe between them, seemingly without limit, as the territory on which they seek to impose themselves is not physical but commercial. As such it is almost infinitely divisible, limited only at the point when the market becomes saturated. So whereas there could have been only one flag flying over the actual territory of British Guyana, Taiwan, or Bangalore, the land itself can play host to any number of oil prospectors, shirt-makers, or call centers.

Powerful corporations are now wielding an unprecedented influence over the countries in which they operate. In 2002, the combined tobacco revenues of the world's three biggest tobacco multinationals—Japan Tobacco, Philip Morris/Altria, and BAT—came to $121 billion. That sum was larger than the total combined gross domestic product (GDP) of 27 developing countries. Poor countries, when offered jobs, revenue, exports, and foreign exchange, are unable to turn down such a package—especially when it is sweetened with a promise of "aid." And when multinational tobacco companies extend loans to small farmers for fertilizer and insecticides, they trap them into a cycle of debt. The anti-smoking lobby group Action on Smoking and Health (ASH) reports claims that several large tobacco companies "exercise overweening influence on tobacco growers" by deciding prices in a restrictive cabal, and punishing growers who try to find a different outlet for their crop. "Growers are effectively squeezed," says ASH, "with many farmers driven deeper in debt to the tobacco companies."

Tobacco companies have tended to support right-wing governments, which is why, in April 1999, when Geoffrey Bible, the president and CEO of Philip Morris, wrote a check for $1,000 to George W. Bush's election campaign, the only surprise was that it was such a modest sum. Doubtless Mr. Bush appreciated the gesture, but in reality the sums passing between tobacco companies and the GOP have been rather larger than that. Many Bush loyalists are also associated with Philip Morris, such as Karl Rove. Rove was a paid political intelligence operative for Philip Morris from 1991 to 1996 and, latterly, the president's leading election strategist. But it wasn't just a cloud of tobacco smoke that clung to him during the latter half of the 1990s. Karl Rove was one of the many Bush appointees who held stock in the company that caused the biggest corporate scandal of George Bush Jr.'s first term in office: Enron.

After Enron, the rules on corporate scandal had to be rewritten from scratch. The story of the explosion of the massive, fast-expanding energy company of the 1990s sent shudders across North America and beyond. And when George Bush was sworn into office as the 43rd president on January 20th, 2001, Karl Rove was in the process of selling between $100,000 and $250,000 of his shareholding in Enron. The connection between the Bush administration and corporate corruption, in other words, goes right the way through from ceiling to floor. Enron and its executives were the single largest contributors to the Texas Governor George W. Bush's election campaign. Enron boss Kenneth Lay was also a member of the "Pioneers"—the affectionate name awarded to any Bush supporter who raised $100,000 from contributions of $1,000 or less. So what went wrong there?

The latest news from Enron, as of April 2005, is that things can only get better. The statement that greets visitors at www.enron.com portrays a company suitably chastened after a bruising encounter with the law, doing its level best to put a brave face on a bad situation. The statement reads: "Enron is in the midst of restructuring various businesses for distribution as ongoing companies to its creditors and liquidating its remaining operations." If ever there were such a thing as corporate contrition, that is probably the nearest we'll get. But such was the scale of Enron's accounting errors that Wall Street's bad books had to be rewritten: the old rules were torn up and shredded at the end of an era that took the process of creative accountancy to new heights—or depths.

And yet, back in February 2005, the disgraced energy firm found itself once again in the spotlight it so wished it could shun, when further revelations broke about the great California power outages of 2000 and 2001. More damaging still, in a country still particularly sensitive about tape recordings of planned illegal activity, the revelations are contained on tape. According to the transcripts, Enron staff actively encouraged power station staff to flick the switches on false pretences at a power plant in Las Vegas, thus creating a power shortage. The aim was to create the conditions necessary to raise energy prices, and—until the scam was discovered—it worked.

The Enron bankruptcy scandal was the biggest corporate scandal of recent times—indeed it was to be the largest corporate bankruptcy in history. When Enron finally crashed, it was one of the ten largest companies in America, hailed as "the perfect new economy company," famous for selling everything while owning nothing. It was, and it did so—for example—by selling electricity it didn't own.

The saga began to unravel in October 2001 when news broke that it had boosted profits and hidden debts totaling over $1 billion by improperly using off-the-books partnerships. It had also manipulated the Texas power market, bribed foreign governments to win contracts abroad and manipulated the California energy market. The inquiry was led by the Department of Justice, the Stock Exchange, and the government's power watchdog, the Federal Energy Regulatory Commission. FERC ensured that, following Enron Corporation's declaration of Chapter 11 bankruptcy (which, under US law, protects the company from its creditors but allows it to continue trading) on December 2nd, 2001, allegations were made that Enron Corporation, through its affiliates, used its market position to distort electric and natural gas markets in the West.

According to A. Larry Elliott and Richard J. Schroth in their book *How Companies Lie*, "The Enron culture was driven by innovation, smart people, and big ideas on the one hand and twisted by financial engineering and greed on the other." Enron was lucky in its choice of friends. Whenever its executives felt themselves hampered by excessive regulation, they could generally rely on a sympathetic ear in the White House, and they used that influence to maximum advantage.

It couldn't last, though. Although skillful PR presented Enron as having a strong economy, it had few real assets and an enormous market capitalization. In 2001, it became known that Enron had mis-reported millions of dollars in earnings. It had masked huge debts by shifting its losses from one limited partnership to another. It was left to the company's auditor to break to Enron executives the unwelcome fact that it had to bear some of the burden of debt itself.

Creditors began knocking on the door, the Securities and Exchange Commission took a keen interest, and, with revelations appearing in the financial press on a daily basis, Enron's stock price dived. On December 2nd, 2001, Enron declared itself bankrupt.

During the previous year, Enron's executives had cashed some $1 billion of stock, taking advantage of the company's $90-a-share high. They also urged employees to invest their pension savings in Enron stock, since the company's rise seemed unassailable. When the company began to subside, though, the workers tried to get their stock out. As Enron's stock slumped to $1, some were left completely broke, with their entire life savings wiped out. That wasn't all, though. It emerged that Arthur Andersen (of which more later) had instructed its own Enron auditors to delete masses of price-sensi-tive papers, even while the Securities and Exchange Commission (SEC), the body that governs the US securities industry, was carry-ing out its inquiries. To this day, further investigations by the Senate, Congress, and Department of Justice are planned.

The political fallout was enormous, too. US Attorney General John Ashcroft had received more than $57,000 from Enron for polit-ical activities. And as we have seen, Kenneth Lay—"Kenny Boy" as he was known to President George Bush Jr.—had been one of his principal fundraisers and friends. Enron had advised Vice President Dick Cheney—indeed Cheney admitted that his staff had met Enron executives five times—when the latter had been framing the admin-istration's energy policy in the spring of 2001. The energy industry was favored with a raft of tax breaks and subsidies, and it seems hard to resist the allegation that energy policy was set with Enron's interests at heart, rather than the nation as a whole.

Kenneth Lay, along with another Enron officer, Jeffrey Skilling, was convicted of conspiracy and securities fraud on May 25, 2006. Lay never did serve time, having suddenly died of a massive heart attack on July 5, 2006. It remains to be seen if these convictions have any impact on the character of the corporate world.

Whiff of Scandal

And yet if anyone had imagined that these corporate shocks would jump-start America into a new era of corporate rectitude, they were sadly deluded. Where Enron led, or was dragged, others followed. The blood-letting climaxed in 2002 when twenty-nine major boardroom scandals emerged. Caught in the headlights were such household favorites as AOL Time Warner ("inflated sales by booking barter deals and ads it sold on behalf of others as revenue to keep its growth rate up and seal the deal"); Merck, which "recorded $12.4 billion in consumer-to-pharmacy co-payments which it never collected;" and Bristol-Myers Squibb, for inflating its 2001 revenue by $1.5 billion by means of "channel stuffing," i.e. "forcing wholesalers to accept more inventory than they can sell to get it off the manufacturer's books."

Suddenly, any company appeared to be within a whiff of scandal. Tyco International was a large, well-established corporation that manufactured a broad range of products from healthcare supplies to alarm systems. In January 2002 Tyco's chief executive, Dennis Kozlowski, resigned. In June he was indicted on charges of evading $1 million in taxes, and giving himself an interest-free loan to spend on paintings by Monet, Renoir, and other masters. He was formally charged on September 12th, 2002, along with former chief financial officer Mark Schwartz and former general counsel Mark Belnick. All three entered an innocent plea.

Kozlowski and Schwartz were also charged with issuing bonuses to themselves and other employees without the approval of Tyco's board of directors. The Tyco Fraud website says that these bonuses acted as "de facto loan forgiveness" for employees who had borrowed company money, or that they were used "to buy the silence of those who suspected the former CEO and CFO of fraud."

Kozlowski, Schwartz, and Belnick were also charged with selling company stock without telling investors, despite being obliged to do so under SEC rules. The three were accused of stealing $600 million of company money. According to the Tyco website, "an internal investigation has concluded that, although accounting errors have occurred, there is no systemic fraud problem. As a show of good faith and in effort to restore confidence in the company, Tyco has spent the past several months replacing its top board members."

Forget Terrorism

Off-balance-sheet loans; inflated capital expenses; "round-trip" deals; improper use of off-the-books partnerships; bribing foreign governments; engaging in network capacity "swaps" with other carriers to inflate revenue and inflating sales by booking barter transactions as revenue: the sheer range of crooked business practices was dazzling. As hysteria mounted, the British satirical magazine *Private Eye* caught the mood of the times in its July 2002 cover, which featured a picture of Osama bin Laden and the caption: "Forget terrorism, I'm going to become an accountant."

Some observers concluded that America, and indeed the global capitalist system, was in terminal decline. They described what they saw as an ethical vacuum at the heart of some of the biggest, plushest, most prestigious names in the business. Meanwhile, how would America—and the capitalist system it dominated—recover from this assault on its financial integrity? Would companies learn their lesson and mend their ways, or would they simply creep back, with their old tricks repackaged and harder to detect? Was an element of deception endemic in any balance sheet, such that only a hopelessly unworldly idealist could quibble if a company was less than straight with its figures?

Whatever the risks, what is certain is that the rewards can be huge. Microsoft is a well-run company that abides strictly by US accountancy and corporate governance laws; but it is the sheer wealth it generates for its owners that shocks: for example William Henry Gates III (also known as Bill) is said to be worth $53 billion, more than he could possibly lavish on his home in Medina, near Seattle in the state of Washington. Just behind him comes Warren Buffett on $46 billion, and languishing at number nine in the list of Forbes's 400 richest Americans is computer boss Michael Dell, aged 41, on $15.5 billion.

Nor is North America the only continent with an abundance of plutocrats. In Malaysia, Robert Kuok, the owner of the *South China Morning Post*, is not complaining about his $7 billion fortune, though at the age of 83 he has had to wait a while to amass that much. In fact, the combined wealth of Southeast Asia's ten richest comes to around $270 billion, and includes Malaysia, Singapore, and Indonesia.

It isn't only Asia and North America. As all British football fans know, Chelsea FC's owner Roman Abramovich is the second richest man in the former Soviet Republic thanks to his $18.7 billion ownership of Sibneft and Russian Aluminum. His wealth is dwarfed only by Mikhail Khodorkovsky, owner of the Yukos group. Khodorkovsky can point to a personal fortune of $15.5 billion, and he currently has plenty of time to count his cash since he fell out of favor with Vladimir Putin in October 2003 and has been sent to prison. Mr. Khodorkovsky's wealth is just above El Salvador's gross domestic product ($14.8 billion), which is ranked 81 in the World Bank's Gross Domestic Product table for 2003, and just less than the Dominican Republic (ranked 80), which has $16.5 billion.

"Their [the top 200 corporations'] combined global employment is only 18.8 million, which is less than a third of one one-hundredth of one percent of the world's people," claim Sarah Anderson and John Cavanagh of Global Policy Forum (GPF).

Such are the fruits of these individuals' labors through remarkably successful business careers. But as Anderson and Cavanagh write, "Not only are the world's largest corporations cutting workers, their CEOs often benefit financially from the job cuts." They go on to explain: "A total of 59 of the Global Top 200 are US firms. Of these, nine laid off at least 3,000 workers in 1995: AT&T, Boeing, Lockheed-Martin, BellSouth, Kmart, Chase Manhattan, GTE, Mobil, and Texaco." After the lay-offs were announced, the stock options for each of these companies increased, which added in value to the stock-holding portfolio of the respective CEOs by a total of $25 million. When did corporate wealth become such a good payer? And how did such vast wealth come to be combined with such a poor record on human rights?

Perhaps we should not be surprised. After all, GPF reports that there are now 40,000 corporations in the world whose activities cross national boundaries. These firms are operating through some 250,000 foreign affiliates. Would anyone be surprised to read that the top 200 corporations control well over a quarter of the world's economic activity, or that cigarette giant Philip Morris, which operates in 170 countries, is larger, in financial terms, than New Zealand? How did this surge in corporate power come about, and how did the corporations come to abandon their social responsibilities?

They've Got a Little List

The Corporate Scandal Sheet run by *Forbes* magazine and its website extends to four pages. A slightly world-weary editor's note at the end of the fourth page admits that the sheet "ceased being updated as of September 2002." By this time, on its own admission, Wall Street had become so enmeshed in vice that it was harder than ever to distinguish between normal and "creative accountancy," as the practice became known. For *Forbes*, at least, enough was enough. Could it be that the scandal-updating staff had become tired, overwrought, or simply desensitized by the successive shock waves that swept Wall Street and the rest of America's financial community during that period?

Of course, it didn't help that President George W. Bush was fighting a global war against terror at the time. In the wake of the cataclysmic breach of homeland security that took place on September 11th, 2001, Bush suddenly found himself fighting fires on several international fronts. It was a jittery time for America, and for the rest of the world, and when the corporate scandal sheet broke, it added to the cloud of uncertainty that seemed to stick to a president who still seemed unable to get his head—let alone his tongue—

round the problems of some distant but extremely rancorous foreign regimes. And yet, here it was, right on his back door: more trouble—in the form of the MCI/Worldcom scandal.

Today, the website of MCI (as Worldcom was renamed in 2004) is an object lesson in corporate optimism. "MCI is a leading provider of IP services, delivering innovative communication solutions for customers around the globe," it declares proudly. A further glance at the website assures us that "MCI is committed to serving customers with integrity and an unwavering commitment to the highest ethical standards."

As well they might. It is not until you search under "Investor Relations" that the first hints of a darker side emerge. The WorldCom Victim Trust website is "the official site for information about the US Securities & Exchange Commission's program to distribute the proceeds of the SEC's successful enforcement action against WorldCom to investors victimized by WorldCom's fraud." Visitors to this page are advised that "If you believe you may qualify for a recovery from the WorldCom Victim Trust, you must file a completed Proof of Claim Form by July 19, 2005."

The case of WorldCom is one of the most notorious. In March 2002, WorldCom, the second largest phone company in the US, was found to have overstated its profits by $3.8 billion over the previous five quarters alone and to have disguised operating expenses as capital expenses; it had also given its founder, Bernard Ebbers, $400 million in off-the-books loans. As the questions mounted, it emerged that WorldCom was sitting on a further $3.3 billion in improperly booked funds, bringing its total restatement up to $7.2 billion, and that it may have had to take a goodwill charge of $50 billion. Former CFO Scott Sullivan and ex-controller David Myers were arrested and criminally charged. Bernie Ebbers was indicted in March 2004.

Friends in High Places

As the allies' push to liberate Iraq gathered pace, all eyes were on who was going to win the contract for equipping the country with the sort of telecommunications system that a newly liberated Arab state deserved. One company that demonstrated both initiative and—in those difficult post-invasion days—no small measure of courage was a Bahrain-based firm called Batelco. Batelco had local contacts and experience in building mobile phone cells throughout the Middle East, and they were not far behind US troops as they pushed deeper into Iraq. They found plenty of work to do, with Iraq's land-lines in disarray. However, despite public acclaim for their services, Batelco fell foul of Iraq's Coalition Provision Authority stricture against companies more than ten percent owned by foreign governments from bidding on civilian cell business in US-occupied Iraq. Did that leave any other more qualified companies? Yes, as a matter of fact, there was one: MCI/WorldCom.

On May 22nd, 2003, *Computer News* restricted itself to a sober statement of the facts. "WorldCom Inc., newly branded as MCI, has won a US government contract to build a Global System for Mobile Communications (GSM) digital cell phone network in Iraq as part of a postwar rebuilding effort, the GSM Association confirmed today." The contract involved building a network of 19 cell towers that can send a wireless signal to anywhere between 5,000 and 10,000 mobile phones. Users will be aid workers and reconstruction officials based around Baghdad. The report went on to say: "The contract authorizes WorldCom to build what will at first be a small network used mostly for humanitarian relief efforts."

Others were not quite so sanguine about the story, nor as happy to see that WorldCom had pulled itself out of the mess it had been in, and seemed to be back on the road to recovery. "We don't understand why MCI would be awarded this business given its status as having committed the largest corporate fraud in history," said AT&T spokesman Jim McGann. "There are many qualified, financially stable companies that could have been awarded that business, including us."

Len Lauer, head of Sprint's wireless division, was another top telecoms executive who professed himself puzzled. "I was curious about it, because the last time I looked, MCI's never built out a wireless network," he said.

What clearly aggravated the onlookers was that, a week prior to this announcement, WorldCom and the Securities and Exchange Commission had reached a final settlement in which the phone company would pay $500 million to victims of its $9 billion accounting scandal, a soon as it had emerged from bankruptcy protection. The fine was the largest ever issued to a non-broker/dealer public company, wiping out the previous record of $10 million against Xerox in 2002.

The Iraq contract incensed WorldCom rivals and government watchdogs who say Washington has been too kind to the company since WorldCom revealed its financial shortfall. Perhaps the company was being rewarded for being good enough to submit itself to the indignity of bankruptcy proceedings. There had to be a good reason why WorldCom had swung the deal, since it was not, strictly speaking, a commercial wireless carrier. "It once resold other wireless carriers' service in the United States but dropped that approach recently," according to press reports.

The WorldCom contract angered plenty in the telecommunications industry who said that the tender was not submitted to open competition. "We were not aware of it until it showed up in some news reports," said a spokesman for Motorola.

Lieutenant Ken McClellan, a Pentagon spokesman, said that WorldCom's experience in Haiti and Afghanistan was "analogous work" to what was needed in Iraq. WorldCom spokeswoman Natasha Haubold emphasized the company's deep relationship with the US military and government, a closeness that few critics had failed to observe. The $500 million was no more than a slap on the wrist, according to observers who pointed out that WorldCom was ranked eighth—its first time ever in the Top Ten—among federal technology contractors in 2002, with $772 million in sales. WorldCom's critics said it was being bailed out by the government, a favor not extended by the all-important General Services Administration to Enron and Arthur Andersen after their scandals emerged. "The $500 million is in a sense, laundered by the taxpayers," said Tom Schatz, president of Citizens Against Government Waste.

Maybe the answer lay elsewhere. In June 2002, just a week before WorldCom's potentially disastrous accounting scandal broke, the

Washington Post reported that WorldCom had contributed $100,000 to a Republican Party fundraising gala featuring George W. Bush. John Ashcroft was said to have received $10,000 from WorldCom as a contribution to his unsuccessful re-election campaign to the Senate in 2000. Trenchant columnist Ted Rall pointed out, "Who needs experience when you have tasty political connections?" He goes on to say:

> Perhaps MCI-WorldCom will overcome its lack of experience, $5.5 billion in post-bankruptcy debt and an extensive criminal record in order to provide the people of occupied Iraq with affordable, crystal-clear cell phone service that never drops calls or loses voicemail for hours at a time. But sleazy back-room deals with Halliburton and MCI-WorldCom belie America's supposed faith in the transparency of free markets and their relationship to spreading democracy. They do more damage to our tattered relationship with the people of Iraq than any suicide bomb. And they prove beyond a reasonable doubt that George W. Bush's commitment to fight corporate fraud is just another lie.

MCI and WorldCom's moral demise was just one among many. But what lessons can the Institute of Business Ethics teach? The London-based institute was established in 1986 to encourage the highest standards of corporate and business behavior and the sharing of best practice. It runs about 30 seminars a year. As part of its Teaching Business Ethics ethos, it uses case studies, questionnaires and inventories, debates and seminars. In one such study, entitled *The Case of the Missing Barrels*, Colin Fisher of Nottingham University Business School gives an account of the consequences following Royal Dutch Shell's admission that it had overstated the oil reserves in its all-important Reserve Replacement Ratio or RRR.

The problem, says Fisher, was that in the late 1990s, Shell was not finding oil fast enough but was under internal pressure to maintain its RRR at artificially high levels. Nor did it help that a feud had broken out between Sir Philip Watts, who was now chairman, and head of exploration Walter van de Vijver.

The scandal broke on January 9th, 2004, when Shell publicly announced that it had vastly overestimated its reserves of crude oil by 20 percent, or 3.9 billion barrels. Shell's stock market lost £2.99 billion in value, and both Watts and van de Vijver were forced to resign.

Shell has done its best since then to defend both its reputation and methods. It has claimed that just because a reserve is de-booked does not mean it doesn't exist, and it goes so far as to claim that 85 percent of the missing barrels will, in the end, prove to have been there all along. Furthermore, say Shell, its approach to internal control is to *manage* risks rather than to *eliminate* them. And in September 2004, Sir Philip Watts announced that he planned to challenge the FSA in the Financial Services and Markets Tribunal, claiming that he had not been allowed to defend himself. After an independent inquiry, Shell was fined £66.29 million by the SEC and £17 million by the FSA, which accused Shell of "unprecedented misconduct" and crucially, a failure to put internal controls in place to prevent misleading information being given to the market.

The Shell case threw up a multitude of ethical issues. Not least among them was an advertisement, in February 2004, caustically described in the magazine *Accountancy Age* as "ambulance-chasing," in which the Baltimore-based law firm of Charles J. Piven explicitly seeks potential claimants for a class action against Shell on the grounds that Shell "deliberately violated accounting rules and guidelines relating to oil and gas reserves, which resulted in a shocking and unprecedented overstatement of oil and gas reserves, the eventual disclosure of which damaged purchasers of Royal Dutch and Shell Transport securities and rocked the investment community."

This is an illustration of another principle motivating corporations: one company's loss is another company's—and usually a law firm's—gain. Wherever a firm is in trouble, another firm stands to benefit from the ensuing trouble. The predatory instinct in the corporate psyche should never be underestimated.

The RRR scandal broke almost ten years after a considerably more serious scandal, the sentencing to death by hanging of nine Ogoni tribespeople in Nigeria. They included the activist Ken Saro-

Wiwa. According to the Movement for the Survival of the Ogoni People (MOSOP), Ogoniland had been producing $30 billion worth of oil for Nigeria, with Shell holding 30 percent as the principal partner. The oil production had severely polluted Ogoniland, though, so Saro-Wiwa had appealed to Shell to look hard at the environmental impact of its work. In response, Shell stopped drilling on Ogoniland, and Saro-Wiwa was charged with murder on trumped-up charges and condemned to death by hanging.

On the morning of November 10th, 1995, the sentence was carried out. "Ken Saro-Wiwa was campaigning for what Greenpeace considers the most basic of human rights: the right for clean air, land, and water. His only crime was his success in bringing his cause to international attention," said Thilo Bode, Executive Director of Greenpeace International. Bode complained: "Shell's call for 'quiet diplomacy' in the eleventh hour…has a hollow ring. Shell had ample opportunity to demonstrate concern over the seventeen months of Ken's incarceration and trial. They chose to maintain their cozy relationship with the military dictatorship to secure oil profits rather than condemn the brutal and unjust arrest and later sentencing of non-violent environmental campaigners."

The murder of Saro-Wiwa was a crime against humanity, but was anyone seriously surprised by Shell's reluctance to act? Certainly few other oil executives would be surprised, given rival oil companies' abysmal record on environmental activities and human rights. Take the case in June 2001 when a lawsuit was filed in Washington DC against ExxonMobil, on account of its activities in the Aceh province of Indonesia. "The Mobil Companies and Defendant PT Arun knew or should have known that their logistical and material support was being used to effectuate the Indonesian military's commission of…human rights atrocities," read the charge, which noted an Amnesty International report that hundreds of local people had been killed by the security forces. "ExxonMobil and PT Arun are therefore liable for the human rights abuses inflicted on the plaintiffs by the Indonesian military," it continued.

Such companies are used to coming under attack, and their defense methods are well honed. Shell, for its part, adopted a genteel policy, claiming on November 14th: "We have no links with the military and have repeatedly spoken out against violence by all parties." It concluded: "We believe the time has come for dialog and reconciliation. We welcome the sentiments of reflection and reconciliation recently expressed by Ken Wiwa [Saro-Wiwa's son] in London. We are prepared to contribute to the debate, and to take positive action with the agreement and support of all the people of Ogoni land." Unfortunately, in the case of Ken Saro-Wiwa, the call for dialog came too late, since he had been hanged four days earlier.

ExxonMobil, in its defense, firmly rebutted the claim in the lawsuit, which had been drawn up by the International Labor Rights Fund. "There is no claim of direct wrongdoing by ExxonMobil [and] the ILRF claims are based on the alleged conduct of the Indonesian military in a civil war," it snapped back. It added, in more mollifying tones: "It is our steadfast hope that the political and economic turmoil in Aceh will be peacefully resolved, so that Indonesia might use its rich base of natural and human resources for the benefit of its people." What progress was being made for human rights in Aceh—and it was precious little—was interrupted by the tsunami of 2004. Both sides may have been allowed a short period of reflection.

Whatever the merits of these complex cases, no chairman or chief executive will stay long in their post if they stop to balance the rights and wrongs of a case. The only response to a charge of wrongdoing is to hire a lawyer or brief your internal PR team, and wait for the scandal to pass over. For home-making celebrity and domestic goddess Martha Stewart, however, that option was not open.

In one of the most notorious cases of its kind, in October 2002, Dr. Sam Waksal, the immunologist who set up the giant drug company ImClone, had pleaded guilty in a New York court to six out of 13 counts of illegal share-dealing. The doomed attempt to off-load surplus stock came ahead of rumors in December 2001 that Erbitux, the company's pioneering cancer drug, had fallen foul of government regulators.

The ImClone share-dealing scandal gripped America—or at least its celebrity-obsessed media community—due to Martha Stewart's presence on the call-sheet. For she had been charged with selling

3,928 shares in ImClone Systems on December 28th, 2001 in order to dodge losses of $45,673 on the stock. Stewart was eventually indicted in 2004 for lying to SEC investigators regarding her communications with Waksal. So it was that, at 6:15 on Friday morning, October 8th, 2004, at the age of 63, Stewart left her close family behind to begin a five-month sentence at Alderson, West Virginia's women's prison. Known locally as "Camp Cupcake," the prison had opened in 1927 and had once housed Billie Holliday as well as Lynette "Squeaky" Fromme and Sara Jane Moore—joint would-be assassins of President Gerald Ford.

In March 2003, meanwhile, in order to settle civil charges, Waksal had agreed to pay $800,000 as a partial resolution of the insider trading case "without admitting or denying the allegations." In June, however, he was sentenced to just over seven years in prison and ordered to pay $4.3 million. He has the distinction of being the first ex-CEO sentenced to jail in the wave of corporate scandals plaguing US companies over the past couple of years.

So ended, or began, one of the oddest sagas in corporate American history. Stewart left prison five months later, having at one stage dropped to her knees to scrub the floor of the filthy staff office. "The experience of the last five months in Alderson, West Virginia, has been life altering and life affirming," she wrote after her release. "Someday, I hope to have the chance to talk more about all that has happened, the extraordinary people I have met here, and all that I have learned."

Dying for Trade

From the case histories described above, it would be easy to argue that corporate scandal is a historical inevitability for most companies: even, to some extent, something as frivolous as a corporate rite of passage.

Martha Stewart's statement was not an example of shameless publicity-seeking. No doubt she was deeply traumatized by the media circus, and the prospect of house arrest at the end of her prison spell did not appeal either, but if she sounded genuinely chastened by the experience of being arrested, charged, and sentenced, she seems to have been in a minority. Most employees of the corporate world would not have dreamed of accepting their guilt, nor of expressing remorse. They would have preferred to leave it to their legal team to prepare the best possible defense, and, most of the time, that would have worked. In the cases involving Shell and ExxonMobil, for example, people's lives were at stake, and those at the sharp end—the people of Aceh and Ogoni—were far from able to seek the advice of highly qualified lawyers. It may be a boardroom scandal in the head offices of Shell or ExxonMobil, but in Nigeria and Indonesia, lives have been lost.

In fact, the Enron scandal resulted in at least one tragic death, too, that of Cliff Baxter, who was vice chairman of Enron before his resignation in May 2001 and had just agreed to testify to Congress about the Enron case. It was said that he had opposed the creation of the limited partnerships which led to so much falsification of Enron's actual financial state, but he was found dead in his car from gunshot wounds, aged 44, and a suicide note was never made public, possibly for fear that it mentioned Enron. Baxter had, it is alleged, expressed concern about his personal safety in the days leading up to his death.

With stories like Enron, the corporation seems to cast a very long shadow. But most companies have learned the lesson that it makes sense to project a strongly moral image, however that may clash with aspects of its corporate behavior. Take a company like Halliburton, for example. "For almost a century, Halliburton has made an indelible impression on the world," proclaims their corporate literature. "From developing breakthrough technologies and constructing monumental infrastructure projects to managing logistics for military operations, Halliburton and our predecessor companies have been leaders in the energy services and engineering and construction industries." Halliburton employs 85,000 people in more than 100 countries. This, says Halliburton, is evidence of its "global presence and extensive, proven capabilities."

Elsewhere on the company website, more evidence is available about where those 85,000 are employed. On January 6th, 2005

Halliburton sanctioned a press release containing a tribute to William "Bill" Bradley, 50, of Galveston, Texas, whose remains had been found near Baghdad earlier in the week. Bradley, a truck driver, had been missing since April 9th the previous year, when his fuel convoy was ambushed by insurgents near Baghdad.

According to Halliburton, "Bill drove trucks all over the United States and his desire to see more of the world brought him to Iraq." According to his family—he is survived by his son, daughter-in-law, and granddaughter—he was a free spirit who loved adventure, new experiences, and motorcycles. "Bill was performing a historic and noble job and his work as a truck driver was an integral part of the reconstruction efforts in Iraq," said Halliburton. "The dedicated efforts of people such as Bill ensure that much needed supplies and equipment are delivered where they need to be. Bill paid the ultimate price while helping his country and the Iraqi people."

He was not the only one. The April 9th attack is referred to as "the deadliest day" for Halliburton employees in the Kuwait/Iraq region. "We do not have any additional details on our remaining missing co-worker, Tim Bell. Halliburton and KBR [the parent company, Kellogg, Brown & Root] continue to cooperate with the authorities." Nor were Bell and Bradley the only Halliburton employees to lose their lives in the region. On March 28th, 2005 came a tribute to Roy Eugene Hyatt, a carpenter foreman at the time of his death. April 25th, 2005 saw details of the lives of Ronald Wade, Lance Taylor, and Sy Lucio, killed when their Chinook helicopter crashed outside Kabul.

"We strongly urge you to respect the privacy of the family during this most difficult time," says the press release. "Halliburton and our subcontractors have lost 62 employees while performing services under our contracts in Kuwait and Iraq."

This criticism is not aimed solely at Halliburton. As the New York-based newspaper *Village Voice* reported on May 5th, 2003, the main instrument of the US in Iraq is not the Pentagon, the US Agency for International Development, or the Army Corps of Engineers, but the Bechtel Group. The claim followed news that the giant international engineering outfit had won a contract worth up to $680 million which gave the company a leading role in rebuilding Iraq, a job which some estimate may end up costing around $100 billion.

Bechtel may be a mighty powerful organization, but it knows the importance of cultivating close ties with politicians. "It is the 17th largest defense contractor, with $1.03 billion in Defense Department deals," said the *Voice*. And it has powerful friends both within and outside government. "Jack Sheehan, a vice president, is on the Defense Policy Board, which advises [then] Secretary of Defense Donald Rumsfeld. Riley Bechtel, the company chairman, is on the President's Export Council...Both Reagan's Secretary of Defense, Caspar Weinberger, and Reagan's Secretary of State, George Shultz, came from Bechtel. Shultz is currently a director. Reagan sent Rumsfeld to Iraq as his special envoy during the early 1980s to encourage Saddam in Iraq's war with Iran."

The war threw up challenges for both companies. On April 4th, 2005 *Forbes* magazine's Peter Elkind reported that federal prosecutors were investigating how Halliburton had sidestepped US sanctions against doing business with Iran as well as a former KBR chairman's alleged involvement in a Nigerian bribery scandal and possible bid-rigging overseas. There was mention of an ugly encounter with the SEC dating back to 1998, focusing on the failure to disclose an accounting change that allowed the company to hit its quarterly earnings targets. Halliburton had settled the case in 2004 after paying a $7.5 million penalty, reflecting the SEC's view that "unacceptable lapses" in Halliburton's cooperation had delayed the investigation. Then there was the company's attempt to cut off promised health benefits for 4,000 retirees, which a federal judge then blocked.

But it didn't end there. According to the website www.halliburtonwatch.org, on June 11th, 2004 the US Department of Justice opened an investigation into an alleged $180 million bribe paid by Halliburton, during Cheney's period as CEO, to the government of Nigeria in exchange for a contract to build a $4 billion natural gas plant in Nigeria's southern delta region. In addition, the FBI began to investigate the army's $7 billion firefighting contract for Iraqi oil wells, which was awarded to Halliburton without competition in March 2003. "An army whistleblower told the FBI that the line between government officials and Halliburton had become so blurred that a perception of conflict of interest existed," says the website. And, as well as the four former employees who allege "systemic" accounting fraud from 1998 to 2001, there was more besides.

If Halliburton's operating record is so lamentable, why then does it continue to win such valuable contracts? It surely can't hurt that it has powerful friends in the White House.

When it was reported on March 25th, 2003 that President Bush had asked for $489.3 million to cover the cost of repairing damage to Iraq's oil facilities, and that much or all of it could go to Halliburton or its subcontractors under the terms of its contract with the army, enemies of Bush were apoplectic with rage. It was the brazenness of the announcement that so infuriated Bush's critics, as if no one would object, or suspect—or be able to reverse the decision. They might even have preferred it if the White House had told a half-truth, if only to acknowledge that they felt a tinge of guilt at the news.

And yet the White House, or at least a part of it, seems somewhat disenchanted with the quality of service they have received. By March 2004, several audits were being prepared by various federal agencies regarding Halliburton's work in Iraq. One claimed in December 2003 that Halliburton had overcharged the Defense Department by $61 million to import gasoline into Iraq from Kuwait. The total overpayment by Halliburton as of April 1st, 2004 was revised up to $167 million. Also in December 2003, a Defense Contract Audit Agency (DCAA) audit claimed that Halliburton repeatedly violated the Federal Acquisition Regulation and submitted a $2.7 billion proposal that "did not contain current, accurate, and complete data regarding subcontract costs." And on January 13th, 2004, the DCAA expressed doubt over Halliburton's "ability to consistently produce well-supported proposals that are acceptable as a basis for negotiation of fair and reasonable prices."

Faced with such incompetence, one wonders that the company can win a single contract. And yet they continue to do just that. Nor, of course, are they alone. Across the world, in Italy, an equally venerable company has been facing a barrage of criticism. The company is Parmalat, famous for producing long-life milk, and details began to emerge in October 2004 of the scale of the fraud with which it had become embroiled.

The scale of this scandal is staggering, even by Italian standards. Parmalat admits that it owes €14.3 billion, which is ten times what it claimed it owed. Trials were being planned for up to 29 employees, from its founder to its chief financial officer and lawyers.

It all started to go wrong in December 2003 when, rather like the beginnings of the Enron scandal, Parmalat found itself in difficulty when settling a €150 million bond payment. If the company was worth almost €4 billion, as it claimed, what was the problem and where was the cash? Parmalat's founder, Calisto Tanzi, made light of the problem, but the doubts remained.

Parmalat then went one better than Enron when its bankers, Bank of America, said it had no evidence of €3.9 billion of holdings. Investigators tried without success to find out if the money ever existed. Forced into administration, Parmalat was forced to sell some of its subsidiaries in order to free up some assets. Meanwhile, it was the investors who had lost out, with shares formerly worth €1.8 billion worthless. Prison sentences may assuage some investors' anger, but only partially.

In Britain, too, scandals have emerged that have dented investor confidence, such as the arms-to-Iraq cover-up, in which British weapons manufacturers were taken to court for trying to smuggle arms out of the country during the 1980s, with the government's tacit approval. Much has changed in corporate circles since then. Would any corporation be so naive again? One farcical incident was the great Dome fiasco which was meant to see in the new year and the new millennium.

Tony Blair's government had invested hugely in the Dome, and the "Dome minister" Peter Mandelson had been marketing it as one of the defining images of the first term of the Blair government. A site was found near Greenwich, the site of the Greenwich Time

Signal, and an area of industrial sludge was cleared in order to create what the government hoped would be a fitting tribute for the new millennium, evoking comparisons with the Festival of Britain of 1951. It was by far the most lavish celebration to be staged across the whole of Europe, with other major cities like Paris and Bonn preferring to put their trust in concerts and light shows.

Even though the mud had been cleared away, the project got bogged down. Soon, Dome ministers were coming and going, and when the Dome eventually opened, the first night party—to which all the great and good were invited—got off to a disastrous start. It was a considerable achievement to persuade several newspaper editors—including some who were decidedly ambivalent about the New Labour government—to forego their editorial limousines and take the Jubilee Line train out to North Greenwich. Less impressive, though, was the delay which kept them standing in line, kicking their heels together for up to two hours. Good will was hard to find after that.

Less impressive still was the content of the Dome itself. What could the government have been thinking? visitors wondered, as they fought to get through a churning mass of retail outlets, which dwarfed any genuine attempt at popular education. The government may have been disappointed that it didn't attract the promised 12 million visitors, but it was crowded enough, with bored and disconsolate children hanging around the fast food stands, wondering if that was all.

In the event, the contrasts with the idealism, wit, and technical brilliance of the Festival of Britain proved to be very unfortunate, and for many, the New Labour experiment foundered from that moment on. And the reason was that the government had been seduced by corporate interests, and had given them too much say in the project.

Maybe the whole project underlined the spent ideological force that governments had now become. If the project had been handled by a company with the wit and sparkle of Nike, say, history might have been very different. The government was unable to generate good publicity for the Dome.

★ ★ ★ ★ ★

What was the fallout from some of the scandals that gripped corporate America? What fate befell the protagonists and were their reputations dented? In the case of Enron, for example, its fading fortunes were inextricably linked with those of another financial giant, the grand old home of accountancy, Arthur Andersen, whose ignominious exit from the Big Five group of major accountants led to them being rebranded the Big Four. The Chicago-based auditing specialist was found to have been complicit, even proactive, in much of the skullduggery of which Enron itself was accused.

What should amaze us more about this whole sordid business? That David Duncan, a former Andersen partner in Houston, pleaded guilty in April 2002 to shredding key documents, or the brazenness with which, just a few months earlier, the company had announced that the two halves of Arthur Andersen Worldwide—Arthur Andersen and Arthur Andersen Consulting—broke off into separate units, with the latter relaunching and rebranding itself as Accenture? Sorry about that, they seemed to be saying. Bit messy, but let's draw a line under it and move on. And most of the financial world did just that.

What's the Problem?

According to the website of the management consultants George S. May International, the following masquerades as justifications for what ends up as corporate fraud:

Everyone else does it.

They'll never miss it.

Nobody will care.

The boss does it.

No one will know.

I don't have time to do it right.

That's close enough.

Some rules were meant to be broken.

It's not my job.

In the light of these excesses, many have asked whether it is in a corporation's genes to behave deceptively. There is a strong case for saying precisely that. Since a successful company advances by being predatory, aggressive, paranoid, and secretive, perhaps it would be naive to expect them to reveal their inner secrets in their financial accounts or any other such sensitive documents.

On the other hand, some deny that the problem is widespread. As James F. Parker, CEO of Southwest Airlines, told *Business Week* on June 24th, 2002: "I think it's unfortunate that the misdeeds of a few have had the effect of creating questions and undermining confidence of business in general."

Or not. Frank Vogl runs his own PR company and is a director of the Washington-based Ethics Resource Center. According to Vogl, it all went wrong in the 1990s. During that decade, "We went from 'greed is good' being said as a joke to people thinking 'greed is good' was a fundamental fact."

Vogl describes US corporations as global leviathans whose fortunes influence the fates of nations. "Damage to the fabric of US business ricochets across the globe," he says, "and hits all economies, and the prospects for the people who live in those economies."

A more extreme point was made recently by author Joel Bakan in his book *The Corporation*. According to Bakan, corporations are psychopathic entities, with no motive—no ethical stance, even—beyond returning a profit for their shareholders. He quotes such grandees as the economist Peter Drucker, whose view is: "If you find an executive who wants to take on social responsibilities, fire him fast."

The hard-ball mantra is descriptive more of Anglo-Saxon economics—or at least it used to be. In Continental Europe, in what is meant to be the rest of the united Europe, they always used to do things slightly differently. Take, for example, the unedifying spectacle of the German Chancellor Helmut Kohl, lecturing a mortified British Prime Minister John Major in 1995 when the Shell corporation seemed determined to dump its oil platform, Brent Spar, in the North Sea.

In Germany, at the time, corporate governance rules were very different from Britain's liberalizing right-wing economic agenda. In Germany, unlike Britain, corporations have a legal responsibility to consider social issues. Corporate social responsibility (CSR) is well established in Germany. A study by the European Monitoring Center on Change, published in January 2005, found that "CSR in Germany goes hand in hand with the national economic and social framework and is considered a fundamental part of their highly regulated and institutionalized industrial relations system." In the UK, by contrast, the picture is of "restricted development of CSR to date" but with "signs of recent activity in this area."

An associated issue is the matter of size. Would it be overcynical to say that the bigger a company gets, the less moral it becomes? It is as if it is an essential condition of growth that it should jettison its ethical baggage. Witness the number of companies which have been roundly criticized, even mocked in the business community for having generous pension arrangements, or those companies in Scandinavia that offer generous maternity or paternity leave. The inevitable conclusion is that ethical behavior is contrary to a company's interests and, commercially speaking, ill-advised.

Companies are limited only by their imaginations. One such is the American firm RiceTec, which is trying to patent basmati rice. According to SAWTEE, the South Asian Watch on Trade, Economics, and Environment, in an article published in February 2004: "The case of the Basmati patent is one among many examples of biopiracy." RiceTec is a biotechnology firm, and it was granted a patent for basmati rice, which it grows and exports from America.

India and Pakistan, in a rare moment of unity, provided evidence that pure basmati rice must come from that region alone, and India provided evidence that not only the grain but also the seeds and plants that produce the grain have been bred and cultivated in India and Pakistan. You can't yet buy RiceTec basmati rice, but you can buy their Jasmati® and Kasmati® rice, and there are still fears that the US Patent and Trademark Office will allow RiceTec to market its own brand as "superior." The case is ongoing.

Furthermore, according to BBC News, "five biotechnology companies—Aventis, Dow, DuPont, Mitsui, Monsanto, and Syngenta—between them own 69 percent of the patents granted on rice, wheat, maize, soy, and sorghum. These staple crops account for almost three-quarters of the world's food supply."

That, at least, was to do with food. Infinitely more tragic and costly was the disaster that befell the Indian city of Bhopal on the night of December 2nd/3rd, 1984, when the Union Carbide plant in the city began leaking 27 tons of the deadly gas methyl isocyanate into the air. None of the six safety systems designed to contain such a leak were operational, allowing the gas to spread throughout Bhopal. "Half a million people were exposed to the gas and 20,000 have died to date as a result of their exposure," says a reporter on the Bhopal Medical Appeal. "More than 120,000 people still suffer from ailments caused by the accident and the subsequent pollution at the plant site. These ailments include blindness, extreme difficulty in breathing, and gynecological disorders." The site has never been properly cleaned up and it continues to poison the residents of Bhopal.

In 1999, local groundwater and well water testing near the site of the accident revealed mercury at levels between 20,000 and six million times those expected. Chemicals that cause cancer, brain-damage, and birth defects were found in the water; trichloroethene, a chemical that has been shown to impair fetal development, was found at levels 50 times higher than EPA safety limits. Testing published in a 2002 report revealed poisons such as 1,3,5 trichlorobenzene, dichloromethane, chloroform, lead, and mercury in the breast milk of nursing women.

In 2001, the Michigan-based chemical corporation Dow Chemical purchased Union Carbide, thereby acquiring its assets and liabilities. "But Dow Chemical has steadfastly refused to clean up the site, provide safe drinking water, compensate the victims, or disclose the composition of the gas leak, information that doctors could use to properly treat the victims."

Incredibly, Union Carbide has yet to be punished for its shocking defects. How can people take action against such corporate encroachment? Not, it seems, by asking the heads of the major industrial democracies—now known as the Group of 8, or G8, which regularly meets to address economic and political issues. The main charge against G8 (to which we return in more detail in Chapter Seven) is that it is no more than a talking shop. Central to the allegation are the activities of the Make Poverty History and Jubilee 2000 organizations. These lobbying groups have been campaigning for some time to make the West rethink its attitude to Third World debt. Africa Action, which has been campaigning for the continent since 1953, is one of several bodies to point out the sheer inactivity and lack of imagination of the world's wealthiest countries. After the G8 summit in June 2003, Africa Action issued a statement lamenting the "stunning failure to make progress on the debt, health, trade, and agriculture issues." Compared to the progress made by the African Union, the G8 was "still a long way off meeting the $25–35 billion required by the UN to halve poverty in Africa by 2015."

Africa Action noted the $10 billion offered by the US for Global Aids programs, but said that the money had not reached its destination. In addition, it noted with alarm that "the G8 continues to spend less than 0.3 percent of their gross national product on aid. In all, the G8 Summit closes with offers of assistance in the range of less than 1 percent of what was spent on the war in Iraq."

The situation with regard to HIV and AIDS was, if anything, even more depressing. The G8 conference had failed to propose any effective progress in the combat and treatment of the epidemic. Africa Action noted "a lost opportunity for progress on the right of African countries to import, produce, and distribute cheap life-saving drugs such as anti-retroviral medicine for AIDS and other life-threatening diseases."

The following year, in June 2004, African countries again appealed to the G8 leaders to ease their burden. After an emotional plea, both for debt relief and for extensive debt cancellation, the G8 rebuffed this offer, making a counter offer which amounted to a two-year extension of the so-called "heavily indebted poor countries initiative," or HIPC.

African leaders reacted with scorn. "All African debt needs to have relief, otherwise whatever we do in other areas will amount to eroding from what we need to have in terms of a flow of resources to be able to move Africa forward," said Nigerian President Olusegun Obasanjo after the meeting.

Meanwhile, recent declines in the stock market reflects a new distrust of the American way of business. Back in 2002, as the ripples from the stock market crash spread across the world, the British writer Edward Chancellor discussed the fate of the stock market in the light of WorldCom scandal and others. "For many years," he wrote, "the US financial and political establishment has lectured the rest of the world on how to conduct its business affairs. Now the once-vaunted Anglo-Saxon way of capitalism is looking distinctly less appealing."

The historical framework that Chancellor describes has deepened since then. We may not be assailed daily with fresh news of corporate blood-letting, but the pain—even if we have become numbed to it—has opened our eyes to something corporeally corrupt about our business institutions. In essence, we are all now living in a post-Enron, post-ImClone, post-WorldCom world. It is only a matter of time before another institutionally corrupt corporation will be dragged down under the weight of debt or accountancy fraud. Equally bleakly, and with a few honorable exceptions, the institutions we used to call the gatekeepers of the system—auditors, stock-market regulators, company analysts, professional fund managers, and investment banks, as well as the business media—have also failed, according to Edward Chancellor, in their policing duty.

Chancellor says that the only way from here is down, and that the stock market will experience a long decline, reflecting a new distrust of the American way of business.

Stock-market bubbles are normally accompanied by national-istic hubris. One thinks of the "bubble economy" of the 1980s, when it was argued that Japanese business success could be explained by its corporate and bureaucratic structures and the innate superior-ity of its workforce. A decade's recession in Japan and the more than two-thirds decline of the Nikkei stock market from its 1989 peak have put an end to such talk. The American bubble of the late 1990s was also rationalized on the basis of the superior flexibility and innovation of the US business world. With their ability to harness new technology and exploit new markets, companies such as Enron and WorldCom were seen as paragons of the US business model.

Joel Bakan, author of *The Corporation*, would no doubt agree with Chancellor when he says that foreign countries have for too long been advised to allow companies to be run for the exclusive bene-fit of their shareholders in the name of "shareholder value." This policy was pursued "regardless of the interests of their employees and customers and the localities where they operated." This was a buyer's market, as well as being something of a jungle. Any com-pany that lagged behind the others was at risk of being bought and plundered by its swifter rivals. The successful company arrived with a battery of management consultants who all had their tool kits and labels marked "market-valued added," "total shareholder return," and "enterprise value added."

A small number of US investment banks became globally dom-inant players during the 1990s. They rated companies on account of their potential to provide a return on an investment. Together with the banks, they talked up new-economy businesses and pre-pared them for public offer on the stock markets. Simultaneously, mergers and acquisitions departments were cheering lustily from the wings for the takeover stakes to be ranked ever higher. In 1999, the value of this takeover bonanza came to more than $1 trillion in Europe and the United States.

Inevitably, after the bubble has burst, the recriminations begin. On February 22nd, 2002, the accountancy group KPMG Consulting reported the results of a study that claimed that one-third of the international takeovers agreed at the peak of the late 1990s were coming apart at the seams. The group had already caused a stir years before in a report which claimed that, for the majority of the 500 biggest takeovers during the boom years, acquisition had not boosted but actually reduced the share price of the partner companies. This new report cast doubt over whether the whole acquisitions strategy could be said to create value for investors even in the long term.

Cream for the Fat Cats

Vodafone, the UK mobile operator, took over its rival Mannesmann in 1999 and lost more than three-quarters of its value over the next three years. And yet Vodafone's boss, Sir Christopher Gent, still received a £10 million bonus for completing the Mannesmann deal. There was more controversy when Vivendi Universal, the French media company, acquired Canada's Seagram in 2000 for $34 billion, and through it Universal Studios. The company's share value plummeted by 70 percent, and its chief executive, Jean-Marie Messier, was forced to resign in July 2002. After another lengthy investigation into further charges of creative accountancy, Vivendi Universal and Jean-Marie Messier were each fined one million euros by French regulators in December 2004. The 15-month investigation found that Messier had "deceived the public."

In the marketplace, the only value shareholders understand is the share price. For example, 3G mobile phone licenses were bought for sums greater than €100 billion when they first came on the market, such was the confidence put in third-generation mobile phone technology. Then the market got cold feet. Suddenly the brand-new marketing, the untried technology, and the lack of clear research into mainstream audience demand led the market to the conclusion that the price paid had been too high. Within a few months of the 3G auctions, the shares of the winning license-holders slid back down to Earth. "Such is the fate," writes Chancellor, "that befalls those who would pursue the shareholder-value grail."

Many in the business community are also beginning to question the enormous disparity between equity-linked CEOs' salaries and the humbler wages of their employees. Business insiders are openly questioning whether it is good business strategy to harness the top executive's paycheck with the company's share price. Is this good news for businesses, investors, or the economy? Stock options as a means of compensation suffer from several flaws, writes Edward Chancellor. "As with all aspects of shareholder value, they involve a confusion of market price and intrinsic value. Why should an executive receive a huge bonus simply because his company's shares are in demand? Does this reflect a genuine contribution to shareholder value or simply the fad of the market?"

Linking the managerial pay packet to corporate equity was, it was felt, dangerously similar to leaving someone with a drinking problem with the keys to a liquor factory. The temptation for management to fix the equity-linked bonus was all too often too strong. At boom times, companies that gave the market what it liked in the form of an annual per-share earnings growth of 15 percent were favored. But in flatter times, this target was clearly unachievable. There were various ways to achieve earnings-growth targets. First, investors would not be given the whole picture about a company's growth: awkward details such as depreciation charges would be overlooked in favor of unofficial and unaudited earnings figures. Also, earnings growth per share could be enhanced by borrowing more to repurchase shares. Another way was for companies to reduce research or investment costs so as to give a misleading impression of sustainable earnings growth. Fourth, many companies went on buying sprees by snapping up less highly valued companies.

The business strategy that these values championed was typified by the behavior of people like Al Dunlap, a ruthless cost-cutter who worked for the British billionaire, the late Sir James Goldsmith, and the Australian media tycoon Kerry Packer. When Dunlap was hired in July 1996 by Sunbeam, a moribund consumer products company, he announced his arrival by letting go of 3,000 of its 12,000 workers and selling off subsidiaries employing another 3,000. He also eliminated all forms of corporate charity and closed 18 factories. The financial payoff was unmistakable: Sunbeam's stock climbed from $12 to $44 in barely a year, but as David Plotz wrote in *Slate* magazine:

> It's easy to hate Dunlap for the wrong reason, which is that he is a brutal, heartless, arrogant bastard. According to *Business Week*, Dunlap skipped the funerals of both his parents, failed to support (or even pay attention to) the child from his first marriage, and refused to help pay for his niece's cancer treatments. But to criticize Dunlap for his cruelty is akin to scolding a lion for killing an antelope. Dunlap lacks conscience? Well, so does the market. If Wall Street were a CEO, it would skip its parents' funerals, too.

Another company, Scott Paper, was worth around $3 billion when Dunlap arrived in mid-1994. In late 1995, when he sold Scott to Kimberly-Clark for $9.4 billion, Dunlap awarded himself a $100 million bonus for the sale. As David Plotz wrote: "Sooner or later—almost certainly sooner—Dunlap will quit Sunbeam, liquidate his stock options, clear a profit of about $100 million, and move on to another high-profile job. Sunbeam will be worth a lot more than it was when Dunlap arrived. It may not be a better company."

So it should have been. In fact, in a classic case of managerial hubris, Dunlap was fired almost two years later when the company's stock price began to decline in line with its poor performance. Suddenly, Dunlap's bullying qualities became negatives. For once, he was out of fashion, the wind turned, and Dunlap was, for a while, out in the cold.

In the same year that the Enron scandal hit the news-stands, customer-relationship-management software developer Broad Vision remembered in April that it had forgotten to include $4 million of expenses for the last quarter of the year 2000. As a result—and the confusion among the accountancy team must have been considerable at this revelation—its January earnings were precisely double what they should have been. Its stock sank 75 percent for 2001, and the company, which had only just been added to the

Standard & Poor 500 index, was removed the following August.

In the financial year 2001 to 2002, what Edward Chancellor called "the shareholder-value obsession" produced Enron, the world's largest bankruptcy, and WorldCom, the world's greatest accounting fraud. In addition, the two largest acquisitions in history—Vodafone by Mannesmann and AOL by Time Warner—destroyed hundreds of billions of dollars of shareholders' funds, but with the markets in decline, could it be that scandals like WorldCom will signal the end for all this corporate excess? Chancellor looks forward to "a new era in which the probity and prudence of management [will be] stressed above its entrepreneurial ability." Alongside that, he hopes that the pursuit of long-term corporate goals will replace an emphasis on short-term share-price appreciation. And, just as Joel Bakan would wish, he expresses the hope that "shareholders' position in the corporate hierarchy [will be] diminished and that of employees and customers enhanced."

The End of the Social Market?

Since Helmut Kohl's impassioned intervention on behalf of the Brent Spar oil platform in 1995, the mounting costs of German unification have continued to put pressure on the Germany economy, and in January 2005, unemployment was measured at just over five million, or 12 percent. In the circumstances, the belt-tightening measures imposed by Peter Hartz, the head of human resources at the German car manufacturer Volkswagen, have caused yells of defiance from some, and a resigned shrug of acceptance from others. His proposals, labeled "Hartz IV," are the biggest overhaul of Germany's generous system in decades, sweeping away many prerogatives and long-established entitlements. The problem is that there are hundreds of thousands of well-qualified people who are eager to work (especially in eastern Germany), but who just cannot find any work, simply because times are hard and there is no work. Instead, some of them are having to work for just one euro an hour in a job that they might well enjoy doing, so long as they were being paid a real wage. Not surprisingly, these people feel extremely wronged by the situation.

Even in France, where unemployment is approaching ten percent, employers are beginning to contemplate the same cost-cutting steps as in Germany. Until now, France has had generous unemployment benefits. In Britain, under Margaret Thatcher's economic heirs, companies which can no longer afford to pay their creditors can simply shut up shop and disappear without paying any reparations. In France, however, the assets must be stripped to compensate the workers—but for how long? A new economic program is being scripted for Jacques Chirac's government by its pragmatic party leader Nicolas Sarkozy. The old certainties may be about to change as the dominant countries of the EU shape up for a war—this time fought with chief executives, not generals. Will the Anglo-Saxon model of "vulture capitalism" prevail, or will the old Franco-German model survive?

Not all countries can afford to take corporate social responsibility so seriously. In China, where 500 million people are peasants, the regions are competing with each other to make themselves attractive to western investments. In that climate, and with such a low-cost economy, there is little incentive to guarantee the rights of workers.

Does big business, then, rule the world? Certainly globalization is becoming the engine that keeps the world turning. And, in theory, its cost savings are defensible. But the savings that big companies make are created on the backs of small and medium-sized companies. They lose, therefore, and the big companies win. One consequence of this is the monoculture that now pervades main streets. In June 2005, the UK-based New Economics Foundation issued a report which claimed that four out of ten of Britain's main streets were "clone towns," made up of chain stores with no regional or local identity. "The individuality of main street shops has been replaced by a monochrome strip of global and national chains," it stated. Many towns had become "somewhere that could easily be mistaken for dozens of bland town centers across the country."

Nevertheless, as long as the cash tills at Boots, W.H. Smith, and Gap are still ringing, the bosses won't be fearing for their jobs.

"Corporate power is now the world's foremost threat to democracy," according to the eco-journalist George Monbiot. He expanded on the point in an article written for the *Guardian* in February 2002: "Such is the institutional power of the corporations that the only people now in a position to hold them to account are other companies. When Amnesty International revealed that Indian police paid by Enron were beating and sexually abusing people living where it wanted to build a power plant, the news was received with horror by campaigners but ignored by almost everyone else. But when institutional shareholders lose their investments, the scandal dominates the headlines all over the world.

Chapter Six: Voices of Dissent

What is the point of dissidence? What use does dissent serve? Against a background of rising capitalist self-confidence, a generation of writers have taken up arms against the forces of globalization. They have denounced corporate tyrants and boardroom corruption. They have railed against the sinister spread of executive power, and the perceived retreat of national boundaries. But have they really achieved anything, or are they merely leaving us better informed—but as impotent as ever? No study of the spread of corporate excess would be complete without taking a hard look at some of its most outspoken critics, to try and answer the question: what are they all talking about?

Modern Dissidents

As the 1980s gave way to the 1990s, consumer warfare replaced martial warfare in the prosperous West. And at the dawn of the 1990s, the technology revolution powered by computers and the internet assumed a prominence not seen before. One of the most talked-about titles to greet readers of the new century was Naomi Klein's *No Logo*. Originally subtitled *Taking Aim at the Brand Bullies*, the book explores—and exposes—the ways today's corporations seek to merge their identities with our sense of self. It was Klein, for example, who revealed that Nike paid Michael Jordan more in 1992 for endorsing its sneakers ($20 million) than the company paid its entire 30,000-strong Indonesian workforce for making them. It was anger at this injustice that made people aim their anger at Nike Town superstores, rather than against governments.

In an interview, Klein maintained: "Even if we don't have a public sphere, even if we've totally bought into this Thatcherite idea that there is no such thing as society, that we're all consumers and investors, suddenly we know that actually you can't place value on human life and you can't commodify seeds, and the depth of the ocean are commons. That's why I'm involved in this, because I think that we need to reclaim the public, the commons."

In her book, she looks at the phenomenon of corporate branding, and at the way in which, for example, the Nike "swoosh" has gone from being just a mark on the side of a sports item to representing sport—or a certain lifestyle. In the process, Nike has taken the decision to remove itself from the process of manufacturing sports shoes, preferring to divert funds towards promoting itself as a brand. Klein discusses ways in which global retailers are invading the common realm. (See for example "Team Nike," otherwise known as the Brazil soccer team.) She also discusses how companies such as Starbucks can put local coffee shops out of business, and how, for example, tobacco companies can have anti-tobacco protesters ejected from events in which they have a commercial interest. She also shows how anyone hoping to join a union in a fast food company or Starbucks might be advised to think again.

Klein also travels to the developing world, to see for herself the working conditions of those who stitch together the shoes, trousers, and dresses that sell so well and for such high prices in the shops of New York, Paris and London. She finds a manufacturing plant in the Philippines called Cavite in which the workers are mostly young women aged from 19 to 25. All have traveled long distances to work there, thus increasing their sense of alienation and powerlessness. If any have contracts, they are deliberately given short-term ones (usually between one and five months) to prevent them being able to claim statutory rights—and to make it more difficult for them to form unions. The workers live crammed into squalid dormitories which, in places, are so dark that white lines have to be drawn to help them distinguish between bed and floor. They work long hours, often up to 12 or more a day, for a few cents per hour. Overtime is compulsory. The women have to take regular pregnancy tests, and face instant dismissal if found to be pregnant.

There are many such terrible stories in Klein's book, though there are also stories of people fighting back, such as the famous McLibel case in which Helen Steel and Dave Morris—an unemployed postman and a community gardener—fought the mighty McDonald's corporation in a court case that lasted an unprecedented 313 days. The McLibel story is an extraordinary and—for those on the same side as the battling duo—inspiring tale. Having been served with a writ for libel by McDonald's, Steel and Morris produced 180 witnesses who told the court about food poisoning, bogus recycling claims, dubious claims about the so-called "nutritional" qualities of McDonald's burgers, and a failure to pay overtime rates. Klein delights in telling the entire story, and it provides a central theme to her book, which is about the empowerment of the individual to take on the might of the corporation. The *Guardian* journalist John Vidal described the case in his 1997 book *McLibel: Burger Culture on Trial*.

Corporate Takeovers

If Klein is concerned with how corporations manipulate consumers, build brands, and exploit workers, British writer George Monbiot—as we saw at the end of Chapter Five—believes that the modern western state is in real danger of being taken over by corporate interests. In the introduction to his *Captive State* (first published 2000), he describes how public bodies are being drawn into—and devalued by—contact with commercial interests. It could be something as apparently minor as the sponsoring of the saddles of the City of London's mounted police, which were printed with the logo of HSBC bank: surely a conflict of interests. Or it could be something more serious. Monbiot cites a company's sponsorship of a fringe meeting at the 1999 Labour Party conference, but a glance at the website of www.sourcewatch.org since *Captive State* was published shows that the habit dies hard. At the 2004 Labour Party conference,

Tesco sponsored the delegates' inaugural drinks party. The financial company Bloomberg, meanwhile, picked up the drinks bill for what was called an "internal reception." Large companies, the legal requirement for which (in Britain, at least) is to maximize shareholder value and profit, are forging close alliances with, and attempting to influence, government—whose duty is to protect the interests of the population generally.

Monbiot also shows how "the provision of hospitals, prisons, and roads in Britain has been deliberately tailored to meet corporate demands rather than public need." He argues that planning permission for urban regeneration projects has been offered to the highest bidder, and that supermarkets ruthlessly suppress competition and control their markets. He also discusses the corporate takeover of Britain's universities and "the resulting distortions of the research and teaching agendas."

Taking a Stand

Klein and Monbiot are far from being the only writers to take on the big corporations. David C. Korten is president and founder of the People-Centered Development Forum, an organization dedicated to advancing people-centered development through a growing citizens' movement towards a just, inclusive, and sustainable society. His book *When Corporations Rule the World* was first published in 1995, and there have been several other titles from a similar angle, more recently *The Post-Corporate World* (1999). *When Corporations Rule the World* is about power, and how globalization, deregulation, and privatization have transferred that away from people and governments and towards financial institutions and corporations. "The result," he writes, "is a global crisis in which the few become wealthy beyond imagination while the many live in dehumanizing poverty and desperation, critical life support systems fail, and the social fabric disintegrates."

Another key text is *The Growth Illusion* by former British government economist Richard Douthwaite, originally published in 1992. Douthwaite is one of many disciples of E.F. Schumacher, whose 1973 book *Small Is Beautiful* argued that the growth of corporatism and the pursuit of profit had reduced economic inefficiency, degraded the environment, and caused a substantial downturn in working conditions. In his seminal work, Douthwaite talked about sustainability and turning the "small is beautiful" principle into an economic reality. The book argues that while growth might be necessary to generate jobs, the development path we are following is not making life better for ourselves or our children. Douthwaite's *The Growth Illusion* is subtitled *How Economic Growth has Enriched the Few, Impoverished the Many, and Endangered the Planet*, and the distinguished environmentalist Edward Goldsmith lends his influence by contributing the foreword.

Dissidents tend to have a narrow constituency, but one or two have broken through and attract a larger than usual audience. One such is John Pilger, who has been winning awards since 1966. His books on Vietnam, Cambodia, and the Middle East have been lauded for his forensic journalistic inquiries. Pilger has developed a style of barracking governments—and it is mostly governments—on matters of foreign policy, so to some extent he could be said to have come from a previous era of political journalism. In fact, Pilger has bridled—something he does quite often—at accusations that his style of journalism is old school, and that he has been overtaken by writers like Klein and Monbiot—and Noreena Hertz (of whom more later).

When asked about this in an interview with Swedish Radio in July 2002, he retorted:

> I think the whole issue of globalization is now only becoming a public issue. And then it's hardly a public issue in terms of the extent of the worldwide protest against globalization. Most people in this country, and in other western countries, are not aware that throughout most of the world—Latin America, especially—there is...a very popular resistance movement against the globalized economy...A lot of the people who are in the broad anti-globalization coalition subscribe to the view that the new rulers of the world are the multinational corporations. I

don't agree. I think it's a combination of state power—with state power still dominant—and the multinational corporations. The two are really wedded together. It's risky to start describing the world as simply run by corporations.

When asked if he felt that governments had already handed over their power to the multinationals, he responded stiffly:

Well, they haven't. The United States government has never been more powerful. Capitalism in the United States depends on subsidy—always has. All the great corporations—the war industries, the great companies like General Electric, Cargill, the food grain corporations, and so on. These are all the beneficiaries of massive government subsidy. [It's] a kind of socialism for the rich. That's centralized state power. And that's state patronage of great capital in the United States—[that] has been the engine room of globalization.

Pilger's TV documentary *The New Rulers of the World* claimed to tell the amazing story of how globalization actually began. It began in Indonesia, with a bloodbath. According to Pilger, historians had always accepted that Suharto rose to power in the mid 1960s in a bloodbath, but what was less known was the role of international capital. Says Pilger: "The film describes how in the wake of the Suharto seizure of power, which was backed by the United States and Britain, some of the most powerful capitalists in the world, the likes of David Rockefeller, convened...a secret meeting in Geneva in 1967, where Suharto's ministers sat across the table from Rockefeller and various other people, like representatives of the Carnegie Foundation and the great banks in the United States." Here, the whole of the Indonesian economy was redesigned—in a week. Different rooms of the hotel were used for separate sections of the economy: one for transport, one for agriculture, and so on.

As with many of Pilger's investigations, it would be farcical if it wasn't so gripping, and if it wasn't told with his trademark gritty earnestness. Pilger continues: "So this was the direct result of the bloodbath in Indonesia the year before in which the United States and Britain had played important, supportive roles. Indonesia then fell under the control of a group called the Joint Inter-Governmental Working Group which was all the main western governments—Japan, Australia, the World Bank, and the IMF. They effectively guided the Suharto economy for many years, determining investment, debt, central bank policy, and so on." And that, says Pilger, was the beginning of Indonesia as the "model pupil" of globalization, as the World Bank described it, until it crashed in flames in 1998.

Pilger would no doubt be reassured to hear—as would many North American dissidents—that no swift retelling of the critics of global capitalism would be complete without mentioning the life, work, and struggles of Howard Zinn. Where Pilger is solemn, Zinn is funny. But he is no joker on the subject of the evils of global capitalism. His landmark book A People's History of the United States, an eye-opening history of the country from the perspective of the disenfranchised, has sold over one million copies since it was first published in 1980 and is a classic of left-wing historiography.

Zinn is an important figure in American political thought. To some he is even the left-wing conscience of the nation. Without doubt he has traveled a long way since his time as a World War II bomber pilot, an event that prefigured and caused his later pacifism. By the time he had moved to Atlanta he had become a leading figure in the early Civil Rights Movement, for which he became the bête noire of both the Southern power establishment and later the FBI. He led student protests from his base at Boston University in the 1960s, and once even flew to Vietnam at the height of the war, where he met the North Vietnamese to try and negotiate the return of some captured American servicemen.

Now in his eighties, Zinn still speaks widely to enthusiastic audiences of all ages. As a teacher and writer, he continues to inspire generations of those who struggle for social and economic justice, expressing vocal support for the writings of younger activists such as Ted Nace. Nace's origins in the radical movement began when he was still at college, in a manner similar to the way in which Michael Moore was stung into action by General Motors' decision to close down the factory in his hometown of Flint, Michigan. In Nace's case, he learned about the plans of several major corporations to develop coal strip mines and other energy projects near his hometown of Dickinson, North Dakota. The result of his investigations developed into his 2003 book *Gangs of America: The Rise of Power and Disabling of Democracy*, a powerful indictment of corporate power that covers an unusually long time-span, from 1267 to 2003.

Another young contender is Noreena Hertz, who has certainly caused a stir on the anti-globalization barricades. Denounced by some as a *fashionista*, and as a mouth for hire, her book *The Silent Takeover*, published in 2001, is a pretty good primer about the new forces that are standing up to capitalism, and the risks of not taking seriously the threat to good governance posed by over-muscled corporate policies. Hertz is described as the Associate Director of the Center of International Business and Management at the Judge Institute of Cambridge University. Seen as a sort of British Naomi Klein, she had the good luck to be photogenic, so much so that she posed for the inside cover of this book on a particularly stressed area of post-industrial landscape. In her thigh-length boots and furry coat, sprawled in an armchair, she was, as one critic pointed out, "more Naomi Campbell than Naomi Klein." Perhaps that is why she has earned a certain amount of derision for her well-meant, robustly argued views.

The Silent Takeover begins with Hertz following some people dressed as pink fairies around the streets of Prague, there to protest against the IMF and World Bank's annual conference in September 2000. As the heiress daughter of the Hertz Rent-a-Car family, she is a former free market evangelist, having worked hard to introduce capitalism into Eastern Europe. Hertz courts trouble from the hard left by asserting: "Capitalism is clearly the best system for generating wealth, and free trade and open capital markets have brought unprecedented economic growth to most if not all of the world." And her views place her at odds with Naomi Klein when, for example, she asserts: "Companies do not tend to lower their standards in their foreign operations, at least not consistently as one might have thought." A *Socialist Worker* critic disparages the book as "Naomi

Klein lite." He ends his review by saying that the book's publication is proof of "how adaptable capitalism is—able to create a marketing niche out of a revolt against the market and advertising."

Reviewing *The Silent Takeover* in the *Guardian*, Howard Davies, chairman of the UK's Financial Services Authority, accuses Hertz of talking rubbish or "globaloney" with her claim that governments are powerless in the face of globalization. Hertz, he writes, "has, in effect, bought into the credo of those she affects most to despise. She implicitly accepts that governments must bow to the dictates of footloose global capital, and that electorates in individual countries cannot make meaningful choices about taxation, public spending, or environmental policies." Davies compares a successful capitalist economy like Germany's, with its high tax rates and high government spending, with the USA's lower tax rates and comparatively low government spending. "Countries may tax energy consumption at radically different rates without seeing all their domestic industry disappear offshore," says Davies. "They can have very different employment protection laws and social benefits. There are still serious and genuine political choices. [And] to argue otherwise, as Hertz does, and to deny that these choices can be made, is to help bring about precisely the alienation between electors and elected that she claims to deplore." He concludes that *The Silent Takeover* is "not just wrongheaded, but dangerous."

For her 2004 book *IOU: The Debt Threat and Why We Must Defuse It*, Hertz is described as "one of the world's leading experts on economic globalization." This book tackled the seemingly intractable problem of Third World debt. Hertz rehearses the tragic statistics: that for every dollar the West gives to developing countries in aid, developing countries pay the West 29 dollars in debt service. But, with the world at the beginning of the new millennium, Hertz says that the global debt crisis threatens us all. The figures are dizzying, and it is surely a good thing that a mainstream author like Hertz is prepared to take them on again, such as sub-Saharan Africa's debt of $200 billion, Brazil's of $223.8 billion, Argentina's of $155 billion. Hertz draws a line between these figures and the deforestation of the Amazon rainforest, and AIDS, and war, terrorism, illiteracy, and death.

But again, not everyone is convinced by her arguments. Another critic is Paul Kingsnorth, deputy editor of the *Ecologist* magazine. Reviewing *IOU: The Debt Threat*, Kingsnorth admits that he could never take seriously someone he describes as "the self-appointed It-girl of the anti-globalization movement." He criticizes her for going soft on her old boss Larry Summer of the World Bank, and he generally dismisses her points as being at least five years old. But the facts, uncomfortable as they are, still deserve to be seen, heard, and read, however many times they have been repeated.

Perhaps it was the sheer breadth and energy of Hertz's offensive that detracted from some of its force—and may have divided the critics in the process. One writer who found considerable success by choosing a slightly narrower focus is the *Atlantic Monthly* correspondent Eric Schlosser, whose 2002 *Fast Food Nation* was published two years before—and possibly proved to be an inspiration to—Morgan Spurlock's film *Supersize Me*. Schlosser's theme is also junk food, but the focus of his attack is broader. He attacks the way the McDonald's Corporation (chiefly), together with Taco Bell, Pizza Hut, and Kentucky Fried Chicken, are threatening to overrun and standardize every main street in the world—echoes of the British "clone towns" we saw in the last chapter. Schlosser pinpoints the power that these huge corporations have, and he discusses their baneful influence over unions such as the meatpackers', and the ways in which they have screwed down cattle farmers in order to get the lowest prices for themselves. Schlosser's assault on the fast food industry is confined mostly to the USA, which could be seen as an example of American self-obsession, but the force of its argument is nonetheless compelling. A *Socialist Action* reviewer called it "a hard-hitting critique of the industrialization of America's and, later, the world's food supply."

In their desire to show a warm, kindly face to the world, the fast food corporations' marketing tools are among the most insidious and aggressive of any corporation. The image of the Ronald McDonald clown is one such example: a blatant attempt to entrap the most vulnerable—and influential—economic group on the planet: children. Schlosser dissects the calorific content of what is really served up on your plate, or in your takeaway carton, and he describes the degrading working conditions that are maintained in some restaurants, and some of the corporations' brazen attempts to restrict the formation and activities of trade unions, or to paying a minimum wage. Both the meatpacking industry and the fast food industry have been staunch and generous supporters of the Republican Party—especially of the more conservative type of Republican—for many years. So when workers are taken ill or injured at work, there are few in Congress willing to bring legal action against the corporations, or to make them look again at their humanitarian responsibilities.

In terms of its power and influence, the fast food industry operates very much like any other corporation, and the behavior of, say, the McDonald's corporation has much in common with that of a global bank or clothing company. William Greider is national affairs correspondent for one of America's most respected liberal journals, *The Nation*, and his books have explored the cost of the corporate and governmental scramble for wealth. In *Secrets of the Temple*, Greider revealed the inner workings of the Federal Reserve, and showed a government institution that was, he said, "in some ways more secretive than the CIA and more powerful than the President or Congress." *One World, Ready or Not* (1998) is a savage critique on the outsourcing of industry much favored by multinationals. And in his most recent book, *The Soul of Capitalism* (2003), he examines how "the greatest wealth-creation engine in the history of the world is failing most of us, why it must be changed, and how intrepid pioneers are beginning to transform it."

The Soul of Capitalism delves into crooked boardroom deals, pension fund embezzlement, the outright theft of stockholder money, and the rampant and abusive way in which employees are hired and fired. He also shows how the lust for cash has eroded family life and social bonds, as well as our natural environment. But as well as railing at the corporations, Greider also looks at the fight-back, at the small voice of reform that is beginning to make itself heard. He even dares to suggest ways in which "American capitalism can be aligned more faithfully and obediently with what people want and need in their lives, with what American society needs for a healthy, balanced, and humane future." He describes a world in which it is in our power to reinvent capitalism to work for the many, not the few.

Dissed on Film

The ground that Greider and Schlosser were treading was not unbroken, of course, but until recently it has been rare for politically committed films to succeed as mainstream theatrical releases in North America. That, though, is precisely what Michael Moore has achieved with a string of searing, opinionated, and highly influential movies aimed directly at the highest offices of power. Ever since the success of the low-budget Roger & Me (1989), in which he attempted to meet Roger Smith, the publicity shy CEO of General Motors, in a vain but heroic attempt to save his local car manufacturing plant in Flint, Michigan, Moore has been dealing with the abuse of corporate power in one way or another. Bowling for Columbine (2002) was an attack on the gun lobby, which included a poignant and ultimately futile encounter with a stiff, elderly Charlton Heston, but it was in the 2004 film Fahrenheit 9/11 that his explosive accusations had most effect. Here, his target was the White House of George W. Bush, and the White House's suspiciously close links to the family of Osama bin Laden.

As ever with Moore, his film was sensation-seeking and (some would say) deeply one-sided, but it burst on the world—initially at the Cannes film festival—at a time when emotion was running high against Bush. Its claim that dozens of members of the bin Laden family had been allowed to take to the skies in the days after 9/11 when every other flight had been grounded was unsubstantiated, as was the implication that the invasion of Iraq was a giant cover-up to obscure the unwelcome facts about the Bush/bin Laden axis, but the film was so high-energy, passionate, and just plain mischievous that it was hard not to welcome it—while also being aware of its provenance.

Moore's polemic got a name check (not exactly in its favor) in the review of another film that came out around the same time, *The Corporation*: the *Independent* described it as "*Fahrenheit 9/11* for people who think." This film was the work of, among others, Joel Bakan, author of the book of the same name, and had an intellectually first-rate cast that included Milton Friedman and Noam Chomsky (more later on him). Bakan's thesis, closely and remorselessly pursued in film as in book, is to anthropomorphize the corporation itself, and then to subject that personality to psychological scrutiny. This approach has been adopted by plenty of others before him, of course, but Bakan perhaps went further—and certainly achieved a higher profile for his claims—by stating that the corporation emerged as a megalomaniac with psychopathic character traits.

Bakan interviews several corporate chief executives, such as Hank McKinnell, CEO of the massive Pfizer drug corporation. He does a serviceable job of representing their views, and even seems to try and find fellow feeling for their views, with quoted remarks such as "Pfizer can be the company which does more good for more people than any other company on this planet." He talks, for example, about the drug Zithromax, a single shot of which Pfizer hopes could prevent up to ten million people a year contracting the debilitating eye disease known as trachoma. But, of course, there is no place on a spreadsheet for pure altruism, and Hank McKinnell concedes that "the marginal cost of our drugs is very low, so if we give away a drug to somebody who wouldn't otherwise buy it, the profit impact of that action on us is just about zero." The very fact that McKinnell chooses to discuss so-called acts of charity with references to hard-edged words like "action" and "impact," and the constant invocation of numbers—"zero," for one—implies that even these apparently benevolent actions have been carefully costed. McKinnell goes so far as to state it explicitly, in fact. "Our primary mission is to sustain the enterprise and that, of course, requires profit." The case could hardly have been stated more plainly, or honestly.

There is a discrepancy between a corporation's aims and its methods. A charitable organization is, or should be, a non-profit-making body. A corporation is the precise opposite, so when Pfizer offered to donate free Zithromax to the organization Médécins Sans Frontières in the impoverished west African country of Mali, it turned down the offer. Pfizer, not surprisingly, was shocked and hurt. But for MSF, the primary aim of its anti-trachoma treatment program had to be continuity. "If Pfizer decides one day to just leave the country or do away with its program or cut back for some reason...we can ensure that the drug remains available for the people that need it in the country." For that reason, MSF preferred to import and pay for a cheaper, generic version of the same drug.

Bakan also points out that Pfizer makes more from so-called vanity drugs—designed to prevent baldness and impotence—than they make from drugs that treat genuinely life-threatening conditions like malaria and tuberculosis, but since 80 percent of the world lives in developing countries, which only make up 20 percent of the world drug market, it would make no economic sense for them to pour resources into producing or developing life-saving drugs. Thus, latest statistics showed that in the year 2000 no drugs were being developed to treat tuberculosis, while there were currently eight patents pending for impotence or erectile dysfunction and seven for baldness.

Pursuing the psychopathic analogy, Bakan writes that the corporation is "singularly self-interested and unable to feel genuine concern for others in any context." The psychologist Dr. Robert Hare added the words "irresponsible," with a "tendency to manipulate," that it was "grandiose," with a "lack of empathy," "asocial tendencies," a "refusal to accept responsibility for its own actions," and an "inability to feel remorse." Human psychopaths, he added, use charm as a mask to disguise their true intentions. The same goes for corporations. They may project an image of social responsibility, but when it comes down to it, "they lack the ability to care about anyone or anything but themselves."

Applying cod psychology to the personality of a corporation may well be described as cheap, or space-filling, or evidence of a trivial mind, but the exercise fits Bakan's thesis, which is to take up cudgels against his old enemy. In any event, Bakan's searing indictment of the corporate psychopathology may have played well in cinemas and to sympathetic listeners, but that box office has to be seen against an even greater voting success in November 2004 when George W. Bush won a re-election victory against a Democratic Party that had failed to find a silver bullet. And, as every boss knows, in America there is a great deal less resentment of the sorts of vastly inflated salaries that arouse scornful "Fat Cat Pay Bonus" stories in the British tabloid press.

Fringe Critics

While Klein, Moore, Bakan, and the like were hitting the big time, other critics of the corporate world (and its interface with the worlds of government and the intelligence community) had been plugging on without such recognition for years—though no less committed. One notable critic is the author Kenn Thomas. His book *The Octopus: Life and Death of Danny Casolaro* (1966) accused the US and UK governments of complicity in the death of the journalist Danny Casolaro and blamed it on a cover-up which he traced back to the Iran-Contra affair scandal. Thomas was for a long time the editor of Steamshovel Press ("All Conspiracy, No Theory"), an authoritative quarterly digest of conspiracy theories. Jim Keith, who died in 1999, was Kenn Thomas's co-writer on *The Octopus*. His other books include *Secret and Suppressed: Banned Ideas and Hidden Histories* (1993), *Mind Control, World Control* (1997), and *Engineering Human Consciousness* (1999). Keith was working on a book about the death of Princess Diana when he died during knee surgery in what supporters claimed were suspicious circumstances. His publisher, Ron Bonds, of IllumiNet Press, died in 2001, apparently from food poisoning. One of Keith's friends, Jerry E. Smith, wrote *HAARP: The Ultimate Weapon of the Conspiracy* in 2001 about a highly secret US government project in Alaska called the High Frequency Active Auroral Research Program. HAARP's proponents claim that it is developing an ionospheric research instrument which will be used "to temporarily excite a limited area of the ionosphere for scientific study." Its critics reckon that the project is a huge superbeam mind-control device.

Other dissident writers include David Ray Griffin, who took a different view of the 9/11 attacks from the White House line (*The New Pearl Harbor: Disturbing Questions About the Bush Administration and 9/11*), as well as Michael C. Ruppert (*Crossing the Rubicon: The Decline of the American Empire at the End of the Age of Oil*). Also look out for Howard Bloom's *Global Brain: The Evolution of the Mass Mind from the Big Bang to the 21st Century*.

The World According to Noam

One commentator who can always be relied on to take a pot shot at almost any incumbent US president is the professor of linguistics at Massachusetts Institute of Technology, Noam Chomsky. Chomsky is a distinguished academic whose political views have, for some long time, placed him well to the left of most US political commentators. Along the way, they have ensured him a devoted following on North American campuses. In a talk on Canadian Radio on US election day 2004, Chomsky decried George Bush's American foreign policy enactments as being imperial, and minted from the same coin as a controversial figure within Nazi German legal circles, Carl Schmitt. But Chomsky's attacks on the government have, some claim, been selective. Critics accuse him of distorting—even, sometimes, of making up—quotations to suit his own ends— charges that Chomsky vigorously denies.

In 2004 Chomsky enraged the hard left by coming out in support of the Democrat presidential candidate John Kerry, albeit while "holding one's nose." In general, though, Chomsky's campaigns have been well to the left of mainstream politics; indeed his critics see him as a self-hating American. In an interview he gave to ZNet, Chomsky criticized the *New York Times* for spreading the impression that Americans were, by and large, happy:

> You look at the Americans they're talking about, it turns out it's not the roughly two-thirds of the population whose incomes are stagnating or declining, it's the people who own stock. So, OK,

they're undoubtedly doing great, except that about one percent of households have about 50 percent of the stock, and it's roughly the same with other assets. Most of the rest is owned by the top ten percent of the population. So sure, America is happy, and America is prosperous, if America means what the *New York Times* means by it. They're the narrow set of elites that they speak for and to.

A Chomsky trilogy—*Secrets, Lies, and Democracy, The Prosperous Few and the Restless Many*, and *What Uncle Sam Really Wants*—was published by a small printing house in 1996. The themes of these books were repeated in a later book, *Hegemony or Survival: America's Quest for Global Dominance* (2003), in which he argues that the current Bush government is seriously undermining international relations and global security, along with familiar Chomsky views on how US policy funds repressive regimes in the name of "encouraging" democracy and how fledgling Central American democracies have been stifled and put down by US policy in the region.

A close ally of Chomsky in political thought was the Palestinian academic Edward Said. When Said died in 2003, his work was not nearly over, but the current of his intellectual ideas had passed into political life. If Monbiot, Hertz, and Klein are the pop end of university dissidents, Said and Chomsky are considerably more substantial academic figures but with just as outspoken political views. Said was a tireless advocate of the cause of the Palestinian people, on whose behalf he wrote a stream of articles and books, passionately advancing their case. His first book to address the subject of his roots, *Orientalism* (1995), was a plea for the western world to see Arabs not as colorful exotics but as real players in a real world. He was also sharply critical of Bush's foreign policy adventures in Iraq, arguing in the *Guardian* on April 20th, 2003 that "US corporations supplied nuclear, chemical, and biological materials for [Saddam's] supposed weapons of mass destruction and then...brazenly erased [details of these transactions] from public record." All of which, he said, "was deliberately obscured by government and media in manufacturing the case for destroying Iraq."

In an article written for the *Al-Hayat* Arabic-language newspaper before war was declared on Iraq, Said talked about the "astonishing clumsiness and failures of US foreign policy." He also criticized the close ties between the White House and Ariel Sharon's government: "So far as the Middle East is concerned, it does seem that since 11 September there has been almost an Israelization of US policy: and in effect Ariel Sharon and his associates have cynically exploited the single-minded attention to 'terrorism' by George Bush and have used that as a cover for their continued failed policy against the Palestinians."

The writers, activists, and essayists presented above represent a small but dynamic dissident community, which is remarkable for the range and diversity of its views. What they seem to share is a marked degree of suspicion. They mistrust the establishment, they question authority, and they resent being told what to say or think. Very few of them would oppose the idea that global capitalism, as it is developing, is a system of thought control. Most acknowledge that capitalism has brought greater prosperity, including better hospitals and schools, to many in the West, in the 50 years from the end of World War II. But, particularly since the end of the Cold War, these writers argue, the beast has evolved. These writers may not all agree on the more lurid theories which abound about global capitalism—for example, that the corporations are actively colluding to wrestle control of the world's finances from the hands of elected governments—but they all agree that capitalism is entering a new, ruthless phase, in which it threatens to consolidate more and more power to itself, to the detriment of us all.

Chapter Seven: Free Trade / Slave Trade

In May 2005, work began on a five-mile wire mesh security fence around the world-famous Gleneagles Hotel and golf course where the G8 summit was to take place in July. The cordon, consisting of about 10,000 panels, was aimed at preventing unauthorized access to the famous Perthshire golfing hotel and its grounds. Extra security would be provided by Group 4 Securicor until Tayside Police assumed overall control. Tayside Police's chief constable Willie Bald was keen to assure reporters that the fence "did not create any significant environmental impact," and that the force had cooperated fully with Scottish Natural Heritage, although the actual impact of the security barrier was more than just a matter of aesthetics.

The G8 is an organization of what is usually described as "the world's leading industrialized countries—and Russia," a definition which must catch in the throat of every self-respecting Russian every time they hear it. Originally known as the G6, its members, France, Germany, Italy, Japan, the UK, and the US, met for the first time at Rambouillet in France in 1975. The idea was for them to meet in a different location every year, where members could discuss "global challenges," and have some time rubbing shoulders away from the glare of the media. Canada joined at the 1976 summit in San Juan, Puerto Rico—not that Puerto Rico was anywhere close to being invited to join the exclusive club. And in 1998, Russia was admitted at the summit held in the suitable post-industrial city of Birmingham, England.

The G8 summits have become almost better known for their security operations than for any declarations or measures that follow from them. The 2001 summit in Genoa was a low point, when street fighting with anti-globalization protesters led to the death of 23-year-old Carlo Giuliani at the hands of local police. Since then, the countries have hidden behind increasingly elaborate stockades, while demonstrators have conceived ever more complex ways of raising the profile of their own causes. If ever there was an illustration of the lack of dialog between the leaders and the led, the G8 summit exemplifies it.

The anger that G8 arouses is perhaps explained, in part, by the implication that its members are the "more developed" countries, thereby raising the suspicion that the group was created to serve their interests at the expense of the "less developed" countries. Other organizations exist which have a more proactive identity, such as free trade organizations. The European Union began that way, when the European Community was born in the shadow of World War II. Originally formed by Belgium, France, Italy, Luxembourg, the Netherlands, and West Germany in 1958, it effectively formed a free trade area, fixing prices and creating economic performance bands. The EU, as it is now known, is not controversial in its own way, but other treaties which it has inspired have proved to be more so.

The whole concept of a free trade area, along with economic liberalization, implies an equality of partnership and opportunity. And yet that pattern is loaded with contradictions, which are shown up most vividly by a free trade area on the other side of the Atlantic that was partly inspired by the European model.

The purpose of NAFTA (North American Free Trade Association) was to dissolve tariffs and what were seen as trade barriers that had grown up over time between the United States, Canada, and Mexico. Canada and the US established an early version of this treaty on bilateral terms in 1988, and the effect of NAFTA was to extend the agreement so as to include Mexico. The terms were worked out by President George Bush Sr., Prime Minister Brian Mulroney of Canada, and Mexico's President Carlos Salinas de Gortari. Preliminary agreement was reached on August 1992, and a signing ceremony was held on December 17th, 1992, although it did not come into effect until January 1st, 1994.

The treaty called for a gradual reduction of the tariffs and customs barriers which, it was claimed, were hampering trade relations. Some were rolled back immediately. Others were allowed longer periods, of up to 15 years, to be repealed. As well as consumer and manufactured goods, it was also designed to open the doors by which US and Canadian banks, insurance companies, telecommunications companies, advertising agencies, and the freight and haulage industry could gain access to profitable Mexican markets. This it achieved, beyond doubt. But the price at which this breakthrough in trade was made is more debatable.

There was, clearly, no comparison between Mexico and the industrial giant on its northern border. So what benefit could economic liberalization bring? It was sold to the country as a trade agreement which promised extra work and job security. But given the huge inequality between the three partner countries, what chance was there for genuine employee security, and how long would it be before the treaty began to impinge on job security and hard-won labor gains such as employment legislation?

As soon as NAFTA went into effect on January 1st, 1993, it eliminated the duty on half of all US goods shipped to Mexico. Further tariffs were phased out over the next 14 years. The loosening effects of the treaty covered the automobile industry, farming, computer construction, and textiles. One important difference between NAFTA and the European Union is that NAFTA law does not override the law in any of its three countries. And yet there was considerable opposition to it, right from the start, from industrial leaders who feared that it would turn Canada and Mexico into branch plant economies, turning out parts cheaply. Nor did the opposition just come from the industrial sector.

The people whose lives are most affected by NAFTA are the factory and farm workers in the NAFTA zone. Large corporations viewed it with favor: for them, there was no loss and much to be gained from lower tariffs. But American labor unions bitterly opposed it, fearing that jobs would be relocated from the US to Mexico.

In 1993, President Bill Clinton, mindful of the success with which his predecessor's trade agreement had been received, promised that NAFTA would create up to 200,000 extra jobs in the US by boosting trade with Mexico. At the time, Mexico was enjoying an economic boom. Two years later, however, the great Mexican banking crisis set in, 8,000 firms went to the wall, and one million jobs were lost. With the economy shrinking by up to a fifth, wages fell by a third, and a fifth of Mexican credit users had fallen behind on loans for cars or homes.

In truth, the treaty had provoked widespread unrest from the start. On January 1st, 1994, launch day for Mexico, an army of 2,000 guerrillas took up arms in protest against the government and seized four towns in the southern state of Chiapas. They called themselves the Ejército Zapatista de Liberación Nacional, the Zapatista army, evoking the name of the charismatic nineteenth-century freedom fighter, Emiliano Zapata. One guerrilla said in a radio interview that while NAFTA opened the door to higher profits for the Mexican ruling classes, it was a "death certificate" for Indian peasants and farmers. American farmers still received subsidies, but none were forthcoming for Indian farmers. Hence many would be forced into bankruptcy. Hence the day of action.

Mexico's then President Carlos Salinas de Gortari sent his troops into Chiapas, but the people responded by storming Mexico City's central government square. The military action was called off.

And yet their efforts were only partially successful. Naturally, as Mexico's economy continued to slow down, North American businesses were not backward in reclaiming Mexico as a resource for cheap labor. By 1995, America's merchandise trade deficit with Mexico had soared to $15 billion. Using the same sums as the Clinton administration had used to calculate the potential gain produced a striking figure: the equivalent of 200,000 North American jobs had been lost.

As William Greider showed in his book *One World, Ready or Not*, the definition of "domestic" or "imported" could be readjusted endlessly by the global manufacturer by switching component production between US and Mexican plants so as to take full advantage of the most desirable trade conditions in either country. So much advantage was taken of NAFTA that the US Commerce Department was, at one stage, forced to issue an advisory memorandum clarifying exactly which parts of a hair dryer had to be manufactured (and where) before it could qualify for NAFTA tax free status by being 50 percent made within either Canada, Mexico, or the United States.

In the case of Canada, the growth in its foreign exports can be attributed, mostly, to its integration with the rest of North America. Canada exports four-fifths of its goods to its southern partner, and imports approximately two-thirds of its total imports from the USA. But the knock-on effects on the rest of the world in our globalized market economy are harder to calculate.

In the modern capitalist world, technological breakthroughs have enabled companies to reach new heights of economic efficiency, reducing costs in the process. The only problem is that as manufacturing output increases, there is no guarantee of finding a market for those goods. "Someone somewhere will have to eat the losses," writes William Greider. "Businesses hope it is not their company."

The rush for profits has degenerated into something more squalid. Since no company wants to be the one left with no chair when the music stops, corporations are being reduced to ever more desperate measures, by closing down factories, for example, or offering massive bulk sales at "unbeatable" prices. The cost-cutting and price-slashing carry on, regardless of the effect this has on the workforce.

What Greider calls "the dirty little secret" about technological revolution is exemplified in the case of Motorola, the multinational telecoms company, which decrees that productive efficiency be doubled every five years. Chrysler had coined the term "stretch goals" to refer to the strenuous reductions in running costs to be implemented by its managers. Chrysler's chief corporate economist, Wynn Van Bussmann, gave an example of this practice. "To develop the K-car in the late seventies and early eighties, it took 54 months and

3,100 people," he said. "A few years later, to develop the Neon took 33 months and 700 people."

Van Bussman was proud of the steep rise in efficiency, but he was also aware that improving that efficiency could not be maintained at that rate indefinitely. Ultimately the music stops and someone jumps—or gets pushed—off.

The problems faced by businesses today—in the NAFTA zone or beyond—are global, and, for the time being, they are outpacing the solutions. "Running a global corporation is like running a government," say A. Larry Elliott and Richard J. Schroth in their book *How Companies Lie*. With 200 locations around the world and 100,000 employees, auditing a global company was never going to be a straightforward matter. First, there are human costs: employees are involved in accidents, in natural disasters, in personal tragedies. Then there are the battles of trade and finance. Companies have evolved ever more creative means with which to disguise either good or bad news. But for a while, during the 1990s, some companies created Byzantine accounting practices that hid the true picture of their financial health. Elliott and Schroth discuss the impact of "alliance partners," the term used by a host of internet companies in preference to conventional partnerships. "Modern corporations manage, or attempt to manage, thousands of shifting and complex business relationships, each with its own revenue, profit, and debt impacts on the value of the company." A big drug company could have between 3,000 and 5,000 of such alliances, whether through researchers, consultants, drug testers, clinics, doctors, hospitals, or hospices. It is this "collaborative" model that lies at the heart of the challenge to conventional forms of governance, for as Enron showed with its "special purpose entities," such arrangements can break down into a multiple of unknowns that succeed on every level except that of healthy commercial practice.

The bull market that made Mexico seem like such an attractive proposition was largely a chimera. The boom was mainly confined to its banking sector, and did not even stretch to all the sectors within that area. "[It was] driven by a single fact of global finance," writes William Greider, "the opportunity to arbitrage the differences in interest rates between the US and foreign financial markets." In other words, a trader could buy on Wall Street at low interest rates, invest in Mexican stocks or short-term government bonds, and bet on the spread, taking advantage of and collecting on a discrepancy of around ten percent between the two countries. This made for a killing on the stock exchange, but it hardly created the conditions for a healthy economy.

In previous centuries, most of the countries in what is now called the developing world were colonies of European powers, who governed them via a relatively transparent hierarchical power structure. Commercial decisions were taken for the sake of the mother country: the overrun workers were the subjects of long-term planning that put the imperial power's interests first. As the imperial era faded, there were many who hoped that post-colonial countries might be able to embrace independence and begin to forge their own destinies. Increasingly, though, it seems that those same countries— Brazil, India or China—have been forced to accept a new form of colonial domination: to be ruled not by the colonial office, but by the headquarters of Nike, Gap, Ford, or Dell.

Black Cotton

The popularity of NAFTA depends on which country is passing judgment on it. In May 2003, President George Bush returned to a familiar theme when he berated the European Union for its short-sightedness in placing limits on genetically modified US grain imports. This moratorium, he said to an audience at the United States Coast Guard Academy, was bad for world trade, and could even lead to the perpetuation of drought and famine in continental Africa. To back up his words, the US had submitted a formal complaint to the World Trade Organization. And yet that policy flies in the face of a case of a similar example of industrial astigmatism, right in America's back yard, which revolves around that trade standard: cotton.

In the northern delta of the Niger River, West African farmers are as reliant on cotton now as they have been for thousands of years. Cotton farming and production employs over two million, and pays for food, clothing, and education for many more. But last year, world cotton prices reached a 30-year low as other innovative man-made fabrics and textiles continued their remorseless encroachment upon what was once a closed market. The result was that cotton prices fell by up to ten percent. This reduction is threatening the livelihoods of Niger's farmers. In some cases, it is even threatening lives as families of 20 or 30 are trying to live on annual earnings of less than $2,000. Survival is at stake. Healthcare facilities—never among the most stable in the world—are in crisis, and the government is unable to allay farmers' fears. One consequence is that people are having to make the awful choice of staying in their villages against an uncertain future, or uprooting themselves by traveling to Europe, in the hope of finding a more stable income. The risk is that the gamble does not pay off. Stuck in a hostile foreign city, unable to pay back the human trafficker who transported them across thousands of miles in barely humane conditions, they face being lured into shabby and squalid working conditions, or being forced to abandon themselves to the European slave trade, and all the obscene compromises that implies.

The United States government has reacted to the current crisis in Western Africa by claiming that it is working hard to promote aid and open trade. It has sent over $40 million to Mali, for example, in money earmarked for educational, health, and development programs. But, as so often with Africa, this is a drop in the bucket. Cotton prices have dropped by two-thirds since 1995: no one is turning down the $40 million, but a lot more than that is required.

What a different story it is in another famous cotton-growing district, the Mississippi Delta. Here, despite the sharp downturn in cotton prices, American cotton growers are not feeling any pinch at all. Why? Well, say American industry spokespeople, the reason lies in the technological advances with which America is blessed. The farmers of Mali have single-bladed ploughs. They use oxen to till their fields, which range in size from 10–20 acres. Such a field could take two weeks to turn, and the cotton on that field will be plucked by hand. By contrast, the cotton farmers of middle America patrol farms with an average acreage of 10,000 or more. Instead of oxen and ploughs, they can call on the services of GPS (global positioning satellite) systems to gauge the right amount of fertilizer to spray on to sprouting seedlings. And they can do all that from the comfort of an air-conditioned tractor, lest the burning heat sully their judgment. North America's cotton growers subsist on an average net household worth of nearly $1 million. The contrast with Mali's impoverished pre-industrial conditions could not be sharper, nor could the consequences for the unfortunate farm workers. But is it all caused by solid economic performance?

In fact, it is the Mali farmers who are the more efficient net producers. American farms have huge maintenance costs. Those tractors are all leveraged—that is, bought on borrowed money—and it costs money to fly a helicopter over the crops in order to dust them with tons of highly expensive fertilizers, defoliants, growth agents, and insecticides. The fields of the Mississippi are costly in terms of their irrigation. And the seed stock they use—genetically modified to resist aphid infestation—is among the most expensive in the world. In fact, it costs 82 cents to produce a pound of cotton in Mississippi. In Mali, the same cotton can be produced for only 23 cents a pound: a quarter of the price. And yet American farmers are seeing their farms expand, while Malians are in a crippling battle for survival. Why so?

The one word missing from this debate so far is subsidies. In 2002, America's 25,000 cotton producers received $3.4 billion in subsidies, and that amount is rising sharply. America's farmers re-elected George Bush Jr. in 2004, and they will not expect him to be any less generous with them than he has demonstrated so far. The effect of this trade-off is that by underwriting the costs of America's black cotton economy, the US is protecting the real price of American cotton on the international market. The more they subsidize, the further world cotton prices sink and the harsher the conditions become for Africa's cotton farmers. In other words, America is itself doing precisely what its president accused European countries of doing: impoverishing families in West Africa and producing circumstances that lead inevitably to famine and drought.

Nor is it just Africa. The NAFTA treaty was designed to stimulate Mexican economic growth—and thereby stem some of the leakage of workers from Mexico into North America. But one of Mexico's main exports is sugar, a product severely restricted by US quotas. At present, the US can import only 7,258 tons of raw sugar. American shoppers buy their sugar at hugely increased prices: something like four times the standard world price. Mexican sugar producers, meanwhile, are facing a very uncertain future. And while America is exporting corn all over the world, Mexican *campesinos* face expulsion from their own land as a consequence of continuing economic recession. No wonder the Zapatistas sensed a whiff of popular insurrection.

Ultimately, it seems, American farmers will never carry the can in the same way that other countries are forced to do, even when their country has entered in a so-called good will treaty with its neighbors. Further south from Mexico, Brazil, the largest country in South America, is straining to put years of woeful economic mismanagement behind it and prove to the world that it is a major economic force. Brazil has welcomed in the bankers of the World Bank and the economists of the International Monetary Fund. It has fought hard to overcome years of chronic political corruption and infighting. And, as if to encourage it, the White House stresses that it looks forward to welcoming Brazil as a full economic trading partner. The United States has gone so far as to lobby for Brazil's inclusion into a free trade area. And yet, away from the declarations, choreographed handshakes, and firm statements of commitment, the US Department of Agriculture is still slapping subsidies and quotas on two-thirds of the citrus fruits that Brazil could export to the United States.

While the United States has strongly criticized the European Union by reporting it to the World Trade Organization, it is clearly in denial of its own bad practices, since it has failed to take action against its own poor record of special tax treatment on profits from certain kinds of exports. The EU has complained, successfully, twice to the WTO, but nothing has changed in American practices. In fact, EU Trade Commissioner Pascal Lamy hinted recently that new import permits probably would be issued by the end of the year. In response, though, there is no softening yet of the American position.

Does international law favor only Americans? NAFTA had decreed that Mexican truckers could drive freely anywhere in the United States. Any Mexican trucker who thinks that this law now applies would be in for an unpleasant shock, though. Fully ten years after being ratified, the law has still to take effect, and Mexican truck drivers must submit to the same controls and limits that restricted them before. Once again, NAFTA has a dispute settlement panel that has consistently found against the United States on account of its failure to observe its obligations under the treaty. It has repeatedly called on the US to comply. And yet, the US drags its feet, and its southern states officials quibble endlessly over the details, arguing that they would be overrun by vagabond Mexican truck drivers in life-threatening rusting hulks charging up and down the highways in search of a new life. And, as ever, the law is imposed one-sidedly.

Another group that opposed NAFTA was America's environmental lobby, and one American who was angrier than most was David Brower, the grand old man of the US environmentalist movement. Brower, then over 80 years old, was a founder of the Sierra Club, Earth Island Institute and Friends of the Earth in the US. He criticized NAFTA for yielding to large-scale corporate interests and removing the hard-won environmental protections passed by Congress in the name of "free trade." His article, written for the *Los Angeles Times* on July 21st, 1996, condemned President Clinton for signing up to NAFTA, which he called "the biggest sellout of American workers in US history."

Three years later, NAFTA was again proving unpopular with the liberal consensus, after Cargill Inc, the country's largest privately held company, won the blessing of the Clinton administration in its bid to acquire the grain-trading operations of its primary rival, Continental Grain Inc. The resulting union places 94 percent of the soybean market and 53 percent of the corn market into one business, and was fiercely opposed by farmers' unions, but to no avail.

As Alexander Cockburn and Jeffrey St. Clair wrote in *CounterPunch* on November 20th, 1999: "How can farmers get a fair price under these circumstances?"

The harsh circumstances had been imposed by treaties such as NAFTA and GATT (General Agreement on Trade Tariffs), both of which had been enthusiastically endorsed by the large corporations at the expense of small or independent farmers. These stories do not make the front page of newspapers like the *New York Times* or *Washington Post* every day, but they are desperately serious, and the agri-conglomerate corporate leaders know it. As Dwayne Andreas, the former CEO of Archer Daniels Midland, said to Reuters: "The food business is far and away the most important business in the world. Everything else is a luxury. Food is what you need to sustain life every day. Food is fuel. You can't run a tractor without fuel and you can't run a human being without it either. Food is the absolute beginning." In other words, said Andreas, agribusiness is more powerful than the oil industry.

Go West (or East)

Not far from Cargill's headquarters in Minneapolis, the cotton that American farmers produce is grown, as it will always be grown, in the dust bowls of Mississippi. The sophisticated tractors they use to reap that cotton may be produced in the Unites States or Europe. But the dumper trucks they use to transport that cotton may well have been put together in a country as far away as China. That process, which is known as outsourcing, is one of the consequences of market globalization, and is still one of the subjects guaranteed to generate the fiercest arguments.

The case for outsourcing can be summarized as follows. At some point in the 1980s, or 1990s, a number of western businesses took advantage of low wage costs in countries of the developing world to redistribute some of its less skilled service and parts contracts. Many such countries have a highly skilled workforce, capable of assembling and manufacturing almost anything. They are educated, motivated, and not particularly unionized. China, India,

Russia, and other eastern European and Asian countries offered such a work force—skilled in engineering, chemistry, and other applied technologies—and countries such as the UK and US were keen to take up the offer. But western countries have had to face considerable flak at home from fiercely protectionist critics who argue that relocating these plants overseas is a one-way process, and that ultimately western industry is contributing to its own impoverishment. As China, for example, continues to flex its economic and industrial muscles, how long can it be before the flow of resources begins to strangle our own industrial productivity? Is it any wonder that California's Governor Arnold Schwarzenegger was cheered by industry leaders when he vetoed a bill which, if passed, would have banned state contractors or agencies from outsourcing jobs offshore?

In December 2004, at the forum of the sixth Shanghai International Industry Fair, the World Trade Organization confirmed that China was in the process of overtaking Japan as the world's third largest merchandise exporter. WTO Director General Supachai Panitchpakdi added that China was also the world's third largest importer, behind the US and Germany but ahead of Japan. He noted that for the past five years, Chinese imports had generally grown faster than its exports, with import growth outpacing export by about an average of five percent each year. "China's strong import growth has provided an important stimulus for export-led growth in the world during the past few years," said the DG proudly. "China's economic boom is potentially an economic boom for the world."

Some conservative academics beg to differ. "Should Americans be concerned about the economic effects of outsourcing? Not particularly," writes Daniel W. Drezner, assistant professor of political science at the University of Chicago and author of *The Sanctions Paradox*. Drezner turns the argument on its head. "The short-term political appeal of protectionism is undeniable. Scapegoating foreigners for domestic business cycles is smart politics, and protecting domestic markets gives leaders the appearance of taking direct, decisive action on the economy."

Drezner is adamant that outsourcing does not starve the domestic economy. In fact, resorting to what he derides as protectionism is a recipe for both long- and short-term decline, he says. And yet the facts remain that outsourcing—relocating parts manufacture to overseas manufacturers or assembly plants—is one of the most controversial of modern day business practices, and shows a company in an unflattering light.

Meanwhile the process continues unabated. The 2005 World Outsourcing Summit, held in February at the Hotel del Coronado in San Diego, California, was the 177th such event to take place, bringing together 400-plus executives and professionals from across the field. Talking points included the forthcoming visit of India's IT Minister Dayanidhi Maran to the US in May 2005 to try and persuade computer chip giant Intel's top brass to choose India over China for its new factory.

The trend is unstoppable. Only two months later they were at it again, this time at the Hotel Westin in Times Square, New York. To some observers it might seem like an act of willing self-destruction, to invest in their employees' future redundancy. But these entrepreneurs embraced the networking opportunities enthusiastically.

On December 5th, 2003, Dr. N. Gregory Mankiw, chairman of President George W. Bush's council of economic advisers, took part in a webchat. When asked for his general feelings about the outsourcing of jobs, his reply—as reproduced on the White House's own website—was succinct, trenchant, and revealing:

Outsourcing is a particular type of international trade. We are used to trade in goods, but trade in services has expanded recently, made possible in large part by advances in telecommunications. Like all forms of international trade, outsourcing benefits an economy overall, though there are also short-term costs as workers are displaced. These costs are real, and the president has policies to help ease the transition—to help people find jobs. But overall, expanding trade is good for economic growth and for American living standards.

The case for outsourcing is that it's easier to assemble a car, computer, or sneaker in a factory where running costs are cheaper. The drawback, as far as the workers are convinced, is that the domestic circumstances of the country being favored with the contract may operate in the company's interests, rather than in the employees'. Social welfare, pay, working conditions: all might take a back-seat to the needs of the client. And in countries where trade unions are less established, vocal, or powerful than in the West, that can lead to goods being produced under conditions of virtual serfdom.

Of course, the argument cuts both ways. Work is flowing in to a country that might need the cash it provides, no matter how ungenerous it seems by western standards. And it is possible that, by opening up a route from, say, East to West, ideas about job security and good employer–employee relations will begin to embed themselves. All that seems a long way away, though, when workers—often mere children—are being forced to work long hours, with almost no time off, for a pittance.

And the big benefit, from the company's point of view, is that as companies trawl the world's markets looking for cheap labor, they can source goods from just about anywhere. With maritime container shipping, goods can be transported from halfway across the world.

To IMFinity and Beyond

Against this background, there seems very little that governments seem able to do when confronted by corporate power. But there are international organizations which are designed to deal with these immensely complex and important issues, and one such is the International Monetary Fund. The IMF was established at Bretton Woods, New Hampshire, in 1944, as America and Britain were beginning to look beyond the immediate needs of World War II at the prospect of a world no longer plagued by war. The IMF was hatched against a world economic context of exchange rates and capital controls. The mission of the IMF was to increase international trade wherever possible by setting rules for currency and tariff rates. It was also designed to grant short-term loans to allow for balance-of-payments adjustments.

For over 25 years, capital controls continued to be lifted until the exchange-rate system collapsed completely in 1971. Then came the oil crisis of 1973. Faced with such a dangerous unevenness in world trade, it was the world's commercial banks that sought to assuage the continuing uncertainty, and the consequential surge in sovereign lending led to the currency crisis of 1982. As George Soros writes in his book *On Globalization*: "Preserving the international banking system became a priority." The world was at a crossroads, but the bankers—led by the IMF—drew up rescue packages, restructured debts, and—broadly speaking—steadied the ship of high finance. At the same time, there was disagreement between central banks and commercial banks. The former leaned on the latter to postpone the settlement dates of their loans. They also required new money, solely in order that debtor countries and banks could keep up with their interest payments. The crisis was resolved, and—in as much as no major defaults occurred—the IMF was seen as having achieved something of an economic miracle. But, as Soros writes: "This was the origin of what came to be seen as a moral hazard: in case of crisis the lenders could look to the IMF for rescue."

A new economic tool was issued, named after the US treasury secretary, Nicholas Brady. These Brady bonds had a smaller yield and a longer maturity date. After the crisis had passed, many countries took advantage of these Brady bonds to reorganize their debts. Mexico became the first country to issue Brady bonds, in 1989. But, again according to George Soros: "On balance, the damage to debtor countries was much greater than to the banks: South America lost a decade of growth."

Economic deregulation continued apace during the 1980s while the international lending crisis worsened. Against a background of continuing uncertainty, the glut of financial instruments that developed at this time changed the face of banking, probably forever. "That," says George Soros, "is when globalization truly took shape."

The big problem, as already mentioned, came down to the

Mexican banking crisis of 1994. The government had borrowed too much, spent too much, and when the currency crashed, it had no recourse but to seek help from the IMF and the US Treasury. Mexico issued "*tesobonos*"—treasury bills denominated in pesos but indexed to the US dollar—and those holding them were paid off, in full. It seemed as though the government had paid its way out of the crisis.

A few years later, though, a fresh crisis took hold of the international banking community. During the emerging market crisis of 1997–9 the IMF was repeatedly called in to administer its harsh medicine in such countries as Thailand, Indonesia, and South Korea. This time, though, the treatment did not work, and the crisis spread until the entire global financial system was in crisis.

George Soros asks if the IMF applied the wrong prescription to the Asian crisis. "Its programs consisted of allowing currencies to fall, raising interest rates to contain the currency decline, and reducing government expenditures to contain the budget deficit." In addition, he records, strict conditions were enforced that exacerbated the banking system and anticipated its collapse. "The prescription had been developed in dealing with excesses in the public sector, but in this case the excesses had occurred in the private sector."

But, as Soros goes on to argue: "It must be asked whether the IMF had much of a choice." Soros's view is that a moratorium should have been introduced, followed by a process of debt reorganization. Then, if the immediate pressure of debt repayments could have been alleviated, it would have been possible to control any currency depreciations while not hoisting interest rates too high. Soros—a man who knows a thing or two about the effects of share price collapses on national economies—claims that the effect of his measures would have had far less profound or damaging effects on national economies. Nevertheless, he admits that even he isn't sure, and that "a moratorium could have damaged the international financial system and spread the contagion." And as he says, since the IMF exists for nothing if not to preserve the financial system, that would have been even more disastrous. So the IMF took no chances. South Korea nearly suffered a moratorium in December

1997, but survived thanks to the intervention of the central banks, which led to a rescheduling of its debt and a restructuring of its credit rating. Still, even this precipitous situation sent shockwaves through the entire banking system, bringing back memories of the banking crisis of 1982. The country that suffered most was Russia, which defaulted in August 1998, at which point the entire international financial system came close to meltdown, a grave situation averted by the mediation of the US Federal Reserve. The IMF, we know now, was instrumental in urging emerging economies to open up their capital markets to western interests. But Soros criticizes the international community for "going too far in that direction." Not surprisingly, when the IMF pressed for capital markets to be opened in Asia, the suggestion coincided with the crisis in the Asian dragon. "Not much has been heard of that proposal since that time," notes Soros.

Selfish? Us?

One result of the credit crisis of 1998 is that rich countries, as never before, were widely perceived as caring only about their interests. The global trade imbalance was growing all the time, and so in November of 2004 an effort was made to bring the bigger economies into line with their less developed trade partners. Meeting in Berlin, the Group of 20 leading rich and emerging market nations managed to agree a set of steps that would reduce the US fiscal deficit, along with reforms aimed at generating growth in Europe and Japan, as well as making the exchange rate more flexible in Asia.

The existence of the G20 is a further sign that countries are waking up to the possibilities of joint action. The group, which is currently chaired by China, claims that it can arrest or even eradicate some of the worst effects of global poverty. Its critics claim that it is a talking shop, in which nothing much gets done while conditions for working people all over the world continue to deteriorate.

It is clear that there is much to be done. The September 11th, 2000 issue of *Business Week* magazine carried the surprising news that around 75 percent of Americans felt business controlled too many aspects of their lives. The tone in the editorial column amounted to surprise at the public support for Al Gore's statement at the Democratic convention that Americans must "stand up and say no" to "Big Tobacco, Big Oil, the big polluters, the pharmaceutical companies, the HMOs."

This view was expressed that same year by a professor of sociology at Boston College, Charles Derber. *Corporation Nation* was written in the light of mergers such as Exxon with Mobil, Citicorp with Travelers, Daimler Benz with Chrysler, BankAmerica with NationsBank, and WorldCom with MCI. Alongside the ascendancy of global corporations, from General Electric to Microsoft to Disney, Derber wrote that we were witnessing a shift of sovereignty that was shaking the roots of American democracy.

"Corporate ascendancy refers to the rise of a new weakened form of democracy in which the powers of average Americans are being transferred to vast institutions with diminishing public accountability," he wrote. "With the government increasingly unresponsive to popular opinion, and corporations almost entirely unaccountable to the public, corporations have begun acquiring new public powers and acting as unelected partners with governments."

He quoted statistics about the power of some corporations, for example that General Motors had annual sales larger than Israel's gross domestic product and that Exxon's annual sales were larger than Poland's GDP. There were 161 countries with annual revenues smaller than Wal-Mart's, and hundreds of subsidiaries of General Electric are bigger than many other nations.

"America's biggest companies—and some huge European and Japanese corporations—are an overwhelming force in our national politics," wrote Derber in his introduction. "Corporations poured almost $2 billion into political campaigns in 1996 alone—only one of many measures of corporate political power. The relation between corporate power and democracy goes largely undiscussed in newspapers, schools, legislatures, and dinner conversations, as does the very nature of the corporation itself, a question that a hundred years ago was at the center of the national consciousness." Derber went on to say that as the corporations get bigger, their influence over our lives continues to grow.

In light of the spread of corporate power, a flood of tiny, grassroots organizations has sprung up to try and present a viable intellectual counterblast. One such is the Program on Corporations, Law, and Democracy or POCLAD. Formed in 1994, POCLAD is a small organization dedicated to thinking up strategies for preventing corporate harm. Its co-director Richard Grossman is convinced that it is corporations that are making all the crucial decisions shaping society. Corporations, he says, are constantly pushing the concept that production has to expand and, to that end, they have managed to get their decision-making to be declared private property:

> We're left with trying to deal with the impacts of the major decisions, trying to make them a little less bad...What's happened is, we've been channeled into regulatory administrative agencies, like the Federal Communications Commission, the Environmental Protection Agency, the Securities Exchange Commission, and the National Labor Relations Board, where we try to make the best of the worst of a bad situation, to make the corporate attacks on life, liberty, property, and democracy a little less bad, usually one attack at a time and usually after the fact, when the harm has been done.

Grossman picks out 1886 as a crucial date in the onward march of corporate America, since it was in that year that corporations were accorded the same status as human beings. "This is prior to African Americans being legal persons, women being legal persons, most men without property being legal persons, debtors, and Native Americans," he says. "One of the things that we stress is that corporations don't have rights. Rights are for people. Corporations only have privileges, and only those that we the people bestow on them." According to Grossman, if we abandon our responsibility, corporations will overpower us. And, he adds: "That's to a large extent what we have done."

Reasons to be Radical

Corporate power relies on several other supranational powers to reinforce its dominance, such as the aforementioned International Monetary Fund, and the World Bank, both of which were created in 1944 at that same conference in Bretton Woods, New Hampshire, and which are now based in Washington DC, within convenient distance of the White House. The World Trade Organization—the other supranational "enforcer"—was formed in 1994 during the "Uruguay Round" of GATT talks. As dictated by the 140 GATT member states, the WTO's remit was to penalize any country that breached WTO directives.

The original brief of the IMF was to promote economic cooperation among nations and to provide short-term loans to member countries. Then came the debt crisis of the 1980s and the vast amounts gambled each day in the international currency markets, since when the IMF has become something like a global pawnbroker, imposing savage conditions alongside emergency loan packages known as SAPS or structural adjustment policies. "The IMF now acts like a global loan shark," according to the San Francisco-based organization Global Exchange, "exerting enormous leverage over the economies of more than sixty countries. These countries have to follow the IMF's policies to get loans, international assistance, and even debt relief. Thus, the IMF decides how much debtor countries can spend on education, health care, and environmental protection. The IMF is one of the most powerful institutions on Earth—yet few know how it works."

Global Exchange proposes ten reasons why the IMF should be opposed. These are:

- **The IMF has created an immoral system of modern-day colonialism that "SAPs" the poor**
  Global Exchange claims that the SAP system imposed by the IMF and the World Trade Organization leave poorer countries with no choice but to reduce spending on health and education, as well as basic food and transportation subsidies. It cites a

recent IMF loan package to Argentina, for example, which led to cuts in salaries for doctors and teachers and reductions in essential social security payments. Countries who take on IMF loans find themselves with no choice but to devalue national currencies in order to make exports cheaper, as well as privatizing national assets and freezing wages. The consequence of these "belt-tightening measures" is an increase in poverty, which in turn weakens the domestic economy and allows multinational corporations to exploit workers and the environment.

- **The IMF serves wealthy countries and Wall Street**
  The IMF is a fundamentally undemocratic organization since it is indisputably true that the IMF is dominated by the decision-making agendas of the wealthier countries in the union. Under the IMF's governing rules, the number of votes each country acquires is not determined by population, size, or even a simple one-country-one-vote principle. The IMF runs a policy in which voting power is determined by the amount of money that has been donated to the organization. The US, therefore, gives the most and has the most votes. This is patently not just unfair, but also means that US interests reign supreme. In an organization in which each dollar means one more vote, the US acquires a massive 18 percent of the voting power while Germany, France, the UK, and the US together control around 38 percent of the IMF votes. Since wealthy countries are never going to vote away their economic advantages, the IMF can be used as a permanent buffer to protect the interests of the wealthy countries and, moreover, to give their vested interests a patina of democratic respectability. The interests of less developed countries are legitimately voted away via an apparently democratic process.

- **The IMF is imposing a fundamentally flawed development model**
  Traditionally, development models have been used in order to assist developing countries to build up their home economies

and then to supply local people with local goods at prices that they can afford. The standard development policy of the IMF, however, is to encourage less developed countries to increase production of high quality, high expense goods and then, ostensibly, to make more money by exporting these goods to the western economies. This is patently absurd as a development argument since it prioritizes exports of "luxury" goods and does not promote sustainable self-reliance and local development. According to figures, over three-quarters of malnourished children in the developing world live in areas in which economic necessity has forced the local farmers to grow food for export alone. Under the economic lending terms imposed by the IMF, farmers no longer receive financial assistance to produce goods for local consumption but, instead, receive massive bank loans to incur debt by providing goods for multinational industries whose financial interests will, supposedly, "help them get rich." Labor costs are now so heavily subsidized within these giant, multinational industries that it becomes impossible for smaller, independent producers to compete. "Free Trade Zones" established by the IMF and the World Bank employ locals at impossibly low wages and then provide housing, much of which is financially attached to the multinational industry. The employees barely make enough money to support themselves, let alone their families, and then end up owing rent to multinational companies. The circle of debt is then increased since the employees are forced to continue working in servitude to the multinationals as they now owe too much back rent ever to be able to pay off the loan or to reduce the debt. This pattern of debt is then repeated in increasing concentric circles, and the cycle of poverty is perpetually increased as governments are then forced to borrow more money from the IMF to pay off the interest on debts whose capital they can never hope to eliminate.

- **The IMF is a secretive institution with no accountability**
  Despite the fact that the workings of the IMF are critical to world development, and that the entire organization is, appar-

ently, funded by the people of the world through international tax regimes, there is not—and there never has been—any kind of transparency in its workings. Local people in less developed countries whose lives are most affected by its workings are never consulted about their needs or desires. Policy is decided behind closed doors in Washington and in the corridors of western banks and seats of government. Despite so much evidence to the contrary, the IMF is still run solely on simple economic principles without recourse to health, education, or labor ministers. And certainly with no reference to environmental ministers. These "external" interests are simply not factored into the design of policy. Bankers, whose interests are based in maximizing profit, are deciding the ultimate policy for people who will probably never open a bank account. And there is no public scrutiny of this process. Anyone whose interest is not purely the maximization of profit is simply not allowed to enter or to witness the debate, let alone make a decision. And no external agency has ever been brought in, even to evaluate the efficiency of the existing process with its extremely narrow terms.

- **IMF policies promote corporate welfare**
Export industries are so heavily subsidized under the terms of the IMF that most local assets and almost all natural resources end up purchased by foreign companies or by companies who intend to export all their goods and services. Public utility companies such as telecommunications, water, and electricity are all sold to multinational companies who work with massive tax breaks and government subsidies. They have no intention of doing anything except making more profit for themselves, and it becomes impossible for local companies to resist these giants, whose mass purchasing power means that they can buy out virtually everything and then export both the product and the profit. For geographical reasons, the effects of this policy are particularly noticeable in South America and the Caribbean—in Guyana, for example, an Asian-owned timber company called Barama acquired the rights to chop down all the local trees in

an area which was 150 percent bigger than all the land which the indigenous people had graciously been permitted to purchase. Barama acquired this land with a promise that they would not have to pay any tax on profit they would make for a period of five years after the purchase date. Similarly, the IMF "forcefully encouraged" Haiti to open its trading doors to the purchase of heavily subsidized rice from US manufacturers. This rice was, naturally, so cheap that not only did Haitians buy it but the market then caused their local industry to collapse. Almost half of the rice now eaten on the island comes from one heavily subsidized US company, called Early Rice.

- **The IMF hurts workers**
  Countries hoping to attract foreign investors are frequently advised by the IMF and World Bank to keep wages down and eliminate union-approved policies such as collective pay bargaining. "Flexibility" is the IMF watchword, especially if this means ceding to corporations the right to hire and fire personnel without contractual obligations. The IMF also encourages corporations to be "flexible" when it comes to statute law, especially if it attempts to impose awkward restrictions in matters such as employment law. Taking Haiti again, the government had previously been bound by law to adjust the minimum wage if inflations went beyond ten percent. However, the government opted for the "flexibility" of IMF pay negotiations, with the result that in January 1998 Haiti's minimum wage stood at $2.40 a day. This policy hurts US workers too. After the Asian financial and economic crisis that created 200 million "newly poor" in South Korea, Indonesia, Thailand, and other countries, IMF financial consultants advised affected countries to go for cheap exports—"export their way out of the crisis." Consequently, the US acquired a considerable amount of cheap Asian steel, and US steel factories shed over 12,000 jobs.

- **The IMF's policies hurt women the most**
  SAPs make it much more difficult for women to meet their

families' basic needs. When education costs rise due to IMF-imposed fees for the use of public services (so-called "user fees"), girls are the first to be withdrawn from schools. User fees at public clinics and hospitals make healthcare unaffordable to those who need it most. The shift to export agriculture also makes it harder for women to feed their families. Women have become more exploited as government workplace regulations are rolled back and sweatshop abuses increase.

- **IMF policies hurt the environment**
  IMF loans and bailout packages are paving the way for natural resource exploitation on a staggering scale. The IMF does not consider the environmental impacts of lending policies, and environmental ministries and groups are not included in policy making. The focus on export growth to earn hard currency to pay back loans has led to an unsustainable liquidation of natural resources. For example, the Ivory Coast's increased reliance on cocoa exports has led to a loss of two-thirds of the country's forests.

- **The IMF bails out rich bankers, creating a moral hazard and greater instability in the global economy**
  The IMF routinely pushes countries to deregulate financial systems. The removal of regulations that might limit speculation has greatly increased capital investment in developing country financial markets. More than $1.5 trillion crosses borders every day. Most of this capital is invested short-term, putting countries at the whim of financial speculators. The Mexican 1995 peso crisis was partly a result of these IMF policies. When the bubble popped, the IMF and US government stepped in to prop up interest and exchange rates, using taxpayer money to bail out Wall Street bankers. Such bailouts encourage investors to continue making risky, speculative bets, thereby increasing the instability of national economies. During the bailout of Asian countries, the IMF required governments to assume the bad debts of private banks, thus making the public pay the costs and

draining yet more resources away from social programs.

- **IMF bailouts deepen, rather than solve, economic crises**
  During financial crises—such as with Mexico in 1995 and South
  Korea, Indonesia, Thailand, Brazil, and Russia in 1997—the IMF
  stepped in as the lender of last resort. Yet the IMF bailouts in the
  Asian financial crisis did not stop the financial panic—rather,
  the crisis deepened and spread to more countries. The policies
  imposed as conditions of these loans were bad medicine, causing layoffs in the short run and undermining development in
  the long run. In South Korea, the IMF sparked a recession by raising interest rates, which led to more bankruptcies and unemployment. Under the IMF-imposed economic reforms after the
  peso bailout in 1995, the number of Mexicans living in extreme
  poverty increased more than 50 percent and the national average minimum wage fell 20 percent.

Does globalization make a company more efficient? Sometimes.
Does globalization make a company a better employer? Take Corus.
Corus is an international metal company, providing steel and alu-
minum products and services to customers worldwide. It has an
annual turnover of $17.5 billion and major operating facilities in the
Netherlands, Germany, France, Norway, and Belgium as well as the
UK. Corus employs 48,300 people in over 40 countries. Its shares are
listed on the London, New York, and Amsterdam stock exchanges,
and it describes itself as "a customer focused, innovative solutions-
driven company." Corus was created in October 1999 when the
Dutch company Koninklijke Hoogovens merged with what used to
be called British Steel.

In the period leading up to June 16th, 2000, Corus announced
that 2,400 jobs were to be scrapped in the UK, presumably as part
of its customer-focused, innovative solutions drive. Just over a
month later, on July 21st, Corus announced a further 1,300 job losses
in the steel-mining strongholds of Port Talbot, Llanwern, and Ebbw
Vale, blaming it on the strong pound, despite the Welsh steel industry's enormous efforts to raise productivity and become one of the

most efficient producers in the world. When the axe falls in the steel industry, it cuts through to the bone.

And consider the Bangladeshi company Spectrum Sweater and Knitting Industries. On April 11th, 2005, its factory in Palash Bari, 18 miles northwest of the capital, Dhaka, collapsed without warning. It was several days before soldiers were able to pull out the bodies of 73 workers who were trapped in the rubble. A further hundred were missing. Of course, labor laws and employers' enforcement should have prevented such a tragic workplace accident. But such is the desire of powerful buyers to cut costs and maximize profit margins that basic safety checks were not carried out. For one thing, the factory was built three years ago on land reclaimed from a swamp, and investigators were speculating within days that the nine-story building itself may have been structurally unsound.

Commenting on the disaster—the worst of its kind in Bangladesh's history—Phil Bloomer, head of Oxfam International's *Make Trade Fair* campaign, said that "employment and working conditions can often be so bad, and wages so low, that jobs can actually make poverty worse." Bloomer said that in many countries, just having a job was not enough to lift workers—particularly women workers—and their families out of poverty, and that this applied not only to Bangladesh but also to Indonesia, Honduras, Morocco— and even the UK. "Too often these women have little alternative but have to work inhumane hours and under precarious conditions that are determined by powerful buyers in global supply chains," he said.

Oxfam and other agencies warn about the implications of chasing short-term profit, for while governments champion so-called "flexible" labor markets as promoting competitiveness—a formula upheld by the International Monetary Fund among others—the consequences can be, as at the Spectrum factory in Bangladesh, that it is not merely the employment practices that are flexible, but the building itself; or in this case, downright shaky.

An editorial in Dhaka's daily *New Age* newspaper on April 13th protested:

It is not enough to suggest that as many as 327 people have

died in garment industry accidents in the last 15 years. Neither is it a good idea merely grieving over such losses of life, though grieving is a natural thing to do. What matters is whether, if at all, the men responsible for such accidents will be brought to justice. Where it is a matter of the building that crumbled…on Monday, one is tempted to ask if in the end the authorities will gather in themselves the courage and the conviction to inform themselves that wrongdoing cannot be allowed to go unpunished.

The question that *New Age* did not ask was whether the authorities had made it too easy, too attractive *not* to build a sweatshop on marshy land. The temptations were obvious, but were the safeguards sufficient?

Governments around the world are clearly failing to enforce labor standards. Foreign and national investors, and buyers for multinational companies, are demanding their orders to be processed faster and cheaper than ever, and the pressure is often unbearable, as some examples from around the world demonstrate.

In Morocco, a law has been passed which should give women workers equal pay, hours, and rights with their male colleagues. However, factory bosses are slow to enforce this, as it means that wages have to rise. Nor have factory inspectors or the country's legal system been swift to implement these measures. Instead, reported violations are widespread.

The Nicaraguan government recently banned labor inspectors from imposing fines on employers who violated labor laws. In Central America there are "*maquila*" or assembly zones with highly demanding compulsory production targets. Workers are forced to work to their physical limits to earn their basic wage, as Naomi Klein revealed in *No Logo*. Meal and toilet breaks are often sacrificed in pursuit of production targets. In Colombia, "overtime" has been redefined more "flexibly" as "beginning after 10 pm."

Indonesia too has a "flexible" labor policy, which consists of thousands of full-time workers, most of them women, being dismissed to be replaced by cheaper, short-term contract workers. As fuel prices in the country rose by 30 percent to comply with IMF repayment conditions, Indonesia's minimum legal wage—which was too low to cover basic requirements like food and housing—was made to look even more insubstantial.

Even in the UK, conditions are hard for home workers. Most—up to 90 percent—are women, and at least half are from ethnic minorities. Oxfam reports that they are "routinely denied their rights to earn the national minimum wage or to receive holiday or overtime pay."

In Cortes, Honduras, the government of president Ricardo Maduro has developed the export-oriented growth strategy that creates jobs, but the scheme is far from even-handed. Instead of constructive pensions schemes, permanent workers can expect to be sacked after about five years, as exhaustion and occupational illness sap their productivity.

As we saw in Chapters Five and Six, the workers do have some backers, though, and high-profile ones at that. One familiar name is Ralph Nader, the campaigning liberal who has twice been blamed for losing the election for the Democrats, first for Al Gore, then for John Kerry. Typical of his style is this letter, written in support of some striking grocery workers at Southland Supermarket in Southern California in February 2004:

> I applaud the thousands of grocery employees in Southern California who are standing up for all workers against all too familiar examples of corporate abuse. For more than 16 weeks, members of the United Food and Commercial Workers have endured extraordinary hardships to fight yet another effort by corporations to break the back of organized labor and diminish its role as standard setter and standard bearer for all working people.
> [The bosses] have used hard-boiled tactics, including selective lockouts and refusal to negotiate in good faith, while sharing profits among closed and opened stores. In contrast, the

Taft-Hartley Act prohibits secondary boycotts by labor that could challenge this profit-sharing and force management to negotiate. Management has locked out employees and used media dollars to convince inconvenienced consumers that this struggle is for a tiny financial gain on the part of greedy strikers.

The truth could not be more different.

Nader lambasted the bosses for shifting health care costs onto workers instead of taking them on themselves, a practice at which he said the United States excelled among industrialized countries. He went on to deride the "tragic race to the bottom" and the part it played in pitting one country against another in the search for ever cheaper labor costs. He concluded: "Why are elected officials so removed from the front lines of this battle for the dignity and daily livelihood of America's workers?"

Tariff Wars

In the battle to reduce trade barriers, the WTO, which replaced GATT in 1995, is of crucial significance. From its headquarters in Geneva, it currently has 148 members, all of whom are required to grant other members "most favored nation" status, in which trade concessions are freely and fully exchanged among members. The WTO's range of activities is wider than those of GATT. GATT only supervised trade in merchandise goods, whereas the WTO extends to the monitoring of services such as telecommunications and banking.

The World Trade Organization was devised to promote free trade by persuading all member states to abolish import tariffs and other such barriers. Globalization could thus be said to be its raison d'être. In its role of overseeing the rules of international trade, it regulates free trade agreements, adjudicates in trade disputes between governments, and sets up trade negotiations. Its decisions are binding on all members, so members must have a pretty strong idea that they are going to win when they bring a matter before the WTO.

Countries which resist its judgments effectively find themselves to be the victims of trade sanctions.

Despite the harsh warnings, WTO meetings have all too often seen sharp disagreement, rather than consent. In December 2003, the WTO ministerial meeting in Cancun collapsed in disarray when they failed to come to any sort of agreement on how to revive trade liberalization negotiations. At the time, the question of subsidies for US cotton farmers was again on the agenda. Import taxes had also been made, several times, but were still not enough and in any case did not extend to other goods like textiles and clothing. Delegates listened again as members from poorer countries complained that farmers from the European Union, Japan, and the US were being protected by trade tariffs. African countries like Benin, Burkina Faso, Chad, and Mali asked the rich countries to cease their subsidies. That matter was not dealt with, nor was the question of whether the WTO should have new rules about foreign investors and price fixing cartels.

There was further controversy when the WTO invited Cambodia and Nepal to join it in September 2003, which prompted the following statement from Oxfam: "At the Cancun ministerial conference, Cambodia will be the first LDC (Least Developed Country) to accede to the World Trade Organization since it was created in 1995. This will be hailed by developed countries as the proof that the WTO can deliver for one of the world's poorest countries. It will also be presented as a satisfactory outcome to the long standing demand by LDC members that accession procedures for LDCs be simplified and streamlined. Unfortunately, this rosy picture is far removed from the truth."

Evidence for that came from comments made by Cambodia's minister of commerce and chief negotiator for accession to the WTO, Cham Prasidh, who said that: "This is a package of concessions and commitments that goes far beyond what is commensurate with the level of development of an LDC like Cambodia. Nonetheless, we do accept the challenges, because we see the benefits of joining the world trading system."

Oxfam was strongly of the opinion that Cambodia reacted to

immense pressure imposed on it by other members of the WTO, making concessions that went far beyond the normal level of commitments made by other LDCs. "For instance," wrote Oxfam, referring to an earlier WTO round of trade talks that had taken place at Doha, "Cambodia has been forced into immediately halting use of affordable generic versions of new medicines, even though the Doha declaration (paragraph 7) allows LDCs to wait until at least 2016 to implement this complicated and far-reaching agreement. Moreover, some of the requirements put upon Cambodia go far beyond what the United States and the European Union are willing to commit to in the present round of negotiations."

The use of generic medicines is always controversial, since member countries are obliged to suspend ordering generic medicines and opt instead for higher-priced medicines available from global companies such as Pfizer.

Oxfam was also concerned about "tariff peaks." Tariff peaks are high tariffs usually defined as three times the national average. In Cambodia, with some 80 percent of the population working in agriculture, the country was only being asked to provide a maximum 60 percent protection to its workers. Compare that with the protection guaranteed for the EU—252 percent—or the US and Canada— 121 and 120 percent respectively.

"There is a very real risk that Cambodia's accession will serve as a template model for the accession of other LDCs and developing countries," wrote Oxfam. "The establishment of a precedent would confirm the trend of demanding increasingly higher levels of commitments of those countries that have not yet entered the WTO. This is in complete contradiction to the WTO principle to provide countries with trade opportunities commensurate with their development needs."

Nor is it only left-leaning bodies that have seen fit to criticize the World Trade Organization. The magazine New American published an opinion by Thomas R. Eddlem on April 3rd, 1995 in which he expressed the view that "GATT/WTO's tyrannical potential can be seen today in the increasingly oppressive features taking shape in the European Union...The nations of the EU are finding they have lost virtually all sovereignty, as domestic policies are increasingly dictated by the shadowy and unaccountable EU authorities in Brussels."

Ten years later, on May 16th, 2005, Eddlem was still weighing into the WTO, this time criticizing the "fervent lobbyists" who favor "phone free trade treaties," He named "huge Wall Street-linked behemoths" like Boeing, Archer Daniels Midland, and Monsanto, and "establishment organizations such as the Business Roundtable, the Council on Foreign Relations, and the Trilateral Commission."

According to Eddlem, when Boeing lobbied Congress for free trade arrangements, it was not doing so in the name of pure free trade, but to increase its own foreign sales—"often at the expense of both free trade principles and the interests of the US taxpayer."

So, continued Eddlem, having forced Congress and some Chinese representatives to sit down together on the WTO's own terms, Boeing won an order from China for $3 billion worth of new airplanes. This was followed by subsequent deals worth a further $5.3 billion. "How does this hurt the American taxpayer?" asks Eddlem. "Payments for the planes were largely guaranteed with US taxpayer dollars through the US Export–Import Bank (Eximbank). If the communist Chinese government reneges on payment, the US taxpayer will be forced to cough up the cash."

The world economy has been revolutionized by technological advances. Trillions of dollars can now travel across the world in split seconds. But is the speed of those transactions matched in any way by similarly impressive improvements in working conditions for real people? If anything, greater globalization has promoted global inequality. There was always a contrast between Europe and Africa, even 200 years ago. But these days the division is sharper, with 83 percent of the world's income in the hands of the richest 20 percent of the world's population. By contrast, the poorest 60 percent in the world receive just 5.6 percent of the world's income. The richest 20 percent of the world's population in northern industrial countries use 70 percent of the world's energy, 75 percent of the world's metals, 85 percent of the world's wood, and 60 percent of the world's food, while producing about 75 percent of the world's environmental pollution.

The World Bank argues that economic growth will help us all. But the famous and much-quoted "trickle-down theory" does not necessarily trickle down to all, and might, by contrast, produce greater than ever disparity between rich and poor. Data shows that between 1960 and 1989, as world trade expanded exponentially, global inequality got significantly worse with the ratio between the richest and poorest 20 percent soaring from 30:1 to 59:1.

According to Global Exchange: "The real function of institutions such as the World Bank is not to promote 'development' but rather to integrate the ruling elites of Third World countries into the global system of rewards and punishments." Direct colonialism is out of fashion these days, but the northern elites still manage to hold sway over Third World governments by promising cash to political or tribal elites in return for putting into practice policies devised in Washington. In Mexico, for example, Mexican governments have pursued the "Washington consensus" of policy reforms devised by the World Bank. This has without doubt created many billionaires, but few of Mexico's population of 85 million are finding life easier than it was 20 years ago. "If the ruling PRI Party did not control the police and military, its blatant corruption and disastrous economic policies would not be tolerated for long," says Global Exchange.

The list of countries ill served by the World Bank is lengthy, from hard-up countries like Somalia, Rwanda, and Mozambique to seemingly rich—if only in natural resources—countries like Ghana, Brazil, and the Philippines. The World Bank has imposed its structural adjustment policies on these countries in order to help them to pay off their foreign debts, but in the process it has pushed wages down for the majority, reduced social services, and made the countries less democratic.

The World Bank's emphasis on expanding exports has been disastrous for the environment, says Global Exchange. The stated aim of expanding exports is to generate more hard currency, whether of dollars or yen. These are then used to secure payments on foreign debts. But invariably, in the search for natural resources to export, countries have been forced to plunder their natural resources. They chop down their forests, thus contributing to the greenhouse effect. They deluge their land with chemicals in order to produce export crops like coffee, tea, and tobacco, which in turn poison their land and water. They tear mineral wealth from the soil, heedless of the cost to human and animal life, and over-fish in coastal and international waters.

As if proof were needed that the model is not the one to follow, it is notable that industrially developed countries spurn the so-called "free market" economic model that they are so keen for Third World countries to adopt. Wealthy countries like the USA, Japan, Germany, the UK, and France—as well as newer members of the rich club like Taiwan and South Korea—prefer a heavily interventionist model in which government takes a central role at managing investments, overseeing trade, and subsidizing certain key economic sectors. According to Global Exchange: "The United States was in many ways the 'mother country' of protectionism, showing other wealthy countries how to do it. Would we have a big electronics industry or nuclear power industry were it not for the massive government subsidy program called the Pentagon?"

Finally, the "globalization-from-above" model has proved unpopular (see Paul Kingsnorth's book *One No, Many Yeses: A Journey to the Heart of the Global Resistance Movement*) and has been rejected by millions of people the world over. From the Zapatistas in Mexico in 1994 to Seattle in 1999, when 50,000 protesters rose up against the World Trade Organization, the grassroots movement demonstrated its hostility to a globalization movement run by wealthy elites and driven by a thirst for ever greater wealth and power. The alternative alliance is made up of human rights activists, trade unions, women's organizations, environmental coalitions, and farmers. It may not have guns and cash, but it does have moral authority.

In late 2002, the World Economic Forum undertook one of the biggest surveys ever conducted of global opinion. Representing 36,000 people from 47 countries, this figure could be extrapolated to represent the views of 1.4 billion people. A vast majority of those in supposedly democratic countries who were questioned—about two in three—said that they did not believe that their country was "governed by the will of the people." So what does that tell us about the value of democracy?

Paul Kingsnorth, who produced that figure in an article written for the *New Internationalist* in November 2004, felt he knew why the answer had been so unmistakable: "It is a simple reason, but one that is not discussed as often as it should be. The reason is this: the global free market and systems of democracy are not, as we are told from all sides, complementary: they are antagonistic. You can have one but, it seems, you cannot have the other. The spread of the free market does not aid the spread of a free politics. Quite the opposite: it eats democracy for breakfast."

The two systems are obviously in opposition. The World Bank is threatened by the demands from alternative voices for greater openness and accountability. Raising wages? Improving health and safety standards in the developing world? Bringing them up to our own standards? These are not solutions that financial leaders are in any mood to hear.

The Global Exchange proposes a solution: "If we could pressure large institutional funds (e.g. university endowments and state worker pension funds) to stop buying World Bank bonds as a way to protest the Bank's destructive policies, we could exert serious pressure on the Bank."

And if we could persuade huge numbers of pigs to spread their wings and float upwards, that would be a memorable day too.

Chapter Eight: The Media Goes Global

On May 16th, 2002 Dan Rather gave an interview to the BBC program *Newsnight* in which he lamented the effect that the attacks on New York City and Washington DC the previous September had had on balanced reporting. Rather's point was that the upsurge of jingoism, and the need to show national unity in the face of the perceived terror threat, had created an atmosphere of intimidation that was blunting the teeth of investigative journalism. "One finds oneself saying: 'I know the right question, but you know what? This is not exactly the right time to ask it,'" he said.

Rather is an institution in American news reporting. He had joined CBS in 1962 and was now almost as revered as Walter Cronkite, his predecessor on CBS News. He felt that the media had been cowed by the after-effects of 9/11, and that dissenting journalism had not regrouped as effectively as, say, the White House or right-wing special interest groups. He blamed "patriotism run amok," which he said prevented him from asking the questions that needed to be asked.

Two years later, Rather was on the spike himself. A documentary, which aired on September 8th, 2004, cast questions over President George W. Bush's army record, claiming that the young George Bush had received special treatment during his time in the Texas Air National Guard, and that he had avoided serving in the Vietnam War. The evidence for these claims had come from former Texas Air National Guard Lieutenant Colonel Bill Burkett. Rather had been an enemy of the right ever since he had trained his journalistic guns on Richard Nixon, but this time he called it wrong.

The documents were forgeries, and it was left to bloggers on the net to reveal it, ironically within hours of CBS putting the documents on its website.

Rather took early retirement on March 9th, 2005, but questions were already being asked about CBS and the sacrosanct nature of TV news. Did this represent the end of the old certainties? For one thing, the demographic that watched CBS news—as well as its rivals on ABC and NBC—is old and getting older, with an average age of 60 or so. Also, and crucially, only 8–9 percent of the all-important 18–34 demographic watches network news. So the CBS crisis could be said to be a storm in a teacup—except it wasn't, because it shows the growing power of an increasingly confident and assertive community of bloggers, many of whom, though far from all, are voluble right-wing Bush supporters.

The press came in for criticism for its treatment of what became known, inevitably, as Rathergate. When it repeated the allegations, USA Today also came under fire from the right-wing lobby group Accuracy in Media for not firing staff. And months after it had been acknowledged beyond doubt that the documents were forgeries, CBS admitted that its credibility had been damaged by the scandal. Rather's supporters criticized CBS for caving in too easily, and accused CBS bosses of being in hock to the White House, but the fact is, the story was wrong, and heads had to roll. It was claimed that Rather had been careless with his facts. Even his illustrious predecessor Walter Cronkite had murmured that he preferred to watch Rather's rival Peter Jennings on ABC. Was it not right that he should go?

Some attacked the president of CBS news division Andrew Heyward, alleging that he was more loyal to corporate interests than to his staff. They contrasted his silence after the event with the attitude of his predecessors—men like Richard Salant, William Leonard and Fred W. Friendly—who stuck up for reporters against incursions from management. In an interview just before he left, Rather didn't comment on this, but said: "I confess that I am concerned that we may be reaching the point where too many members of the press fear being labeled unpatriotic or partisan if they challenge the actions or decisions of political leaders of any persuasion."

Against that sort of background, it doesn't seem to matter whose side the bosses are on. Rather pointed to the blizzard of blogs, all competing shrilly for attention. "What the country doesn't need, particularly just now," said the 73-year-old, "is a press that's docile— never mind obsequious or intimidated. I don't agree with those who say, 'Dan, it's already happened,' but I do recognize there's some danger."

Profit over Principle?

If the problem lay anywhere, perhaps it was budgetary rather than directly political. CBS had seen its program-making budget slashed over the years, to the point where its ability to report the news accurately was becoming an issue. Also, the diminution of its TV audience from a high of 50 million led to many asking just how much of a force evening news still was, at a time when many of its target viewers were still at work, rather than sitting comfortably on their sofas at home. The three big networks had failed to represent—or to keep up with—the reality of American life in the 21st century. And it was for this that they were being punished.

CBS is now one of several players in a shrinking media market. In an age of apparently booming media outlets, the number of owners has shrunk sharply. And that cannot be good for democracy. In 1983, 50 corporations owned most of the US media operation. By 1992, that number had shrunk to below 24. In September 1999, CBS was bought by Viacom and so, by 2000, it was six. And so it keeps going: by 2004, the number stood at five— Warner, Disney, Rupert Murdoch's News Corporation, Bertelsmann of Germany, and Viacom.

Those media conglomerates tend to lean to the right, since their bosses are chasing closer links with government leaders. In 1989, for example, News Corporation formed HarperCollins out of Harper & Row and Collins book publishers. In 1993, Murdoch gained a controlling interest in the Asian satellite TV service Star TV. Keen to promote his own interests in Asia, particularly in China's burgeoning media market, in 1998 Murdoch ordered HarperCollins to quash the autobiography of Chris Patten, Hong Kong's last governor and a prominent critic of the communist China government.

When we pick up a newspaper or magazine, or turn to a TV or radio station, we may not realize whose vested interests we are buying into. The ABC network, for example, is owned by the Disney corporation, which refused to handle Michael Moore's documentary film *Fahrenheit 9/11*. News Corporation owns the right-leaning Fox News, as well as a tranche of television stations, 20th Century Fox Studios, and five British newspapers.

Never has so much power been concentrated in so few hands. And rarely have the press come under so much fire. In January 2005, a third journalist was exposed as having been paid by the White House to deliver Bush-friendly pro-marriage propaganda on the pages of a respected American newspaper. Michael McManus's column on Ethics and Religion is syndicated across 50 newspapers in the US. It was similar to the scandal of foreign correspondent Jack Kelley, which erupted when he stood down from *USA Today* after it emerged that he had been making up quotes from stories all over the world. A *USA Today* internal report found that his dishonest reporting dated back to 1991. The scandal of Jack Kelley's false reporting led directly to the resignation of editor Karen Jurgensen, and to her replacement by Ken Paulson.

"There is, in this media-saturated age, a new genre of journalist—the reporter as media performer," said *USA Today* in a wide-ranging self-critique aimed at bringing journalists back down to where they belonged. But the genie is out of the bag. Journalists are becoming part of the news themselves. In February 2005, it emerged that "Jeff Gannon," who until then had been a part of the White House press pack, had been paid by a Republican front organization to throw "soft-ball" questions at the Bush administration. And yet, wrote Paul Harris of the *Observer*: "If, during the Clinton administration, a fake reporter from a Democrat front organization, using a false name, had been exposed as attending White House press conferences it would have been a national scandal...With 'Gannon' and Bush there has been no such outcry. The mainstream media has approached the story warily, while right-wing organizations such as Fox News have largely ignored it."

The result, says Harris, is that there is now a dangerous vacuum in American reporting, which is being filled by bloggers of both political persuasion and several in between, precisely those "guys sitting in their living room in their pajamas, writing" who are so derided by blog-hostile defenders of professional journalism. But the bloggers have been proved right, many times over, ever since Matt Drudge—whose Drudge report is now essential reading for all political reporters—struck gold with the first report of the Monica Lewinsky scandal on January 17th, 1998, a story which, incidentally, *Newsweek* had all but quashed.

Speaking at the Global News Forum 2000 symposium in Barcelona, media commentator Robert McChesney pointed to the "hyper-commercialism of content as the traditional barrier between the creative and editorial side and the commercial side has collapsed." He went on: "The structure we currently have in the global system, especially in the United States but increasingly around the world, works directly against the needs of democratic journalism and a democratic society."

Everywhere, conflicts of interest are the new news story. NBC News, for example, is owned by General Electric. GE has global business interests in defense contracting and nuclear power. Can NBC report the facts without fear of censorship? Or is it not inevitable that, among certain broadcasters, news will receive a low priority where profits are involved?

The first and quickest players to capitalize on the trend towards globalization were American media organizations such as Time Warner and CNN. When Viacom took over CBS in September 1999, to create a company worth more than $66 billion, Sumner Redstone, Viacom's chief executive, made no effort to conceal his delight. "The creation of this formidable media giant marks the beginning of a new era of explosive growth domestically and around the world. Our future is without limit," he declared gleefully.

Merger Mania

And yet mergers, like marriages, have honeymoon periods, and the marriage doesn't necessarily settle down happily ever after—for example in June 2005, Viacom's board of directors approved separating its more mature businesses, such as CBS and its radio division, from its faster-growing cable TV networks, even though it had bought CBS (for $40 billion) only in 1999. Nevertheless, the quest for size and profits continues unabated in today's global economy. Globalization has presented these corporations with further opportunities for growth, and the large companies have responded to globalization in a variety of ways. To some, the problem concerns which flag you are seen to be flying, and it was clear which flag they did not want to be seen to be holding. "We do not want to be viewed as an American company," said AOL-Time Warner's Gerald Levin. Others, such as Bertelsmann CEO Thomas Middelhoff, seem to be trying to belong to two different countries at the same time. "I'm an American with a German passport," he said in 1998. Middelhoff also said: "We're not foreign. We're international," as if his company were able to avoid any national or parochial issue altogether. The only media chief who seemed to recognize any sort of national boundary pattern was Frank Biondi, the former chairman of Vivendi's Universal Studios, who said of the new class of super-mergers that 99 percent of their success would be derived from how they pursued their business overseas—or "successful execution offshore" as he put it.

Once upon a time, it was considered unacceptable for a media company to be owned in a different country from that in which it broadcast. But that sort of sentimental talk is mostly outdated. Bertelsmann owns 15 percent of the US book-publishing and music markets. Dominant players in the media industry are themselves parts of huge global media conglomerates. From January to June 2000, the volume of merger deals in global media, the internet, and the telecoms business topped $300 billion. That was three times the figure for the same period in the previous year. Company mergers were definitely flavor of the year.

In brief, the global media market is now divided up among seven multinational corporations: Disney, AOL-Time Warner, Sony, News Corporation, Viacom, Vivendi, and Bertelsmann. All these companies have changed beyond recognition in as little as 15 years. Sony used to be strictly involved in electronics, Bertelsmann was originally a Bible printing company. Now they all rank among the largest 300 non-financial firms in the world. Only three could really be called US-based firms, but between them they own the entire Hollywood studio system and all the US television networks bar one. Add to that the world of book and magazine production, all or most of the global cable TV market, and a vast chunk of European terrestrial TV, and one begins to see what a huge amount of global business this really is. And the super-merger season is not over yet. Partners have to be found while there are still available partners. If the giants don't merge with other giants, they risk becoming dinosaurs.

Rupert Murdoch's News International's satellite TV services are ranged across Asia through Europe and Latin America. His Star TV has continental domination over Asia with a total 30 channels in seven languages. Phoenix TV, 45-percent-owned by Murdoch, has a penetration of 45 million homes and enjoyed an advertising revenue growth of 80 percent in 2001. Altogether, News Corporation's considerable portfolio now includes Twentieth Century Fox films, the Fox TV network, the publishers HarperCollins, TV stations, cable TV channels, magazines, over 130 newspapers, and professional sport teams.

Who Benefits?

So who benefits from the emergence of these global media players? Lawrence K. Grossman was president of NBC News from 1984 to 1988. He says that in the television business of today: "You have, again, a paradoxical situation, where we get many, many more channels, many more news outlets on the air, owned by fewer and fewer multimedia global corporations. Where news used to be the major centerpiece of a broadcast operation, it's now very minor and relatively insignificant in terms of the balance sheet of Time Warner,

Turner, Disney, ABC, Viacom, CBS, GE, NBC. News is just a small player in those companies. So the whole set of priorities and focus becomes very different."

Grossman criticized the effect that mergers had on local broadcasting in the United States. The problem, he said in 2001 in conversation with Harry Kreisler (*Conversations with History*, Institute of International Studies, UC Berkeley), was:

> the major networks, which had strong, long traditions as responsible broadcasters, partly because of the government policy of operating in the public interest, were sold to outsiders, in a sense. To General Electric, in the case of NBC; in the case of CBS, to somebody who owned an investment portfolio, Larry Tisch, who saw the front-loaded losses that news was taking and said, "Why do we need all of that? Why do we need to spend all that money? It's interfering with our bottom line."

Grossman goes on to say:

> The most costly thing in putting on nightly news programs is covering the hard news. And besides, people are getting CNN and getting the news elsewhere. But it was very cheap to put on prime-time 'news magazines,' which really are a misnomer—they're basically non-fiction entertainment magazines. And so you get the idea: in order to attract an audience, in order to attract advertisers which follow the audience, instead of presenting hard news about government and about finance and about international affairs, we focus more on the entertainment aspects of news. And so it has been moving in that direction.

Grossman's final charge relates to the regard in which news is held by the media organizations' new owners:

> While you get many more channels that you can tune in to see news happening, what is happening now is you get fewer and fewer news-gathering operations. They're all feeding off of the

same syndicated news reporting services. And one of the consequences of that is the misreporting of election night, because instead of having every network do its own analysis of the voting returns, for example, they pooled the coverage, they had one voter news service reporting, and that was mistaken, and they all fell into the same trap.

Fair and Balanced?

In July 2004, a film opened at box offices in America that was a surprising hit. Called *Outfoxed*, Robert Greenwald's documentary told the story of Rupert Murdoch's dominance of the media. Cooperating with the organization MoveOn.org, the film painted a portrait of the media group that controlled much of the airwaves, at the whim of Rupert Murdoch. *Outfoxed* offered an unblinking look at Fox News, and what it called "the dangers of ever-enlarging corporations taking control of the public's right to know."

The film also talked to former Fox news producers, reporters, bookers, and writers who revealed what it was like to be persuaded to adopt a "right-wing" point of view at the price of losing their jobs. Robert Greenwald's documentary did not pretend to be impartial. The Fox News Channel was launched in 1996 with the slogan of "fair and balanced" reporting, which was intended as a goad to the "liberal consensus" of CNN, CBS, or the *New York Times*. Fox regards itself as promoting the other side of the argument, in apparent contradiction to the other networks and the propaganda of which they themselves seem only dimly aware. "Mr. Greenwald's film challenges this notion," said A.O. Scott in the *New York Times*, "and methodically works to disarm the ready-made accusation that it is outfoxing Fox by stooping to its methods...The story [former employees] tell is of the systematic and deliberate dismantling of journalistic norms, and of an outfit that has become not merely a voice of conservatism but a cheerleader for the Republican Party." So much for Fox's famous "fair and balanced" reporting.

Rob Mackie in the *Guardian* enjoyed it too:

There's no Michael Moore-style entertainment here: it's a straightforward indictment of the station whose CEO Roger Ailes was media strategist for Nixon, Reagan, and Bush 1, and which labels itself "Fair & Balanced" onscreen. There's a lot of Fox footage (with Republicans accounting for 83 percent of its guests) [which] includes a shockingly aggressive interview with a war dissenter (the phrase "shut up" seems to be a popular interviewer's gambit) and a nauseatingly sycophantic interview with Bush Jr. from a man whose wife is an active Bush campaigner—no problem for a Fox political journalist, apparently. Kerry coverage concentrates on his "flip-flopping." He is also said to look "a bit French."

Murdoch has certainly done his homework. Under the banner of "market difference," he has created a channel, Fox, which is markedly different from other channels. In its 2005 report, the US-based Project for Excellence in Journalism commented about cable TV: "Republicans have tended to congregate in one place: Fox." The report commented on cable TV in general: "For now, the content of cable news is measurably thinner, more opinionated, and less densely sourced than other forms of national news." And in July 2004, Fox News faced being taken to the Federal Trade Commission when its claim that it was "fair and balanced" backfired. Two pressure groups—the liberal internet-based group MoveOn.org and the historically non-partisan Common Cause—alleged that Fox News had "deliberately and consistently distorted and twisted to promote the Republican Party of the US and an extreme right-wing viewpoint."

MoveOn.org claimed that the Fox Network managers told line producers and correspondents to target their news coverage "in a way that specifically promotes the positions of the Bush Administration and the Republican Party." They accused the network of making "no effort whatsoever to achieve any semblance of balance on its many interview shows." And they accused the network's coverage of current events of being "grossly distorted and biased." MoveOn.org's study of the newscast *Special Report with Brit*

Hume for the latter half of 2003 found that conservative guests out-numbered progressive guests five to one. In 2002, a similar study found that conservative guests had outnumbered progressive ones by 14 to one. In short, the channel is nationalistic, chauvinistic, and right-wing, and generally panders to the worst prejudices of its viewers. And yet the advertisers still flock to promote their wares on this channel, and the tills keep ringing.

The Republican Party receives much valuable support from another sector: Christian TV channels. In October 2004, news emerged that, as it has been doing since 1992, the Christian Coalition was to distribute 30 million "voter guides," which purported to advise voters about the ethical stance of the two candidates, George Bush and John Kerry. These guides were distributed nationally at churches, shopping malls, and other public locations.

The massive voting power of Christian America obviously worried a lot of observers. "These guides are clearly partisan, almost always supporting the Republican campaign," said Barry Lynn, executive director of Americans United for the Separation of Church and State. "They make the Republican look like a candidate for sainthood and the Democratic candidates look like they belong in the house of horrors wax museum."

But they must have done their job, marshalling support among a population that is said to consist of 25 percent white evangelicals. Among Republicans, about four in ten described themselves as evangelicals. Topics on which "guidance" was provided included—in rather lurid wording—"unrestricted abortion on demand," "adoption of children by homosexuals," "permanent elimination of death duties," and "federal firearms registration and licensing of gun owners."

Embedding

The quality of the news we are all fed is also compromised by the new practice of "embedding." An "embed"—from the word embedded—usually means a news reporter who works within one side in an armed struggle. On the one hand the journalist is being protected by the army—this came to mean the allied forces led by the US and UK forces in the second Gulf War. The drawback of this, in terms of journalistic neutrality or integrity, is that they are dependent on the army for all their stories, and cannot go off on their own. For many western journalists, the army press officer is their sole source. Their impartiality is thus heavily compromised. There may be perfectly good reasons for this, as in a warlike situation it is simply not safe.

There are, of course, Middle East specialists like the journalist Robert Fisk who—even when he is not actually physically present at the front line—are scathing about the process by which journalists take press releases from, say, the Pentagon and simply recycle them as news, but not all independent reporters take that line. In an article written for the UK *Press Gazette* in November 2004, the UK Channel 4 news presenter Alex Thomson argued forcefully that embeds were an inevitable part of the war operation. "From Operation Desert Storm in 1991 onwards, through the invasion and occupation of Iraq to the reinvasion of Falluja last week, the world has come to accept the Pentagon war-fighting doctrine of overwhelming force as normal," he wrote.

The embed has emerged since 9/11, and along the way the traditional "war hack" has largely disappeared in war-torn areas like Iraq. In those days, war correspondents were somewhere between hitch-hikers and travel writers, trying to charm their way into a military unit for a while so that they could report on all the strange sights they saw. These days, it's invitation only. As Thomson says, the modern-day war reporter has little choice except to "Go embedded or face the—often lethal—consequences."

The problem is that the argument has become so polarized. In Iraq, the Americans see themselves as liberators, but to many Iraqis they are merely crusaders in modern battledress. And up until now the insurgents have, by and large, ignored the temptation to hire journalists to present their case for them.

In 2003, Saddam Hussein used western reporters to show the effects of allied bombs on Iraqi children, so, to a limited extent, western audiences who watched TV were shown the other half of the picture and could judge that against the carefully staged

British/US media briefings. The problem, as Thomson says, is that "Saddam bore as much relationship to al-Qaeda as Pluto does to wind-surfing." There is an ideological clash taking place, and Islamic fundamentalists are not taking the trouble to give briefings to western hacks. That suits the White House just fine. From their point of view, the less the public gets to know about the aims and motives of al-Qaeda the better. But journalists know in their gut that they're not telling the whole story. And that doesn't do their conscience any good.

"Many viewers," says Thomson, "appear to think the media still have some kind of conferred neutrality. That the press badge can still act a bit like the Red Crescent...Well, those days have well and truly gone." Thomson argues that even embeds can tell a version of the truth. And that their images or words can be haunting, evocative, persuasive. There is much in these reports, he says, which we would not otherwise have known, which some of us might have preferred not to know, and which a democratic society should know. "For the first time Falluja brought military embeds hard up against bad news for the Pentagon—and the news sometimes still got past the censor."

There were a record number of journalists killed in 2004—the worst for a decade. In all, 129 died—bombed, killed in accidents, or in some other way. They died in Iraq, India, the Philippines, and Sri Lanka, among 34 countries. But it wasn't lone intrepid western journalists. More often than not it was local reporters, cameramen, and photographers trying to get a picture, or sticking their heads up at the wrong moment.

The advent of al-Jazeera, the world's first pan-Arab news agency and the leading Arab TV station, has done a lot to change attitudes to press. al-Jazeera has been all but banned from Iraq by the pro-US government, but this curb on press freedom is bound to be overturned in time. Alex Thomson is not the only journalist who argues that, in time, with sufficient cooperation between news organizations and local reporters, even insurgents will open up to journalists, and then the whole embed situation will become not one- but two-sided.

In April 2003 the Washington-based organization Excellence in Journalism published a report called "Embedded Reporters: What Are Americans Getting?" It found: "The embedded coverage is largely anecdotal. It's both exciting and dull, combat focused, and mostly live and unedited. Much of it lacks context but it is usually rich in detail. It has all the virtues and vices of reporting only what you can see." It then went on to list five findings in particular:

- In an age when the press is often criticized for being too inter-pretive, the overwhelming majority of the embedded stories studied, 94 percent, were primarily factual in nature.

- Most of the embedded reports studied—six out of ten—were live and unedited accounts.

- Viewers were hearing mostly from reporters, not directly from soldiers or other sources. In eight out of ten stories we heard from reporters only.

- This is battle coverage. Nearly half of the embedded reports— 47 percent—described military action or the results.

- While dramatic, the coverage is not graphic. Not a single story examined showed pictures of people being hit by fired weapons.

The Price of Independence

Journalists might be entitled to think that "embedding" themselves at least guarantees them security from injury at the hands of one party in a conflict, but what happens to those journalists who still attempt to undertake the difficult and hazardous business of reporting independently on the war? On April 8th, 2003, Reuters cor-respondents Taras Protsyuk and Jose Couso of the Spanish network Telecinco were killed when an American tank fired an explosive shell at the Palestine Hotel, where most non-embedded interna-tional reporters in Baghdad were based. Three other journalists were injured. Survivors said that the tank seemed to pick its target carefully, and they vigorously denied that the tank had been fired on. On the same day, a bomb hit the al-Jazeera Arabic-language news agency building, killing one of its cameraman. The headquarters of Abu Dhabi TV was also hit. Reporters had enough to worry about when being shot by insurgents or hostile fire. To find themselves being fired on by US forces must have been doubly alarming. Two days later, on April 10th, UK Prime Minister Tony Blair announced the launch of a new, allied-sponsored TV station, "Towards Freedom," which would broadcast one hour daily from the US flying TV station Commando Solo—a specially equipped Hercules aircraft fitted with a television studio.

Still, at least some debate was held over the coverage of the war later in the month when UK Air Marshal Brian Burridge attacked the lurid reporting style of the war for being high on conjecture but low on analysis. In the rush to provide telling pictures, he accused news programs and the media of turning the war into "reality TV." That argument should not conceal how dangerous war-reporting still is. The organization Reporters Without Borders reports that in the first six months of 2005, 27 reporters were killed, 110 were imprisoned, and 76 "cyberdissidents" imprisoned.

On April 7th, 2003, the Committee for the Protection of Journalists wrote an open letter to the then Allied Commander Tommy Franks to say that it was "deeply concerned about two recent incidents in which US forces allegedly interfered with and mistreated journalists working in Iraq." The letter followed reports that non-embedded journalists had been attacked by American forces. The letter concludes: "While we recognize that embedded journalists have been given special access to coalition troops, we are extremely concerned by these reports of harassment and violence against independent journalists."

Pentagon spokesperson Victoria Clarke told the Associated Press on April 9th: "We've had conversations over the last couple of days [with] news organizations eager to get their people unilaterally into Baghdad." The message seemed to be: don't do it. "We are saying it is not a safe place; you should not be there," she said.

Never Just Black and White

In the past, the media has been at the forefront in raising issues of outsiders, minorities, and discrimination. Ideally, it should help us to make sense of a complex, constantly changing world, and our view of the world is shaped by the choices it makes. The problem is that if the media itself is in a state of crisis, there is a risk that the stories and values they publish will be tinged by that uncertainty. But there is evidence that, here too, they are beginning to lose their nerve.

In 2005 the Canadian organization Media Awareness Network argued that members of ethnic and "visible" minorities were still inadequately represented in entertainment and news media in the US and Canada, and that portrayals of minorities are "often stereotypical and demeaning."

Canada's small immigrant population has proportionately fewer members in prison than the general population, but they have been overwhelmingly portrayed in the media in negative terms. In a survey of three major Toronto papers conducted by York University's Dr. Frances Henry, she found that, over four months in 1997, 54 percent of all articles in the *Toronto Sun* that contained the word "Jamaican" were about criminal activity, while 46 percent of stories on drug offences in all three papers referred to East Asian and Vietnamese "drug gangs."

Nor is this stereotyping limited to crime. The Canadian Nation of Immigrants Project reports that "newspapers over-represent immigrants in stories about sports and entertainment, and under-represent them in politics and business coverage." On the other hand, it is hard for the mainstream media not to see white males as authority figures, while marginalizing the expertise of members of minorities. "Approximately 90 percent of all experts featured in US news stories are white," reports the Media Awareness Network. "When minority experts are called upon, it's typically in response to minority community matters, drugs, and crime."

The media has always been responsible for promoting ethnic stereotypes. In Britain, the man generally referred to as the "fiery

British preacher Abu Hamza al-Masri" has become something of a hate figure for those on the right, frequently referred to in tabloid newspapers the *Sun* or the *Daily Mail* as "Captain Hook" on account of his prosthetic hand.

In 2002, the University of Adelaide decided to take positive action in order to challenge the increasingly negative western perceptions of Islam that had emerged since the attacks on the Pentagon and the Twin Towers. The university's four-week course, called "Questioning Western Perceptions of Islam," was developed by its Center for Professional and Continuing Education and presented by Dr. Arthur Saniotis, an anthropologist with extensive experience in Islam and Muslim cultures. "A major aim of this course will be to challenge misconceptions of Islam and Muslims in general, and to give an informed understanding of Islam and its relationship with the West," said Dr. Saniotis. "By drawing from historical and anthropological sources, this course will offer the participants an opportunity to question taken-for-granted notions of 'otherness' and how they are often conveyed in xenophobia and intolerance."

It appears that Australia still has much to learn. John Howard, who was re-elected as prime minister in October 2004, was accused of "playing the race card" with his calls for a points system for economic immigrants. His election adviser Lynton Crosbie went on to advise Michael Howard, the leader of Britain's Conservative Party that lost in the general election of May 2005.

Death in Brief

On June 24th, 2002, a 20-carriage passenger train crashed into a cargo train in central Tanzania after rolling out of control for 20 miles. In all, some 200 people were killed, but the story merited only a 102-word write-up in the "In Brief" column of the London *Times*. Of course, stories of remote interest will always be lower down the news agenda than national disasters, but it adds to the impression that the news organizations care little for "other" people.

Another case of media simplification is so-called "compassion fatigue," which the charity VSO (Voluntary Service Overseas) highlighted in a report called *The Live Aid Legacy*. The report, published in January 2002, draws attention to the awkward balancing act the media undertakes, caught between depicting the horror of the consequences of famine and leaving the British public with a view of Africa as a continent permanently in the grip of famine and unable to move forward from there. The international development charity claimed that eight percent of the British public "believe the developing world exists in a permanent state of disaster." And much of the blame for this, said VSO, lay with the media, which has not managed to break away from the gripping and unforgettable images of the Ethiopian tragedy that led to so much well-intentioned famine relief work in Africa in the 1980s.

"We commonly use images of famine and western aid that are 16 years out of date and relate to only a tiny minority of people in the developing world," the report says, comparing that with the actual experience of VSO staff overseas who are living in circumstances that clash with preconceptions in the West.

"The Live Aid images that were once such a force for good have left a legacy that hangs like a cloud over our relationship with the developing world," said VSO's chief executive, Mark Goldring. "There is an urgent need to rebalance the picture. We must ensure that nurturing this grotesque lack of reality—that most of the world is one block of disadvantaged, poverty-stricken people—is not the legacy of our generation."

After 9/11

Is the consumer well served by the media? While it's true that there are plenty of alternative information sources out there, the consumer—whether of print or electronic media—has some searching to do to find non-mainstream viewpoints, and when it comes to TV or radio, the choices are fairly stark. With determination, and some pre-existing knowledge, the seeker of alternative truths can find the perspective they seek, but without any such help, they are in a limited market.

After 9/11, many wondered which truths were being propagated, and by whom. Among the American media, the sense of horror and victimization was so acute that one would have had to search long and hard to find any dissenting view. There were very few broadcasters or periodicals that did not sign up to the general view that innocent America had been hit below by the belt by the incarnation of Satan: and within days Fox, ABC, CBS, NBC, and CNN had signed up to the general hysteria, and were running stories that al-Qaeda was planning any number of even more audacious attacks on America. There was a generalized feeling, too, that anyone with dark skin and a beard might be a Muslim terror suspect, a suspicion that the American media, and similar organizations in the UK, did little to impede. The UK *Sun*—a Murdoch-owned newspaper with a notably inscrutable moral core—and the left-wing *Daily Mirror* rated as honorable exceptions among the UK tabloid pack when neither signed up to the lynch mob mentality.

Writing in the weekly English language *Al-Ahram* newspaper on May 9th, Muqtedar Khan, assistant professor of political science and director of the International Studies Program at Adrian College, asked why "US policies in the aftermath of 9/11 have subverted and compromised the inalienability of democratic and human rights by making them seem like luxuries that can be afforded only under secure conditions." The US, said Khan, being the world's most prominent democracy, was sending the wrong signal to the rest of the world. "It is suggesting that in moments of crisis and insecurity even the most powerful of states cannot afford to protect democracy, human rights, and international law. Most other nations are far more insecure and often in crisis; how can we then demand that they adhere to international norms and protect the civil and political rights of their citizens?"

It was, if anything, the horror of 9/11 that encouraged some people to try to get behind the headlines and the jingoism. Instead of going after the terrorists with guns, some people tried to pursue alternative points of view in order to understand them, rather than simply confront them. This was difficult in the United States, where a limited number of broadcasters controlled most of the broadcast media, but in Britain, newsagents reported increased sales of the *Irish Times*. The perspective was worlds away from the Murdoch-owned London *Times*.

There was also, inevitably, a surge of interest in alternative websites such as Salon.com, and the ZNet site, which can be found at zmag.org. That site is just one of many packed with interviews, book reviews, magazine articles, recommended links to other sites, reports of anti-corporate or anti-governmental activities around the world, and other news stories which serve the community of dissidents. Another is Indymedia.org—a vast dragnet of resources from correspondents across the world. Definitions of such concepts as "freedom" and "independence" are notoriously hard to clarify, especially on the web where many self-appointed truth-seekers are harnessing the resources of the internet to serve their own extremist points of view, but for those with the time to sift the various perspectives, the effort is well worth while. Mediachannel.org—"the global network for democratic media"—is another site that has been campaigning to present what it sees as a more balanced point of view. These sites' outsider status gives them a freedom that other media sources sometimes lack.

In the US, the mainstream media has worked consistently to marginalize alternative points of view. The organization FAIR (Fairness and Accuracy In Reporting) has been studying examples of media bias and censorship since 1986. FAIR aims to scrutinize media practices that marginalize public interest, to expose neglected news stories, and to defend working journalists when they are muzzled. FAIR states: "Almost all media that reach a large audience in the United States are owned by for-profit corporations—institutions that by law are obligated to put the profits of their investors ahead of all other considerations. The goal of maximizing profits is often in conflict with the practice of responsible journalism."

Their "Fear and Favor" report, released in March 2005, chronicled literally hundreds of examples of reporters being "leaned on" by PR agencies, advertisers, media owners, and governments. *USA Today* noted concerns that grisly Iraq images were putting off advertisers. There were also numerous examples of advertorial copy disguised as real news, which were easier to get into smaller local newspapers.

FAIR reports one such violation in the case of news and entertainment programs being featured on network "news magazine" shows where the broadcaster has a particular interest. According to the May 14th, 2004 issue of the *Los Angeles Times*, the NBC News program had no scruples about championing the programs of another NBC unit. "Despite criticism that NBC's news programs have been turned into brazen marketing tools for several of the network's prime-time series finales," the *Times* reported, "the management of the combined company seems delighted with the promotional firepower of its enterprise." The *Times* cited, among other things, a two-hour special that went out on May 5th, 2004, devoted to the final episode of the sitcom *Friends*, as well as generous coverage of the NBC sitcom *Frasier* and the Donald Trump "reality" show *The Apprentice*.

FAIR also notes examples of government pressure. For example, when celebrity reporter Kitty Kelley was promoting her critical book about the Bush family, the *New York Times* reported, on September 9th, 2004, that a White House official had put a call in to NBC News president Neal Shapiro to try and persuade the network not to do interviews with her. The investigation by CBS on April 28th, 2004 of abuse and torture at Abu Ghraib prison was also delayed for two weeks in response to a request by the Pentagon.

One consequence of the 9/11 attacks was that the news channels had to gear up to meet the wall-to-wall coverage that the public required in the immediate aftermath of the event. Advertisers—in the US especially, but also in Europe—were reluctant to book space as they did not want to see their products associated in potential purchasers' minds with the national tragedy. And, as the war effort stepped up and US forces were sent into Afghanistan, the process of following the forces was hugely expensive. To compound the problem, the public was beginning to switch off, and from the all-important advertisers' point of view, that was even worse news for broadcasters. Hauling camera crews around remote places, paying for satellite up-links, and budgeting for the health and safety insurance costs all raised the bill significantly. And, to make things worse, war fatigue soon claimed TV audiences. Broadcasters must have been delighted when viewers voted with their feet, preferring to "veg out" in front of a raft of escapist movies or low-budget reality shows like *Big Brother*.

On April 4th, 2000 the author Norman Solomon wrote an article for ZNet about the recent merger news between America Online and Time Warner, claiming: "To an unprecedented extent, large numbers of American reporters and editors now work for just a few huge corporate employers—a situation that hardly encourages unconstrained scrutiny of media conglomerates as they assume unparalleled importance in public life. Like the Viacom-CBS merger, the joining of AOL and Time Warner puts a lot more journalists in an awkward position: on the payrolls of media outlets that are very newsworthy as major economic and social forces."

"Not only are most major media owned by corporations, these companies are becoming larger and fewer in number as the biggest ones absorb their rivals," says FAIR. "This concentration of ownership tends to reduce the diversity of media voices and puts great power in the hands of a few companies. As news outlets fall into the hands of large conglomerates with holdings in many industries, conflicts of interest inevitably interfere with newsgathering."

Inevitably, media organizations have turned into mini-guerrilla units in a bid to block the big guys getting their way. One such is Adbusters.org, a spirited bunch of radicals who exist to put a spoke in the corporate wheel, either by *not* participating (not buying the products, not watching the adverts, not joining the groups and clubs that promote unbridled consumerism) or by actively disrupting and interfering with poster sites, rewriting the message to reflect what they see as a deeper truth that is concealed by layers of corporate misinformation. Poster sites and billboards are targeted and very pointedly rewritten, either by the use of graffiti or with jarring images.

In 2002 Canada's Campaign for Press and Broadcasting Freedom reported a similarly disturbing pattern to that reported by FAIR: the concentration of media ownership in Canada's newspaper industry was progressing "at an alarming pace." In 1970, said CCPBF, the Special Senate Committee on Mass Media noted that the three biggest newspaper chains had boosted their share of daily circulation from 25 percent in 1958 to 45 percent. By 1980, that figure had risen to 57 percent.

In Canadian television, 60 percent of viewers receive all their programming from a mere five corporations. In cable TV, three companies control 68 percent of the market, twice the 1983 figure. The total revenue from the radio industry is in the hands of ten companies—up 50 percent on the last decade.

"Globally, the story is very similar," reports the CCPBF. "Time Warner Communications, AT&T, MCI, British Telecom, News Corporation, Sony, General Electric, Bertlesmann, Microsoft, and Disney Corp are among just a handful of companies which control the vast majority of the world's media and communications sector. Furthermore, international trade and investment agreements are making it increasingly difficult for governments to effectively regulate media ownership even if the political will is there."

It pointed out that negotiations with the World Trade Organization could further reduce the capacity of governments to control foreign investment, safeguard domestic companies, develop public service broadcasting, and block takeovers and mergers in the media and communications sector. "The likely result will be yet further concentration and conglomeration," wrote CCPBF, adding that it was clearly incompatible with a healthy democracy to allow "a handful of powerful and often politically ambitious media owners to set the news and information agenda—we run the risk of limiting the diversity and range of opinion given public expression."

More than 50 years ago, former Canadian press baron Lord Beaverbrook was honest enough to tell the British Royal Commission on the Press that he ran the *Daily Express* "purely for propaganda and no other object." John Bassett, former publisher of the *Toronto Telegram*, was once asked whether he used his newspaper to advance his own conservative political views. "Of course," replied Bassett. "Why else would you want to own a newspaper?" Conrad Black, who purchased the *Jerusalem Post* in 1989, urged the then moderate newspaper to swing to the right, the better to reflect his own views. (The editor resigned, citing editorial interference, and 190 staff jobs were eventually cut.)

Murdoch's Fox was not the only news organization accused of showing favoritism. On October 31st, 2001, *Washington Post* reporter Howard Kurtz wrote a front-page story in which he alleged: "The chairman of CNN has ordered his staff to balance images of civilian devastation in Afghan cities with reminders that the Taliban harbors murderous terrorists, saying it 'seems perverse to focus too much on the casualties or hardship in Afghanistan.'" The story went on: "In a memo to his international correspondents, Walter Isaacson said: 'As we get good reports from Taliban-controlled Afghanistan, we must redouble our efforts to make sure we do not seem to be simply reporting from their vantage or perspective. We must talk about how the Taliban are using civilian shields and how the Taliban have harbored the terrorists responsible for killing close to 5,000 innocent people.'"

The statement was made in the light of US warplanes firing bombs at residential areas, a Red Cross warehouse, and a senior citizens' center, producing widespread casualties. "I want to make sure we're not used as a propaganda platform," Isaacson said. "We're entering a period in which there's a lot more reporting and video from Taliban-controlled Afghanistan. You want to make sure people understand that when they see civilian suffering there, it's in the context of a terrorist attack that caused enormous suffering in the United States."

The message that the CNN head was stressing was that CNN's cameras should not be seen as unwittingly spreading the message of resistance from the Taliban. It did not seem to have occurred to him, however, that there could be other interests at stake, and that the viewpoint which they were expressing could be any closer to home.

Some correspondents had expressed concern that their reports might be seen as thinly disguised propaganda, especially after MSNBC and Fox News yielded to then National Security Adviser Condoleezza Rice's request not to show any more Osama bin Laden videotapes, either live or unedited. CNN showed only brief excerpts.

CNN's editorial processes came in for criticism from other broadcasters. Jim Murphy, executive producer of the CBS Evening News, said of the CNN instructions: "I wouldn't order anybody to do anything like that. Our reporters are smart enough to know it always has to be put in context." NBC News vice president Bill Wheatley adopted a similar position, saying: "I'd give the American public more credit, frankly. I'm not sure it makes sense to say every single time you see any pictures from Afghanistan, 'This is as a result of September 11th.' No one's made any secret of that."

Perhaps inevitably, though, Fox News vice president John Moody came to the rescue of the CNN directive. "Americans need to remember what started this," he said. "I think people need a certain amount of context or they obsess on the last 15 minutes of history. A lot of Americans did die." Kurtz pointed out that the cable networks carried American flag logos, and several hours of speeches and briefings every day by President Bush, Donald Rumsfeld, Tom Ridge, Ari Fleischer, and other administration figures. "Few viewers complain about this coverage being one-sided," wrote Kurtz.

With Taliban leaders courting world sympathy after the bomb damage—and receiving it in plenty from the Arab and Islamic world—the Pentagon was still denying that Afghan casualties were anywhere near as big as the thousands claimed by the Taliban. In fact, CNN was criticized during the first Gulf War over its reporter Peter Arnett's coverage of the effects of the War inside Baghdad.

Arnett, an ex-CNN reporter, became one of the second Gulf War's more celebrated casualties when he was sacked from his three reporting jobs—NBC News, the MSNBC cable channel, and National Geographic Explorer—after giving an interview to Iraqi TV in which he said that the US's initial war plan had failed. This seemed to bear out the prophecies of the author Phillip Knightley, whose book on war reporting and truth, entitled *The First Casualty*, has been reissued several times under different, updated titles since 1975. Knightley feared that Gulf War II could spell the end for the war correspondent "as an objective, independent person trying to find out what is going on."

Knightley was no admirer of the embed system, telling BBC News Online: "The Pentagon has been out to get Peter Arnett ever since he reported from Baghdad in Gulf War I. It hates war correspondents being there and has pressurized all their employers to withdraw them. This is the new Pentagon. No more Mr. Nice Guy. Report it our way or we'll get you."

Left or Right?

The media is dominated by powerful corporate interests. Every word they report is scrutinized by the proprietor's office. If the proprietor's office approves, it goes through. If the proprietor's office does not, it will either be referred back for rewriting, or balanced out, to the point of being neutralized, by an opposing point of view. The aim of this so-called balance is not to present an open forum, since media barons do not become media barons by proclaiming their interest in open debate. Rather, the small group of plutocrats who control each of these media organizations are people of very firm views that more often than not are well to the right of the political center.

Right-wingers relished the sight of the *New York Times*, CBS News, the *Washington Post*, ABC News, and NBC News failing in their bid to prevent the re-election of George W. Bush. The problem, they say, is that the Old Media no longer enjoys the monopoly over political news that it used to have. But that has to be balanced against Rupert Murdoch and Fox News, which were tireless in their campaign to see the president re-elected. Are the real issues then being reduced and simplified in terms of a phony left–right debate? What is clear is that there is a tendency for each side—left and right—to reduce their opponents' viewpoints to ever more simplified versions.

An illustration of how loosely such terms as left and right have come to be defined these days was provided by Matt Taibbi of the *New York Press* on February 25th, 2005. He noted a report on Fox News of a visit to France's Institute for Political Sciences in Paris earlier in the month by Secretary of State Condoleezza Rice. The Fox reporter, James Rosen, had said, almost in passing: "Speaking to one of France's leading left-wing political science academies, Secretary of State Condoleezza Rice urged old Europe to put aside the old differences over Iraq…" As Taibbi points out, the Fondation Nationale des Sciences Politiques "is so left-wing that it claims [the recently departed administrator of Iraq] Paul Bremer as one of its graduates. Other graduates include Jacques Chirac, François Mitterand, Georges Pompidou, and Boutros-Boutros Ghali. What Rosen was obviously trying to say was that Rice was speaking to a bunch of recalcitrant Europeans. Left-wing is becoming a synonym for not American."

The media has enormous influence over our lives, together with a proven ability and desire to shape our attitudes and perceptions. Over the past two decades there has been a trend towards entertainment rather than to allowing us to deal with difficult or challenging issues. The "dumbing-down" argument is a clear example of this, with reality shows achieving such high ratings that executives have been taking resources away from so-called serious programming and diverting it to "eye candy" programs that look attractive but are mere distractions. Serious issues like the future of Medicaid in the US or the state of hospitals in the UK have been ignored or swept under the carpet. In the 1960s, media theorists such as the Canadian Marshall McLuhan were still attracted to the possibilities that the novelty of TV offered to the inhabitants of the global village. By the 1980s, however, the dream had gone sour. In his 1986 book *Amusing Ourselves to Death*, the chair of the Department of Culture and Communications at New York University, Neil Postman (1931–2003), regretted the decline of the printed word and bemoaned the ascendancy of TV, and its tendency to present everything—from murder to politics or the weather—as entertainment. Postman foresaw the shriveling of public discourse and feared that TV would degrade our conception of what constituted news, political debate, art, or even religious thought.

The tragedy is that the tabloid formula peddled by TV has been enthusiastically adopted by the printed media too. Television now sets the agenda from Europe to North America, reducing newspapers and magazines to the role of commentators on whichever minor celebrities are parading themselves on the small screen. The loss, society's loss, is a sense of proportion. Everything these days, it seems, is about having fun.

Conclusion

For whatever reasons, the desire to run the world is always viewed as sinister. It is the main motive for a large number of super villains in works of fiction. In real life, one has only to remember the aims of Adolf Hitler and his Third Reich to find the same evil intent. There have been empires throughout history, where the home nation conquers and governs other nations, often far removed geographically. Was the Roman empire deemed to be evil? Was the Ottoman empire evil? Was the British empire evil? The answer to all of these is a resounding "yes" if you happened to be a foreigner under their strict control. There is something secure about a nation; its borders are defined and any attempt to reduce them in size is always met with extreme resistance. Attempts to take over a nation are always met with similar resistance, even if the aggressor is successful. Nationalism is often stronger than religion. It unites its people with a desire to defend the very soil they stand on as if they were actually born from that soil.

When nations come together through mutual, peaceful consent, there still exists the friction at the borders. It is significant that the great attempts at amalgamation of nations occurred as a direct result of the two world wars of the 20th century. After the first, the League of Nations attempted to bring former aggressors together and eliminate the need for future wars. This failed as a result of the United States Senate refusing to ratify the treaty President Wilson had worked so hard to obtain. After World War II, the United Nations was created with similar intentions. American support was forthcoming for this attempt and it still operates to this day, but there are the inevitable signs of friction and resistance to acting as one global community. Nationalist interests always override internationalist concerns. Military alliances and shared security form stronger bonds than do economic ones, since commercial competition in finance and trade is often carried out along the lines of active daily warfare with campaigns and business strategies based on ancient theories of battle.

National borders are ignored when it comes to the activities of multinational corporations. Without the diplomatic restrictions of nations, these giant corporations are able to invade other countries and seize foreign market shares with a ruthlessness common to the empire-building of old. They are able to operate in all areas of commerce and control all stages of the distribution, from cheap slave labor manufacturing in the developing world to the affluent consumer driven markets of the West. These corporations are often financially bigger than the countries they exploit. To repeat the fact given in the introduction and within the book, of the largest 100 economies, 51 are multinational corporations and only 49 are countries.

Are these giant corporations deemed to be evil in their global acquisitions in the same way that the Roman, Ottoman, and British empires were before them? Again, the answer is a resounding "yes" if you are one of their slaves, being exploited for the pay differentials that always exist. Yet proponents of globalization defend the merits of providing employment and access to foreign markets which wouldn't normally exist. Exploitation is nothing more than getting the best deal on pricing structures. However, it is the unscrupulous drive for maximizing profits that offends a lot of the world's more vocal elements. Violent demonstrations against the G8 and similar groups that attempt to manage the world economy are very visible signs of discontent at the way the world is really being run.

But is it being run at all? Or do we really exist in a random chaotic soup of international relationships that are only partially manageable? The frequency of wars is a worrying indicator that that may be the case. Human attempts to run the world are nothing more than vain attempts to rise above the spirit of nationalism. It is a theory that is not held by conspiracists. They are willing to believe that secret groups have mastered the art of global management and have been doing it for as long as can be remembered...by those in the know. This secret knowledge is as much the allure of secret societies as anything that can be gained from wearing religious robes. Why do they have to operate behind the scenes? Why are their identities hidden from prying eyes? Again, it is because there is the sinister element to it all. People are not supposed to be able to rule the world. It is just too big. Alexander the Great ruled over all that he could see, but his reign did not last long and his empire fragmented on his death.

Critics will point out that before there were nations, there were tribes, and that the strongest bond that unites a people is tribal. A person is a Tutsi before he is a Rwandan, before he is an African, before he is a citizen of the world. The predominance of the stars and stripes flag over American state flags indicates that the process can evolve over time. Perhaps the leap from United States to United Nations is too great. If this is the case then surely a continental identity would be next above that of nationality. The most advanced attempt at this is in Europe, where common legislation and a common currency combine with the partial removal of borders. The experiment is currently entering what looks like its terminal phase with too many nations involved. Again, national frictions exist.

Multinational corporations will continue to amalgamate until they reach a point of obesity when they start to expire. It is almost as if there is a natural limit to how large an organization can get, like microbes in a Petri dish. Trying to sift through corporate activities for signs of hidden puppet masters is a difficult task, since the constant movement of funds around the world leads to degrees of secrecy that can only really be justified if something sinister is going on. Eventually the real reasons come out and directors disappear with millions of dollars. If you're looking for evidence of the people who are trying to run the world, do not look for the fictional super villains and their evil plots. Instead, look for the signs of hidden regulation, control, and punishment. Those are the footprints of power. Look for the people who use advanced surveillance methods to catch the fraudsters. Look for the people who influence the politicians over the very long term and are not subject to the vagaries of short-term election successes. Look for the constancy throughout changes of administration. Look for the directors of the multinationals who meet with competitors in different surround-ings, even if it involves urination in the woodlands of Bohemian Grove. But ultimately, look for the people who wear suits and not flowing robes.

Bibliography

PART ONE

Allen, Gary, and Larry Abraham, *None Dare Call It Conspiracy*, Vine House, 1990

Armstrong, Hamilton Fish, and Allen Dulles, *Can We Be Neutral?* Ayer Co. Pub, 1977

Bamford, James, *Body of Secrets*, Random House, 2001

Brzezinski, Zbigniew, *Alternative to Partition*, McGraw-Hill, 1965

Carter, Jimmy, *I'll Never Lie to You*, Ballantine Books, 1976

Carter, Jimmy, *Why Not The Best?*, Corgi, 1976

Domhoff, William G., *The Bohemian Grove and Other Retreats*, Harper & Row, 1974

Epperson, A. Ralph, *The Unseen Hand: An Introduction to the Conspiratorial View of History*, Publius Press, 1985

Griffin, Edward G., *The Creature from Jekyll Island*, American Opinion Publishing, Inc., 1995

Hager, Nicky, *Secret Power: New Zealand's Role in the International Spy Network*, Craig Potton, 1996

House, Edward Mandell, *Philip Dru: Administrator*, Robert Welch University Press, 1998

Kissinger, Henry, *Nuclear Weapons and Foreign Policy*, W.W. Norton, 1969

McCoy, Alfred, *The Politics of Heroin: CIA Complicity in the Drug Trade*, Lawrence Hill, 2003

Quigley, Carroll, *Tragedy and Hope*, The Macmillan Company, 1966
   The Anglo-American Establishment, Books in Focus, 1982

Reeves, John, *The Rothschilds, the Financial Rulers of Nations*, University Press of the Pacific, 2003

Robertson, Pat, *The New World Order*, Word Inc., 1991

Robison, John, *Proofs of a Conspiracy Against All of the Religions and Governments of Europe, Carried on in the Secret Meetings of the Free Masons, Illuminati, and Reading Societies*, Cadell, 1798

Ronson, Jon, *Them*, Picador, 2001

Rosenbaum, Ron, 'The Last Secrets of Skull and Bones', *Esquire* magazine, September 1977

Shea, Robert and Robert Anton Wilson, *The Illuminatus! Trilogy*, Constable & Robinson, 1997

Schulzinger, Robert D., *The Wise Men of Foreign Affairs*, Columbia University Press, 1984

Skousen, W. Cleon, *The Naked Capitalist*, Buccaneer Books, 1998

Stauffer, Vernon, *New England and the Bavarian Illuminati*, Russell and Russell, 1967

Wala, Michael, *The Council on Foreign Relations and American Foreign Policy in the Early Cold War*, Berghann Books, 1994

PART TWO

Bakan, Joel, *The Corporation*, Simon & Schuster/Constable, 2004

Bloom, Howard, *Global Brain: The Evolution of the Mass Mind from the Big Bang to the 21st Century*, John Wiley & Sons, 2000

Chomsky, Noam, *Hegemony or Survival: America's Quest for Global Dominance*, Penguin Books, 2004

  What Uncle Sam Really Wants, Pluto Press, 2003

  The Chomsky Trilogy, Odonian Press, 1996

Derber, Charles, *Corporation Nation*, St. Martin's Press, 1998

Douthwaite, Richard, *The Growth Illusion: How Economic Growth has Enriched the Few, Impoverished the Many, and Endangered the Planet*, New Society Publishers/Green Books, 1999

Drezner, Daniel W., *The Sanctions Paradox: Economic Statecraft and International Relations*, Cambridge University Press, 1999

Elliott, Larry A. and Richard J. Schroth, *How Companies Lie*, Crown Business/Nicholas Brealey Publishing, 2002

Friedman, Thomas, *The World is Flat*, Allen Lane/Farrar Strauss Giroux, 2005

Greider, William, *One World, Ready Or Not*, Simon & Schuster, 1998

  The Soul of Capitalism, Simon & Schuster, 2003

Griffin, David C., *The New Pearl Harbor: Disturbing Questions About the Bush Administration and 9/11*, Interlink/Arris Books, 2004

Hertz, Noreena, *IOU: The Debt Threat and Why We Must Defuse It*, 4th Estate, 2004

  Silent Takeover: Global Capitalism and the Death of Democracy, Arrow, 2002

Keith, Jim, *Mass Control: Engineering Human Consciousness*, Adventures Unlimited Press, 2003

Kingsnorth, Paul, *One No, Many Yeses: A Journey to the Heart of the Global Resistance Movement*, Free Press, 2003

Klein, Naomi, *No Logo: Taking Aim at the Brand Bullies*, Flamingo, 2000

Knightley, Phillip, *The First Casualty: The War Correspondent as Hero, Propagandist, and Myth-maker from the Crimea to the Gulf War II*, Andre Deutsch, 2003

Korten, David C., *When Corporations Rule the World*, Earthscan, 1996

Lindstrom, Martin and Patricia B. Seybold, *Brandchild*, Kogan Page, 2003

Monbiot, George, *Captive State*, Macmillan, 2000

Nace, Ted, *Gangs of America: The Rise of Corporate Power and the Disabling of Democracy*, Berrett-Koehler Publishers Inc., 2003

Postman, Neil, *Amusing Ourselves to Death: Public Discourse in the Age of Show Business*, Viking, 1985

Ralston Saul, John, *The Collapse of Globalism and the Rebirth of Nationalism*, Atlantic Books, 2005

Said, Edward, *Orientalism: Western Conceptions of the Orient*, Penguin Books, 1995

Schlosser, Eric, *Fast Food Nation*, Houghton Mifflin/Allen Lane, 2001

Schumacher, E.F., *Small Is Beautiful*, HarperCollins, 1974

Smith, Jerry E., *HAARP: The Ultimate Weapon of the Conspiracy*, Adventures Unlimited Press, 1998

Soros, George, *George Soros on Globalization*, PublicAffairs, 2002

Stonor Saunders, Frances, *Who Paid the Piper? The CIA and the Cultural Cold War*, Granta Books, 1999

Thomas, Kenn, *The Octopus: Life and Death of Danny Casolaro*, Feral House, 1966

Vidal, John, *McLibel: Burger Culture on Trial*, Pan, 1997

Zinn, Howard, *A People's History of the United States*, Longman/New Press, 2003

Index